YOU ONLY
LIVE
TWICE

a memoir in
two genders

**JAY
DEFAZIO**

Editor: Melissa Rudder
Senior Editor: Laurie Knight
Cover Design: Kristina Edstrom
Author photo: Amanda Tangredi

PRIDE & JOY
— *publishing* —

An Imprint for GracePoint Publishing (www.GracePointPublishing.com)

GracePoint Matrix, LLC   SAN # 991-6032

624 S. Cascade Ave, Suite 201, Colorado Springs, CO 80903
www.GracePointMatrix.com Email: Admin@GracePointMatrix.com

A Library of Congress Control Number has been requested and is pending.
ISBN: (Paperback) 978-1-961347-85-4
eISBN: 978-1-966346-62-3

Books may be purchased for educational, business, or sales promotional use.
For distribution queries contact Sales@IPGbook.com
For non-retail bulk order requests contact Orders@GracePointPublishing.com
Printed in U.S.A

CONTENT WARNING

This memoir contains descriptions of mental health crises, suicide attempts, psychiatric hospitalization, domestic violence, emotional abuse, childhood sexual abuse, substance abuse and alcoholism, pregnancy loss and stillbirth, medical procedures related to gender transition, and experiences within the criminal justice system.

If you find certain content disturbing or triggering, please take care of yourself while reading.

Table of Contents

Dear Reader,

You are not a mistake. You are not an abomination. You are not a sin. You are neither sick, disgusting, nor disturbed. You are not responsible for making others happy, proud, or justified in their ignorance, fear, and hate.

You are not crazy. You are not a freak.

You are beautiful; you are loved; your life has purpose. The world needs you; I need you. No matter where you are in your journey to authenticity, there will always be another person a few steps behind you facing a challenge you've already overcome. You have the power to turn and extend a hand, to offer your shared experience to lift that person, to let your presence be the proof that we are all growing and evolving, and no situation or person stays exactly the same.

The circumstances that come with the labels can, at times, feel heavy and insurmountable. At various points, it's not unusual to experience fear, loneliness, or even despair. When systems, institutions, and individuals turn against us, we sometimes turn against ourselves, and our world becomes small. Our focus becomes narrow and inward facing. Our self-criticism grows like a cancer, screaming into our conscious awareness while creeping silently into our subconscious to undermine various parts of our lives.

But it doesn't have to be that way.

If you are somewhere in the downward spiral, I'm writing this for you: This painful place is not where you are destined to remain. It is simply one part of the journey, perhaps the very worst part for sure, but not a life sentence. Change is not just imminent, it's guaranteed. The best part is that *you* get to write your narrative.

This book represents many years of my own personal journey. If my progress were plotted out on a graph, it would look like the wild scribblings of a toddler with erratic peaks and dips indicating trial and error, huge plummets where mistakes were made, and even some flat lines marking the times I completely gave up trying at all because even the involuntary act of breathing was too much.

Sprinkled throughout that messy graph, I could plot all the times help was offered by my therapists, doctors, friends, family, and others on a similar journey. Nearly all of it was solid advice, real tried-and-true tips that would have undoubtedly been useful to me in the moment—had I been ready to hear any of it.

So, before you read the words I've written in these pages, I want to acknowledge not just the importance of right timing but the fact that right timing has a unique meaning for each person.

Condensing years of someone's life into a few hundred pages of words can make it look unrealistically simple when it was anything but. I can assure you; I do not have all the answers. The struggles still arrive in waves big and small; I've just learned how to paddle downstream or in the worst cases, how to get back into the boat.

My hope and my purpose for sharing this material is that each person who reads it can pick out a few nuggets of something helpful, comforting, and relevant to their own uniquely timed journey. Take what you need and leave the rest.

If you don't like where you are at this moment, if it feels too big, too painful, too uncertain, know that this book is my way of holding space for you: acknowledging, validating, loving, and encouraging. Change is guaranteed; it's happening with every breath, even in the moments when breathing feels like more than you can handle.

Jay

Part One
What Am I?

PROLOGUE

I *step out of the shower and onto the fuzzy blue bath rug, wiggle the water off my toes, and sink them into the polyester pile. It's nice and dry, the upside of being first in line for the shower. After a few passes with the towel and one last shuffle in the blue fluff, I am dry enough to step forward onto cold linoleum. I wrap the towel tightly around my waist, twist the corner and tuck it in to hold it in place, the way my dad does. After my last shower, my mom told me I need to start wrapping it high up under my armpits like her, to cover my chest... but I don't want to. It feels dumb and my chest isn't big like hers anyway, thank God.*

I reach for the fat pink comb and move closer to the counter to study my nine-year-old reflection. Everyone talks about how much I look like my dad. We have the same blondish-brown hair color, the same blue eyes, and the same pug nose. My little brother and sister have brown hair and dark brown eyes like my mom, which makes me happy because I like being the only one who looks like dad.

Tiny trails of water run down my back as I start the annoying process of combing through tangles. My hair is a little more than shoulder-length and wavy. I hate the way it looks, hate dealing with it. But I get to work combing as quickly and as painlessly as possible. Water droplets pelt the plastic shower curtain behind me with each pass.

When it's done, I check my reflection again and notice how different my hair looks when wet and slicked back. Something is familiar. I suddenly recognized my dad's hairline. I grab the comb and set it like a point then carefully drag it backwards, creating a side-part, like his. After a few swoops across the crown, it looks just like his black-and-white senior photo from high school—the one where he was wearing a sports coat, and his hair was slicked down with something he called Dippity-Do. It's one of my favorite photos of him. My hair is too long, though, so I quickly comb it behind my ears and try to adjust my position in front of the mirror until the long strands are mostly hidden behind my neck.

Wow.

It's hard to stop staring. I examine my defined brow line, blue eyes the shape of my dad's, and a nose that looks too fat to be girly. Ugh.

I turn just a few degrees to the left and examine my jawline. It's straight and hard just like the raised collarbones on my flat chest. I cross my arms, stretch and contort to make my shoulders look broad and strong before returning my attention back to the face in the mirror.

I keep staring at my hair, eyes, nose, jaw, hair, eyes, nose, jaw… Over and over until my brain delivers a distinct and lasting understanding: I make a really ugly girl, but I make a pretty decent-looking boy.

My gaze shifts from admiration to searching, looking for something girly, anything at all. I shake my hair out of its hiding place behind my neck, but it doesn't help. My eyebrows are boy, my nose is a blob, my jaw is hard, and my smile is gone.

I drop the pink comb on the counter and turn to go. A white nightgown with tiny blue flowers and ruffled sleeves hangs on the doorknob waiting for me. I toss it over my shoulder and rewrap my towel at armpit level before making my way to the bedroom I share with my sister.

CHAPTER ONE

The First Communion dress was a nightmare, and I wanted zero part of it. But there was no choice; I had to wear it. That's the rules. At least my mom agreed to my request for one that stopped at the knee and didn't resemble a wedding gown like some of the other ones in the catalog. It still came with a stupid veil though. And white lace gloves. And white sandals with heels. *Ugh.*

"Okay let's get a picture then we need to get going," Mom announced as she finished pinning the veil to my head. I smelled my dad's cologne seconds before he entered the living room. "We're supposed to be early so they can line up," she reminded him.

"You look pretty!" The words clanged into my ears like an insult. I was smart enough to know I wasn't pretty (and didn't aspire to be), so why did they insist on saying that? Did they think I was stupid or blind? I felt ridiculous in this outfit, and the last thing I wanted was to be photographed in it.

There were more compliments when we arrived at the church. The moms collectively ooohed and awwed and fussed over the whole group. I glared with envy at the boys in their suits. They had nothing pinned to their heads, no stupid gloves, and they didn't have to sit with their knees together or worry about wobbling on unsteady shoes. Plus, the neckties and sport coats were so cool. I wanted to dress like that, to look like my dad or my grandpa. But I didn't say so. I sensed it was weird, shameful, and unspeakable, although I had no idea why. It's just as well; there was probably no good answer anyway. Or it's a because-that's-how-it-is answer like when I asked why girls can't be altar boys.

I took my place in the procession and kept my eyes locked straight ahead in an attempt to ignore the stares, smiles, and camera flashes. We filed into the first two rows, girls first then boys. I glanced across the aisle and saw my family in our normal spot: third pew from the front. That's where we sat every single Sunday. My mom said it was so we could see better and pay attention. It definitely worked: My eyes were always drawn to the statues, stained glass, and giant crucifix that hovered above the center aisle.

The first reading was about to begin so I settled in for what was going to be a longer-than-usual mass. Like any other Sunday, I flipped to the correct page of the missalette to follow along, but within seconds my attention drifted up to the big crucifix. I felt really sad for Jesus and couldn't make sense of the whole thing, even when I watched the movie on TV at Easter. As I studied the sculpture, scenes replayed in my mind: the men jamming thorns onto his head, whipping him, and then hammering nails into his hands and feet. God was supposed to be his father but let that happen to him. My dad would never do that to me, that's one thing I did know for certain.

I heard things like Jesus died for our sins, Jesus died and opened up heaven for everyone, or Jesus was doing the will of God. One of my religion teachers said Jesus loved us so much he willingly took on that suffering. Couldn't those things have been done without all the blood and cruelty? Jesus never killed or tortured anyone.

None of this made sense to me. My continuous *why* questioning eventually dead-ended with "because that's what we believe." So, I stopped asking questions and just followed the rules, even the painful ones like going to confession.

I hated confession. There was a whole script to memorize, and it was really embarrassing to tell stuff to the priest.

"What are your sins?

"Ummmm, I told some lies."

"Mmm hmm, and what else?"

"Uh, I fought with my brother."

"Ahh, and what else?"

What else? I was seven. *What else is there?* I wondered.

So, I'd make up some super generic stuff like, "I wasn't nice to people." Then I'd receive my sentence of ten Hail Marys and ten Our Fathers and attempt to recite them in my head without losing count and without peeking through my closed eyelids at the statue of bloody crucified Jesus hanging over the altar.

The church organ began to play, signaling it was communion time. I was suddenly nervous, my stomach felt uneasy. I really didn't want to eat that dumb wafer. The religion teachers let us try an unconsecrated one last weekend. It tasted like Styrofoam. I was dreading the wine too because I didn't want to drink out of the same cup as 200 other people. Sure, they wiped the edge with a cloth after each person but what about the germs and saliva that backwashed into the wine? Outside of church, I wasn't supposed to drink after other people unless it was my parents but sometimes even that wasn't allowed if one of them was sick.

It was my turn, I held out my cupped hand. There was no way I was letting the priest put the wafer on my tongue. I didn't think it was possible for him to do that without his fingertip also touching my tongue. The wine barely touched my lips, I don't think I even opened my mouth really.

I made my way back to the pew and knelt down, the wafer still in my mouth. The teacher's words replayed in my ears: "Don't chew the host, it's disrespectful! It's the body of Christ. Let it dissolve on your tongue."

"The body of Christ" was another thing I didn't understand. Well, I thought I did at first. I thought it was the symbol of Jesus like we were remembering the Last Supper, but the teacher very sternly said it is *not* a symbol; it is the actual, literal body of Christ because the priest turns it into that during the consecration.

How? Why?

In a family where the men hunted deer and squirrel, I never once feared we would someday eat my dog or cat. I don't even recall questioning it or even considering it; we loved our pets, and they would never be on the dinner table. *But we eat Jesus? We are the cause of his torture and violent death! And then we made him into bread and wine and ate him? Not once, but every week for 2,000 years?*

The final song started, and we filed out of the pews and into the aisle behind the priest and altar boys. The communion wafer was still on my tongue, and I wasn't sure what to do. It hadn't dissolved, it just became soggy. I tried to swallow it, but it stuck to the roof of my mouth. Somehow this seemed more disrespectful than chewing, but I did as I was told.

Despite so much confusion and fear, going to mass was oddly comforting because I was doing the physical actions of a good person: I kneeled, stood, sat, recited, sang, closed my eyes, bowed my head. The adults smiled and approved. God smiled and approved. And then we all got to have donuts and punch in the church hall.

This was the formula I applied to the first forty years of my life: Do what's expected even if it makes you suffer. Don't argue. Don't question, even when it doesn't make sense. Follow the rules even when it feels counterintuitive. Make God happy. And by all means, don't screw up and go to hell.

CHAPTER TWO

My mom kissed me goodbye, shut the door, and headed to the living room window to watch me make the long walk to the bus stop. The sun had only been up for about twenty minutes, same as me, and I wondered if it was as tired.

After a few breaths of damp morning air, I fell into a rhythm with the sound of my footsteps and the swish-swish of my jacket against the red three-ring binder tucked under my arm. The narrow, blacktopped access road delivered me to Rural Route 20.

A quick glance over my shoulder to the faraway living room window reminded me that my mom was watching. I heard her voice in my head as I prepared to cross the big road to the safety of Mrs. Greene's gravel driveway: *Look both ways before you cross, left, right, and then left again... run, don't walk!*

Mrs. Greene's daughters were waiting too but they didn't acknowledge me; they were in high school, and I was a little kid. Those two worlds had no connection unless you were siblings. But it's okay, I didn't like to talk anyway.

My parents always told people I was shy, which was really embarrassing and not at all helpful. Thank God they didn't walk me down here in the mornings. My dad was already at work and my mom had to stay at the house with my little brother and baby sister.

Gravel popped and crunched under my shoes as I found a good spot to wait—not too close to the Greenes and not too close to the road. I peered up Route 20 and saw the big yellow bus in the distance, a tiny dot.

Its driver was a man older than my parents, maybe not quite as old as my grandparents, it was hard to tell. He was tall and skinny with hunched shoulders, a long face, big ears, and dark, tan leathery skin. His name was Homer.

I really liked that name and wished it were my own. I had an old lady name because I was named after Gram, my mom's mom. No one else had my name, and when I saw one of those racks in the drugstore that has personalized magnets or stickers or pencils, my name was never there.

I complained to my mom once for choosing my name and she told me I should be ashamed for saying that, since it was Gram's name. I thought that proved my point entirely! But then she reminded me that it was also *her* middle name. So, I gave up the argument.

Air brakes hissed to a stop, the bus door opened, and my stomach churned in protest. This bus was too crowded for a seven-year-old. Most of the kids went to middle school or high school and did not like sharing their seats.

I moved carefully down the aisle looking for any sign of green vinyl, avoiding eye contact with the sandy-haired junior high kid in a comfortable slouch, knees pressed into the seat ahead of him.

"Hey little one, where are you going?" he asked softly as I passed by, pretending not to hear. I spotted a few inches of open seat ahead, next to two girls hovered over a *Teen Beat* magazine. Hoping they wouldn't notice, I carefully perched the smallest possible amount of my butt on the edge, my feet and knees still in the aisle.

The girl closest to me shrieked as if I had eight hairy legs and just descended from the ceiling. Her voice blasted me back into the aisle, "MOVE!"

The bus began to roll forward and my legs stiffened in an effort to keep me upright. The next seat held one silently reading occupant, scooted to the aisle-side with lots of room between himself and the window. Stopping next to him I stared until he looked up.

"This seat is saved," he said, and returned to his book. The bus picked up speed, and I frantically looked through the loud sea of teenagers. I looked back toward the front of the bus, hoping something would miraculously appear, but I was met with Homer's scowling face in the big rectangular mirror above the steering wheel.

His baritone "Sit down!" pinned me like high beam headlights until a warm hand gently grabbed mine. The sandy-haired teenager guided me back to his seat, taking the window side as usual. When I was seated, he scooted close to me.

I already know his name, it's Evan. He told me several bus rides ago, after offering to share his seat. I thought it was really nice of him at the time; he had soft eyes and smiled a lot. He made the same offer the next day too. I don't know how many days there were before the day he put his hand on my leg. I pushed it away and kept looking straight ahead.

His face was close to mine and his mouth was moving. Words were coming out in a quiet, calming tone but I didn't hear them. He moved his hand back and started petting my thigh. Just like today, there were no empty seats around me, nowhere to go. I stared straight ahead, like a statue, and waited for my school to appear.

A loud burst of laughter startled me out of the bad memory. A boy across the aisle was pointing at us and cackling, saying something to Evan about his "little girlfriend."

I didn't make eye contact with him or with Evan, who was, like last time, too close to my face. I took my red three-ring binder and made a wall separating my legs from his, my left hand resting on top of the binder to keep it standing upright.

He mistook this as an offering and put his hand on mine, stroking it gently. I pulled away which sent my binder to the floor with a loud smack before it slid under the seat in front of us, gone forever. I struggled to swallow. Tears would not leave my eyes but had instead opted for the safer route down the back of my throat.

Evan retrieved my binder from the floor, brushed off the dirt and set it flat like the top bread of a sandwich on the back of his hand that came to rest on my leg. His mouth kept moving, his words were soft.

Soon his hand moved further up my thigh. Way up to places where it definitely didn't belong, until I made myself disappear— staring out the bus windshield, looking at the road, imagining turning the big steering wheel with each curve, listening to the brakes, and watching Homer's leathery face in the mirror.

Occasionally he picked up the CB radio and talked to other bus drivers. For a moment I caught him grinning. I strained my ears to hear his voice. When he was silent, I wondered what he was thinking. His face was serious and droopy eyed like an old hound dog. *I loved hound dogs.*

I studied every wrinkle on his forehead and the shape of his big old ears—like two wide-open cupboard doors. They were long too. For a second, I wondered if he was related to me because I had relatives with big, long ears. I bet he chewed tobacco; his big boney chin and jaw seemed built for spitting. I listened for another CB call and waited for his smile… and waited for my school to appear from around one of those curves I was steering in my head.

I waited until the bus came to a complete stop before leaving my seat… waited for the door to fully open… *walk, don't run… form a straight line…* took my seat and sat quietly with my eyes on the teacher.

CHAPTER THREE

"Well do you have a little boyfriend yet?" My grandma waited for my answer with a big smile on her face.

We'd just finished a big family dinner and moved from my grandparents' dining room to the living room. Side conversations stopped and all eyes in the room were on me now.

I bashfully shook my head no and sunk down further into the couch between my mom and dad. I hated being the center of attention. The school year had just started so there were plenty of other questions for Grandma to ask.

"Do you like your teacher? What's her name?"

Now that was something I could answer. Boys never caught my attention the way my teacher did. She was an attractive young woman with long, blonde hair pulled back in a ponytail, and I was content to stare at her all day. Her name was Ms. Phipps although my grandpa jokingly called her Ms. Hips. He was always being silly in an effort to make us laugh. Fortunately, the sexual innuendo went over my head.

The concept of a boyfriend, of *liking* a boy, was unimaginable. There was nothing creepy in the fact my grandma asked, as I suppose the idea of it was considered cute. But for me it became one of many expectations and assumptions at the forefront of my childhood. It was one in a long list of questions about my school day.

After being asked a couple more times about this thing called a boyfriend, I felt obliged to pick one. By "pick" I mean mentally pick, not actually talk or interact with someone.

On the playground one afternoon, I scanned my options and noticed a boy with white hair and glasses who seemed to be the leader of whatever the kids were playing. He stood on the merry-go-round like a daredevil, perfectly upright without holding onto the bars as it spun. He was the only kid in the class with white hair and it stood in stark contrast to the thick black rims of his glasses. I made a mental note of his name and over the next few days studied his behavior.

On the next visit to Grandma's house, I was ready for the interrogation; all I had to do was wait. When dinner was over, Grandma and my mom did the cleaning up before joining the men and kids in the living room. My brother and I had already emptied a box of cars onto the floor and began to line them up on the braided oval rug like a racetrack. Grandma settled into her comfy chair with the evening newspaper and started talking with the adults. *Good, she forgot,* I thought to myself as I positioned another car on the track. The reprieve only lasted a few minutes.

"How's school?" Her words blared out like the loudspeaker announcer of our soon-to-be race.

"Good." I backed a '69 Charger into an empty lane.

"Do you have a little boyfriend yet?" There was a grin in her words, but I didn't look up from the track.

"Yeah."

"You do?! What's his name?!" I heard the rustle of a hastily closed newspaper like static on the imaginary loudspeaker.

"Chad."

"Chad? Is he cute? What's he look like?" She sounded really happy about this news.

I lined up another car. "He has white hair. And black glasses."

My grandpa was deep in conversation with my dad, but Grandma was not about to have him miss out. "Did you hear that?" she shouted at him. "She has a little boyfriend named Chad!"

I couldn't resist sneaking a side glance at my grandpa to see his reaction. He raised an eyebrow and said, "Ahhh." He was a man of few words, but his tone told me this was a positive reaction.

Grandma was thrilled. I felt a sense of accomplishment and planned to keep this boyfriend, which was an easy task considering he was completely oblivious.

I understood that a *boyfriend* was something girls were *supposed* to have, like lip gloss or cute shoes, although I had no interest in those things either. Luckily my good Catholic upbringing kept me well-versed in doing what I was told and not asking questions, especially when it didn't make sense.

As I progressed through elementary school and gained a small circle of friends, I learned how the boyfriend-girlfriend dynamic worked. It was based upon physical appearance first, then behavior, then friend groups.

Once you identified a potential partner, you never approached them directly. You had to send in your best friend to talk with their best friend. If the other party agreed, then it was filtered back through the best friends and made official. Being a couple involved physical interaction such as sitting next to each other during school assemblies, being chased on the playground (if you were the girl), and sharing a bus seat on field trips so you could secretly hold hands beneath a coat or backpack. If you were daring enough, you played Kissing Catchers during recess.

I didn't fare well in this area of social development. My wavy mess of blonde hair, jeans, T-shirts, and sneakers set me apart from other girls. I ranked high in behavior though; I never got in trouble and always shared my belongings with others. I had a good friend group too, so usually once a year I got matched with someone for a few days.

It was easy to live in the drama and gossip of a ten-year-old's world and *talk* about boys despite feeling uninterested. It was like choosing a puppy, and I knew how to do that thanks to a book from the library. The cutest one is always the obvious choice, but you have to take your time and interact with the whole litter, being careful not to pick one that's too aggressive or too shy, not too hyper or too lethargic. You look for one that appears relatively healthy, seems friendly, and shows some interest in you as well.

Nevertheless, in fifth grade, I made a critical error in agreeing to be the girlfriend of Oscar. He was friendly but just different enough to be stereotyped as a little bit of an oddball. I felt like an oddball too; I just kept a lower profile. Oscar didn't follow the protocol of having one of his friends ask one of my friends and so forth. He just passed me a note that said "I like you. Do you like me? Will you be my girlfriend?" Below that were two squares, one next to the word *yes* and one next to the word *no*. Underneath was the instruction: Check yes or no.

I didn't want to be his girlfriend, but I also didn't dislike him as a friend. Yet there were only two options in his multiple-choice note. It was a nice gesture to say he liked me, so it felt kind of mean to say no. So, I just said yes and figured it wasn't a big deal. But I guess it was a big deal to Oscar because he wasted no time telling *everyone*.

"You're going out with *Oscar*?? Hahahahaha!" I heard it over and over. They didn't hide the jokes and laughter from Oscar either. I felt bad for him and didn't really understand why the other kids liked to pick on him. The only things that made him different—that I knew of anyway—were that he was shorter than nearly all of the other boys, although not by much; and his parents looked a lot older than everyone else's parents. But he was the youngest kid of a big family so how could they not be older?

The whole situation was embarrassing, but I didn't know how to break up without hurting his feelings. I mostly tried to avoid him when possible and shrug off the teasing. But eventually the criticism was too much for me and I cracked one day during recess.

"I don't even like him. I don't want to be his girlfriend," I angrily shot back at a laughing classmate. I didn't know my admission would set the breakup into motion.

From a distance I saw someone excitedly delivering the news to Oscar. The look of hurt and embarrassment on his face made me feel queasy. Several minutes later he quietly approached me and asked, "Why did you break up? I thought you liked me."

Face to face with the visual impact of my actions, I was overwhelmed with guilt and shame. Upsetting people and confrontations were two things I avoided at all costs.

"I'm sorry, I do like you. We don't have to break up." And just like that I put myself right back into the situation I'd regretted from the beginning.

It was a cycle: Kids would begin teasing me again, I'd eventually snap and tell someone I didn't like him, he'd find out and confront me with hurt feelings, I'd agree to be his girlfriend again. The whole scenario repeated a few times over the course of fifth and sixth grade leaving me confused and frustrated each time. *How do I get myself in these situations? How do I not hurt someone's feelings and still keep myself out of the line of fire?*

CHAPTER FOUR

Saturday mornings in the '70s were dedicated to cartoons. I was all in, and so was my dad. He didn't get up as early as my brother and me, but he'd usually join us in time for the *Looney Tunes* hour.

My love of art was probably born out of my connection to animated characters. I wanted so badly to be part of the Flintstones family. I'd imagine working one of the dinosaurs at the rock quarry or driving a car with stone wheels. My favorite episodes were the ones that included Pebbles' babysitter, Ann Margrock. She definitely got my attention although it would be decades before I understood why.

No matter what cartoon I watched, I closely identified with two things: a male character that I wanted to be (Speed Racer, Fred from Scooby Doo, Superman, Robin, Hong Kong Phooey, and Shroeder, the piano-playing friend of Charlie Brown) and an irresistibly cute animal that I wanted to be friends with (Garfield, Odie, Snoopy, Captain Caveman, and all 101 Dalmatians).

I wanted to interact with these characters so badly that it was nearly overwhelming at times. "Don't you wish Snoopy was real? If I could have one wish, that's what I'd want," I said to my parents.

One day I sat next to my mom while she talked on the phone. She had a habit of doodling on a little notepad during calls. I watched her draw spirals, squiggly lines, and then as if by magic she turned a simple square into a three-dimensional box with an open lid. My mind was blown. I could barely contain myself waiting for her to get off the phone.

"How did you do that? I want to do it, show me!"

"Okay, okay. It's like this…" I watched her draw a square, then another overlapping square. "Then you connect the lines like this." And just like before, the three-dimensional, clear box appeared.

I practiced a few times with her guidance, and it worked, but I wanted to be able to do it on my own. That was more of a struggle when I had to remember where to add the diagonal lines. In frustration, I flipped through the notepad for a blank page. I stopped on a drawing of the Mickey Mouse Club logo.

"Who did that?" I asked, shocked.

"I did." My mom laughed. "But it's not that good, I was just doodling."

I thought it was amazing. It was the first time I'd ever considered drawing a cartoon character. I tried drawing my own Mickey Mouse, but it looked nothing like him. He has those big round ears, but his nose and mouth were very difficult to get right. I was quickly frustrated.

"Draw Snoopy!" I said to my mom, as if she were a street artist taking requests.

"I can't draw Snoopy. You draw him," she encouraged. But it was too hard to translate the image in my mind to something on paper.

"I can't do it," I whined.

She got up and went to the stack of newspapers at the end of the kitchen table, shuffled through the pile, and returned with the Sunday Comics.

"Here. Here's Snoopy, you can look at this and draw him," she said, folding the page neatly next to my notepad. "Keep trying, you'll get it."

So, I did. I erased and tried again, erased and tried again, sometimes erasing a hole in the paper. Like Mickey Mouse, Snoopy is deceptively difficult to draw. His head seems like an easy shape but if it's not exact, it's very obvious.

I paused on my Snoopy efforts and jumped to another comic strip, Dagwood. He looked pretty straightforward. I carefully copied each line and curve. When the last mark was made, I put my pencil down and sat back to examine my work.

Wow, I did that?

I'd been so focused on each detail that it seemed Dagwood appeared by surprise or magic. The satisfaction was exhilarating.

More than that, I loved seeing a cartoon character on my notepad right there in my kitchen. The characters still weren't real, but it was as close as I could get. My parents were impressed too and eventually had to buy me a sketchbook as I worked my way through the Sunday Comics.

"Wow! That's really good—it looks just like the picture," they'd say. Whenever their friends or my grandparents came to visit, my parents would inevitably call me into their conversation with the instruction, "Go get your sketchbook and show everyone your drawings."

Nothing felt as good as their words, reactions, and the individual attention that came with it. Yet somehow when those moments passed, my inner critic would take over. I'd pick up the same drawing a few hours or a day later and see only inaccuracies and mistakes. It never looked as good as when I'd finished it. When I voiced this complaint to my parents and pointed out the imperfections they responded as any good parent would.

"It's a great drawing, I couldn't do that!" my mom would say.

"You're a perfectionist… you have a good eye for detail," my dad added.

The kindness and love that came with their words felt good, but it just wouldn't stick. My brain slammed the door on those comments. The critic in my head said they were lying to avoid hurting my feelings. Or that they were my parents, so they had to be nice. Or that they refused to see what I was seeing. The only thing standing between my drawings and the garbage can was the fear of getting in trouble for throwing them away.

Luckily, I found a way to deal with the critical noise in my head: Start a new drawing. Getting lost in the process of drawing something else meant there wasn't time to pick apart one I'd finished. After the Sunday Comics characters, I moved on to referencing my little sister's coloring books.

By this time my parents had given me a set of colored pencils. I drew full color reproductions of Scooby Doo, the Care Bears, the Fox and the Hound, and other Disney characters. Each one was taped on the wall above my sister's bed in the room we shared.

I cautiously attempted to branch out. I tried drawing objects or scenes, but the results weren't great, in my perfectionistic opinion. I had an unyielding drive to do things *right* and to not make mistakes—two things that are contrary to creativity, but I didn't know that.

When I wanted to draw a landscape or a room I was immediately stuck. I couldn't figure out how to draw depth or perspective. *The line needs to go through the paper, how does that work? It's not possible.* So, I stuck to my cartoons or silly doodles, which became all the more interesting when I learned to combine them with humor.

One afternoon my best friend Samantha came over and brought a new comic book. We flipped through the story quickly and got right to our favorite part: the mail order novelty page. It was an obsession we shared and each time one of us had a new comic, we'd hover over the last page together reading about each item, giggling and making wish lists.

"My mom is never going to let me order the Sea Monkeys. I even asked for it for Christmas and she said no." This was an ongoing battle for me.

"I know, my mom won't let me order them either," Samantha groaned. "She said it's all fake."

"Whatever. My mom said the same, but they can't be. Look, they come with a bowl and food and all kinds of stuff. They have to be real, or they wouldn't sell it."

"EXACTLY. Look how cute they are…"

We moved on down the list: electric hand buzzers, fake dog poop, X-ray glasses, and more.

"Look, the fake severed finger is free! You just pay shipping and handling. That was in the last issue, and I showed my mom, she won't even let me order that either! She's all like, 'It's not free if you have to pay for it.'" I mocked her words sarcastically.

Samantha rolled her eyes and commiserated. "Yeah, my mom said the same thing. But you know what? I'm saving my money and ordering the fake dog poop anyway. I don't care. She can't stop me. I only need about seventy cents more." Samantha often had change in her purse or allowance money, and I knew she was serious. I cheered her on. Someone needed to make a stand against the moms, once and for all.

"Hey, we should make our own catalog of stuff. Wouldn't that be funny?" I said. The idea just popped into my head randomly.

Samantha closed the comic. "Make our own? Like what, draw it?"

"Yeah, I have construction paper and pens and stuff. And my dad has this hole puncher thing that puts holes in paper. We could punch the pages and tie them together with string, you know, like a book. A catalog."

Samantha was on board. We gathered all the stuff and took over the kitchen table. For the rest of the evening, we drew a ridiculous assortment of items, laughing hysterically at each creation. When it was finished, we hole-punched it, tied it with yarn, and called it a masterpiece.

It was a great way to loosen up and be funny. My drawings were messy and chaotic because we were inventing things like light-up sunglasses, silly wigs, and strange underwear. I didn't have the pressure of trying to draw from reference photos and make things realistic. Besides, Samantha was drawing too, and she wasn't hung up on details. If our creations got a laugh, it was a success.

CHAPTER FIVE

O ne day when you grow up and have a husband and kids…" was something I heard relatively often in my young life from either my mom, or aunt, or a grandparent. I didn't like thinking about having a husband, but it was the expectation: Girls grow up, get married, have kids. They usually stay home and raise them too, although that part seemed negotiable.

Despite swearing it off, somehow, I knew I'd grow up and have kids of my own. I just couldn't handle thinking about how it requires another person and the stuff you have *to do* with that person to make it a reality.

At one of my family's weekly trips to the public library, I stumbled upon some books about how babies are made. I checked my surroundings and secretively pulled one from the shelf. I was genuinely curious about babies growing inside someone's body. My mom had just given birth to my little sister a year or two earlier, so it was kind of relevant.

I don't remember how I got that book and one other to the checkout desk or what I said to my parents. But when we got home, I tucked them under my arm and headed for my room.

"Do you want to read those together?" my mom asked as I was making my exit.

"NOPE. I'm good," I said quickly before shutting the door. Her question on its own was embarrassing to me. I was steeped in shame when it came to talking about the human body. The names of body parts made me cringe. Even the word *pregnant* was uncomfortable. Maybe my discomfort came from the hatred of my own body, I don't know. But what I did know was that the birds and the bees didn't need to be a talk when it could be an independent study.

The books were jarring to say the least, but I made it through despite being pretty disturbed by the black-and-white photographs. I was mortified for the poor woman. There she was under bright lights with her legs wide open and a bunch of people staring at her business. The next photos were close-ups of the baby in various stages of being born. I wasn't even sure what I was looking at in the one captioned, "crowning." It was clearer in the next one though. The baby's head looked way too big to be coming out like that.

When it was fully out it didn't even look like any baby I'd seen, not even my little sister. It was covered with gunk, and they'd put it right on top of the mom's naked chest! I could understand why she appeared to be crying really hard. But she was so upset that I guess she didn't notice how slimy the baby was; she was hugging it anyway.

It was a lot of info to take in, that's for sure. At some point my mom stopped by my room to ask how I was doing and if I wanted to talk about the books. My answer was still *no*. Probably always would be, as far as I was concerned. Babies and toddlers were cute, and I liked making them laugh, but I wanted no part of the process.

I stuck this topic way back on a shelf in my mind. It would only resurface when a movie or TV show was depicting a woman in labor, knees up, pushing and yelling. The discomfort and embarrassment were so strong I'd have to leave the room, even if my parents weren't watching with me.

Hearing my peers talk about the mechanics of sex didn't fare much better and like many other things in my world it was confusing and made no sense. The church rule was loud and clear though: Sex was to be saved for the wedding night.

The wedding night. That was a whole other set of fears, shame, and confusion. I couldn't understand how two people could have all of their clothes off and be comfortable. On TV it was always dark when a couple was in bed together. That was a little comforting and seemed a bit more reasonable when I thought about it. *Maybe in total darkness it could be okay. Maybe. If I have to do this when I'm an adult, the lights will definitely be off. But how will I get to the bed and under the covers before being seen?*

Sex involved embarrassing sounds too, mostly made by the woman. I learned this because our neighbors had HBO, and the high point of a sleepover was staying up really late and watching an R-rated movie with "sexual situations" in the rating description. Preferably it was also a horror movie. Like my friends, I was drawn to these things out of curiosity and the rush of doing something forbidden. The sex scenes were intriguing for sure but always triggered a little panic when I thought about growing up some day and being in those situations.

My sex education continued with Girl Scouts.

Samantha's mom was the troop leader and local cookie sale organizer, so every time I visited Samantha's house during cookie season, we'd grab a couple boxes and head upstairs to the attic. It was going to be her bedroom once her dad cleaned it out and fixed it up. Until then she was stuck sharing a small room with her little sister. We were not concerned with waiting on the room to be finished before occupying it though. We'd find a little clearing in the stacks of boxes and settle in with our cookies to lazily pass the time.

The attic also contained adult magazines, which wasn't unusual in the '80s. Most kids' parents had at least a few stashed in a dresser drawer somewhere. Like the cookies, we helped ourselves. While Samantha skimmed the issues for any sign of a penis (a futile effort in *Hustler* and *Playboy*) I perused at a much more leisurely pace.

Being just ten or eleven years old it was very educational. Years of Catholic indoctrination kept it from being sexually stimulating. In fact, when my friend's older cousin told us Cyndi Lauper's hit song "She Bop" was about masturbation, I was unimpressed. I really didn't understand the hype for that activity. The church said it was a sin and God sees everything so why would anyone even try?

Up until that point I'd never seen a naked woman aside from a few family members. But on a handful of summer afternoons with only time to kill and plenty of cookies, I could study the female figure at length. I'd never given any thought to the wide variation in human bodies: curves, leg shapes and lengths, different breast sizes and shapes, the broad range of color and diameters of areolas, and even the differing amounts and styles of pubic hair.

****

The next summer, while staying with my cousin for a week, I had a similar experience, but with pages and pages of nude men.

My cousin Dee was four years older and allowed to stay home alone while my aunt worked. One afternoon I was sprawled out on the living room floor like a starfish, bored and staring at the ceiling while Dee washed dishes in the kitchen. One of my outstretched arms inadvertently came to rest under the couch. My hand hit something: a pile of magazines. I pulled one out expecting to see a woman on the front but to my surprise it was a man on the cover of a magazine called *Playgirl*.

I wasted no time turning the page and was completely mesmerized by what I saw. The variety was impressive. Many times, the penises didn't even match the body of their owners: a big bodybuilder with a small one and a scrawny guy with what could pass for a third arm. It was quite the learning experience.

While I definitely appreciated the female body, with the exception of my own, I still had an obsession with penises. "I want a tail like Daddy," I declared to my mom when I was two years old.

I don't remember saying the words, but the sentiment took up permanent residence in my head.

A couple years after that request, I settled in with my parents to watch the weekly *Incredible Hulk* TV series. The opening sequence was a montage set to dramatic background music. *"Don't make me angry, Mr. McGee. You wouldn't like me when I'm angry,"* Dr. Banner warned. Cut to a close-up of his eyes turning green, his body enlarging into giant muscled green limbs, his clothes splitting into rags. I asked what I thought was a very reasonable question: "Does the Hulk's penis turn green and get big when he changes into the Hulk?"

If my parents were amused by my question they hid it well. I remember the abrupt answer being something along the lines of *Don't ask that kind of stuff.* I took their words to heart and never asked another penis-related question again. I'd try to figure it all out in my head from then on.

And so, I looked through every issue over the course of my week-long stay. Dee didn't care, they were old news to her. (We didn't mention it to my aunt.) It was the highlight of my trip aside from seeing *E.T.* at the drive-in theater. On one hand it was very much like the experience of looking at the female magazines back at Samantha's: not sexually stimulating, just fascinatingly educational. It was a whole new understanding of the human body.

On the other hand, it was a completely different experience. I had studied everything about the women—their faces, their hair style, their hands—wondering if the women were nice or funny. What did their voices sound like? Did they smell like perfume and powdered makeup? What kind of cars did they drive? What were their favorite songs?

With the men in *Playgirl,* I never read the bios and didn't consider anything about them as individuals aside from taking notice of what was between their legs. They simply had the part I was missing.

CHAPTER SIX

W hat are you doing in there? Hurry up, I'm waiting to get in the shower!" My mom banged on the bathroom door and jiggled the locked doorknob. Both noises startled me, causing me to flinch and work faster. The knot in my throat made it hard to swallow. Slam-spinning the toilet paper roll, I tore a wad free and continued wiping the floor.

Sitting down to pee had always felt weird, embarrassing somehow. I'd always wanted to pee standing up. So, on this particular day I figured I'd put the seat up and do it. No one would be the wiser. I'd just have to stand more over the toilet than in front of it... Bad idea. There was pee everywhere: on my legs, down the outside of the bowl, and on the floor.

Experiences in public restrooms didn't fare much better. My elementary school was an old 1920s schoolhouse. The girls' restroom was one large room with three small toilets lined up on one wall completely in the open with no dividers or doors. Each bathroom break was a line of girls watching three other girls use the toilet. I had way too much body shame to deal with such absurdity. I opted instead to train my bladder to hold eight hours' worth of urine.

The mother of all bathroom traumas happened in April of 1983, just four months shy of my twelfth birthday. Like any other day, I got off the school bus, speed-walked my full bladder up the long access road to our house and made a beeline for the toilet. In the swift motion of dropping my pants and sitting, I saw a bloody mess where the white cotton of my underwear was supposed to be. Through the leg holes I saw a large blackish-red stain on the inside of my jeans.

I knew what this was all about. I knew it was going to happen at some point, but it was still a shock. There was so much blood. It was gross and alarming and weird. I was too angry to cry so I just sat there for a long time, fuming, trying to devise a plan for how to make this *not* my reality. I didn't want to tell my mom. It was far too embarrassing, and I was never comfortable with this type of conversation.

Just a few years prior she had told me my older cousin started her period. I wanted to rip the words out of my ears. Why did I need to know that? And I guess now, in the same way, she would find it necessary to announce *my* misfortune to the family tree.

This whole thing is bullshit! I thought, still on the toilet. Pin prick tingles in my legs signaled I'd been sitting there for a while. I continued to silently rant in my head. *What do I even say to my mom? No way am I going to say the word* period *or any form of the word* menstruation. *Hell no. I don't even want to say the word* pad*! Why does she even have to know? Can I keep it a secret? No, because I don't have older sisters, and I don't have money or the ability to buy stupid PADS... oh my God that word again! I have to tell her. Oh great, and there's that pact I made with Samantha that whoever started first would tell the other one. Yeah, that's not happening either. Fuck fuck FUCK...*

I have no idea how long I actually stayed in the bathroom that day. The memory feels like it was an hour or two. In reality, it was probably twenty minutes. There was no way to disappear, no way to walk out of there. I was trapped by this stupid body and its stupid functions.

With no alternative I grabbed a washcloth and started the process of removing blood from my body. With a towel wrapped firmly around my waist I went to the closed door and yelled for my mom. Within a few short seconds she rattled the locked doorknob, "What? What's wrong?" I turned the lock and opened the door about two inches, just enough space to whisper the dreaded words: "I need pads. And underwear and jeans."

She asked if I needed help, and the *NO* was out of my mouth before she finished her sentence. She disappeared for a few minutes and returned with fresh clothes and a section of the previous week's newspaper. Through the narrow opening of the door, she said there were pads in the cabinet below the sink. She instructed me to put the newspaper in the cabinet and whenever I needed to throw away a used pad I was supposed to tear off a half page of newspaper and wrap it up before putting it into the garbage can.

Later that evening my first disposal came with the angry realization that my dad would know every time this happened to me because he would see big wads of newspaper-rolled pads in the garbage. He wouldn't think it was my mom; obviously he had the inside info on her situation, but he would totally know it was me. I wished for instant death that day. And every twenty-eight days thereafter.

A few months later Samantha came over to spend the night. She brought her overnight bag into my room, shut the door, and flopped onto the bed. With a big sigh she announced, "Well, I have something to tell you." She didn't actually say anything but pulled a neatly wrapped pad from her overnight bag and held it up like a smug lawyer producing the murder weapon at trial. She rolled her eyes, a look of annoyed embarrassment on her face. I didn't react but calmly responded, "Yeah I started in April."

"WHAT?!" If she had been a cartoon, her head would have blown off her neck like a rocket. I couldn't contain a laugh, seeing the animation play out in my mind. But it was not the right reaction at all. She was actually pissed. I think she tried to physically kick me.

"You TURD! You didn't tell me? We promised!" She folded her arms and flopped back against the wall, turning her head away from me.

"I'm sorry!" I whined. "It was too embarrassing!" She remained silent; her head still turned away. Part of me held out hope that her anger was playful like it was in other situations when we jokingly antagonized each other. It was quickly becoming clear to me that this was not the case. I really did break our pact. "Please don't be mad, I'm sorry. I couldn't say it; it was friggin' AWFUL! Like really really horrible, I wanted to be dead."

"Yeah, ya think? I didn't really look forward to coming over here and telling you, but I DID. I kept my end of the deal!" She looked away again, still fuming.

I felt terrible. I don't know why but I believed our experiences were totally different—mine far more traumatic somehow, thus excusing me from the pact. But a pact is a pact, and I'd selfishly let her down. I hadn't considered the hours of dread she must have experienced before coming over, not to mention packing up the stupid pads.

Shit, I'd have to tell her the newspaper disposal rule and then inform my mom.

Samantha eventually forgave me. It was the first time I really hurt her feelings, and I wouldn't forget it. However, the confusion stayed with me as well. I never expected her to be embarrassed and annoyed. I thought normal girls like her were more or less unfazed by periods. Sure, we'd long ago discussed the embarrassment and shared dread—that's how the pact came about in the first place. And we'd both read *Are You There God, It's Me Margaret.*

From my perspective, Samantha easily embraced all of the requirements of being a girl: carrying a purse, hair accessories, wearing pastel outfits and cute shoes, dresses, nail polish, and a whole host of other things. Consequently, those were all things I railed against and wanted no part of.

We were complete opposites that way, yet we were similar in our struggles with self-image. "At least your mom doesn't cut your hair," she'd say to me, complaining about her latest cut.

"Yeah, but sometimes she lets my grandma cut my bangs and that never goes well."

"You're lucky though. I wish I had blonde hair and blue eyes like you. My hair is basic old brown and there's so much iron in our water that it gets a weird texture," Samantha countered.

"I hate my hair, it's stupid. At least you're not fat. See this fat roll?" I gestured to my stomach. "My doctor called it a spare tire! I hate her. And speaking of bad haircuts, hers is the worst ever." I was irritated at the memory but laughed at my doctor's expense.

"What?!" Samantha was equal parts angry on my behalf and amused by my comment. She chuckled and said, "What a bitch. Is she skinny?"

"Hell no! And she's ugly too. She needs to worry about her own spare tire."

Weight was always a topic that loomed over us. Not just in our conversations, but everywhere and in everything around us. Our moms and grandmas crash dieted; it was the topic of TV shows and magazine stories. Samantha was not overweight as far as I could tell; she looked normal to me. But our bodies were starting to change with puberty, maybe that was the issue. Sometimes it's just a comment, like my doctor's, that skews a person's entire perspective and scars them forever.

"School pictures are tomorrow. What are you wearing?" I asked.

"Well…" Samantha sounded irritated, "I was going to wear that pink and white jumper, you know the one I wore to church Sunday?" I nodded affirmatively. "Until my aunt told me I looked like a giant Good & Plenty candy!"

"What the hell?" We were back in the familiar space of being angry but unable to stifle our laughter at the ridiculousness of the comment.

"Uh, yeah. She has no business criticizing anyone. You've seen the outfits she wears plus she doesn't even have enough sense to put on a friggin' bra before she leaves the house. Anyway, what are you wearing?"

"I don't know. It's between my E.T. shirt and my Pac-Man shirt, I haven't decided. And jeans, of course," I answered.

Samantha grinned. "Maybe you should wear your bandana and piss off your mom."

She was referring to the famous fifth grade class picture fight between me and my mom. I was determined to wear what I wanted: jeans, a Harley Davidson T-shirt, my knock off converse tennis shoes, and a red and blue bandana around my head. It wasn't the kind of bandana girls wear to keep their hair in place; it was a red handkerchief and a blue one rolled tight like ropes and braided together. And it was the primary point of contention.

My mom angrily conceded, "Well fine then! You want to look silly? Go ahead. You're gonna look like Willie Nelson in that photo and every one of your classmates will have a copy of it forever!"

The photo came back months later and I'm right there in the front row looking like a young Willie Nelson fan. In my opinion the outfit was the best thing I had going for me; it was my round face, spare tire, and tangled mess of hair that ruined the picture for me.

CHAPTER SEVEN

Eighth grade school year was off to a shitty start. To begin with, I'd just arrived in Kentucky two days prior. My dad's job change required us to move six hours away from our home and family in West Virginia. The only thing I knew about Kentucky was fried chicken and horses. My parents knew nobody; it was as if we'd landed on an island of strangers.

I'd been accustomed to starting school after Labor Day, so it was a shock to my system to step onto a crowded school bus on August 17. It took a while to find an empty seat, but once I did, I was promptly insulted by a boy who I believed to be just as "fat and ugly" as he said I was.

The school was unimpressive. It was a long single-floor building that stretched out in the shape of a T, like a prison. Starting with homeroom and throughout seven class periods I endured the embarrassment of each teacher stumbling over my last name. Students would snicker and whisper while I was forced to offer the correct pronunciation aloud. And once was never sufficient because inevitably the teacher would feel the need to give it a second attempt, which would still be wrong. I would have been content to let them say it wrong but without fail, they would say it as a question, requiring me to repeat it again.

Every class had assigned seats in alphabetical order, which meant the mouthy kid on my bus was always one or two seats behind me all day long. He'd kick the back of my desk or push it with his feet. If I turned to look at him or even turned my head to look out the window, he angrily told me to turn around. I day-dreamed of punching him in the face.

I missed my old school back home. There were jerks there too but at least I had enough friends and acquaintances to balance it out. It was just different here. I looked around and saw cliques of popular girls with big, permed hair and popular guys with parachute pants. Even the quiet kids seemed to stick together. I tried to figure out which kids might be most like me: awkward, slightly over-weight, and unable to afford name-brand clothes. But even those kids were closed off.

Very quickly I embraced being a loner. I felt grumpy most days and was determined no one would ever replace my best friend in West Virginia anyway so why bother. My parents told me it was a shitty attitude, and I wouldn't make friends with that mindset. *Duh. That's the point,* I thought. But to my parents' credit they recognized how difficult the move was for me and did what they could to make things better.

They gave me my own room or at least room/space instead of making me share with my little sister. I had the back half of the L-shaped downstairs family room. There was a door near my bed that opened to the backyard and small patio space. A more confident and social thirteen-year-old could have taken full advantage of the ability to sneak out, but I was basically a grumpy old troll. My parents had nothing to worry about.

It wasn't so bad having a room that connected to the TV room. We never had TVs in our bedrooms—not even my parents—so this was as close as I'd get. After school I'd come home, grab a snack, and head downstairs to turn on MTV or VH1 and watch music videos until dinnertime. I'd also start a letter to Samantha. We wrote to each other daily, and if my parents couldn't afford anything else at least they made it a priority to have plenty of stamps on hand at all times.

One evening, a couple of months into my new surroundings, I was stretched out on the floor of my room listening to music and writing to Samantha. It was routine to go back and proofread for mistakes or anything I may have forgotten to talk about before sealing the envelope. After this particular proofing something stood out to me. It wasn't just in this one letter, but the realization was that it was happening in all of the letters. We both adopted the habit of signing off with "love ya and miss ya like crazy," which is not a big deal between best friends, but my feelings were morphing into something else, and I couldn't make sense of it.

The questionable part of this particular letter was near the end when I said the song I was currently listening to made me think of her and I wrote out a couple lines of lyrics. It was a popular love song about missing someone. Why were love songs making me think of my best friend? Why did I spend much of the last paragraph of the letters telling her how much I missed her?

Samantha never responded to those things directly and probably didn't notice. She didn't send me song lyrics back. I'm sure to her it was nothing outside of the realm of normal best friendship. But something on my end was clearly off and I began to panic internally.

I closed up the letter, went to bed, and stared up at the ceiling. My brain started to string together a series of thoughts that shook me to my core:

You're acting like her boyfriend! Gross! You're weird. You're going to hell. Moving to Kentucky is your punishment, you did this. This is all YOUR fault for having these weird feelings toward your best friend. You're sick. This miserable life, 300 miles away from your family and friends is YOUR fault.

It was the worst epiphany ever. Through muffled sobs I begged God to forgive me. I chanted a litany of apologies. I tried to reason with God. *No, see I'm not weird! I've never wanted to kiss her, and I still don't! I can't be... weird. I don't feel this way toward any of my other female friends. If I were… weird, I'd like all of the girls, and I'd want to kiss them, but I don't. Not even Samantha, I have no desire to kiss her at all!*

I was thirteen. What exactly did I know about being "weird" or gay? My mind immediately went to what my mom had told me years prior: "Gay people are sick in the head; there's something wrong with them." She told me that Catholics don't believe in being gay; it's against our religion. It's a sin. Her disgust was evident, and I felt ashamed just hearing the explanation.

There were no gay people on TV, no gay talk show hosts. God help you if you were in rural West Virginia and gay. Samantha's family was much more forward-thinking and accepting than my conservative family. She had a second or third cousin, a thirty-something man named Jim, who was gay. I met him a couple of times when I tagged along with her to family events or to her grandma's house. I knew *gay* meant he liked men and not women, but he didn't seem unusual or any different than any other person. Eventually Jim decided to leave West Virginia. He moved to a place called Homosassa, Florida. People in our rural town found it quite funny and appropriate that he went to live in "Homo's asses, Florida," as they liked to call it.

Being gay could never EVER be an option.

CHAPTER EIGHT

Between my visit to West Virginia and her extended visit in Kentucky, I spent most of the summer before high school with Samantha. I was happy and laughing and life felt fun for the first time in almost a year. We passed the time watching music videos, listening to records by Prince and Culture Club, reading Stephen King novels, and eating. Lots of eating. Sometimes we took walks if the humidity wasn't insufferable.

I wasn't thinking about God during this time. I don't know if I censored my letters after having that mental breakdown back in the fall, but I believed and accepted that living in Kentucky was a punishment from God for my sins. I loved Samantha but not in an "in love with" kind of way. I didn't look at her and feel any kind of physical attraction; however, I did like sitting in close proximity to her. Sometimes I wondered if it meant I was weird or abnormal but that line of thinking always made me question why I seemed more like a boy than a girl, a thought that set off alarms of eternity in hell. It was better to not think about any of this stuff if at all possible.

After Samantha returned home, the reality of high school was only a few short weeks away and anxiety was creeping in. I remembered the cruel kids on the bus and in my classes. What if ninth grade was a repeat of the horrible eighth grade experience? I still looked in the mirror every day and hated the fat ugly reflection staring back at me. Why did I always seem to forget how awful I looked until I saw a mirror? It was always a disappointment. The same thing happened when I saw my eighth-grade school photo. I hated it so much that I begged my mom not to send it out to family members.

The thought of another year of cruel insults and rejection was too much. I needed to blend in and become invisible.

My grandparents were preparing to visit and take us shopping for school clothes. When money was tight, they always helped keep us clothed. There was a shopping trip before school started, one in the winter, and one in the spring.

Instead of my usual blue jeans, T-shirts, and sneakers I decided to pick out girly clothes and shoes. I asked for makeup and a stupid purse. I'd have to figure out how to choose and maintain a hairstyle too.

I needed my parents to not think I was weird and to not think I was too attached to Samantha. I needed my peers to not think I was a fat, disgusting tomboy with a ridiculous last name. I just wanted to be invisible, to meet the basic criteria of "female," and blend into the crowd.

As soon as the school year started, I realized that being feminine was a whole lot of *work*. The clothes were uncomfortable and there was way too much prep time required before leaving the house. Applying makeup was the least annoying part simply because I loved art. Hair styling, on the other hand, was complete and total bullshit. Before each hair appointment, I would find a photo in a magazine of some celebrity or model, tear it out, and take it to the salon with me. I'd show the stylist and explain exactly what I wanted only to walk out of there looking nothing like the photo.

Even if the stylist got it pretty close, I could never make it look like that on my own. The next day I'd shower and as the water hit my hair the panic would set in. By the time I was dressed and had the hair dryer plugged in, I'd be overwhelmed with the task at hand. If I were lucky enough to get one side of my head looking similar to what the stylist had done, then it was guaranteed the other side—

usually my left since I'm right-handed—would be all kinds of wrong.

I didn't understand how women did this every day.

Every Sunday morning my mom woke up two hours before we had to leave for church so she could shower and do her hair and makeup. Now I was attempting to do the same thing every weekday before school. But why did it have to be like this? Didn't women like to sleep?

I was so envious of my dad and brother who could roll out of bed and be showered, dressed, and out the door in fifteen minutes. They never had to preheat a curling iron or spend an extra three minutes in the shower waiting for their deep conditioner to work. They never left the house with mascara in their eyes or uneven foundation. They didn't have to coordinate shoes and accessories and fill their lungs with hair spray. They never had a panic attack wondering if they forgot to unplug the curling iron.

Being a girl felt ridiculous. I was checking the boxes, going through the motions to fix my external appearance, yet every day it felt like a failed magic trick. But unlike the magic kit I got for Christmas one year, I couldn't give up and throw myself in the back of the closet to wait for trash day. As tempting as it was, it wasn't an option.

So, I went through my school days trying to be invisible. Instead of talking to other people I carried an extra notebook and wrote to Samantha. My attitude hadn't changed since the previous year, I still didn't want new friends. But I was also a rule-follower and raised to not be rude so on the rare occasion some other kid spoke to me, I answered. This is how I became friends with Terry.

We were assigned seats next to one another in freshman English. I had noticed him in eighth grade because he always wore a black Members Only jacket zipped all the way to the top as far as it would zip. It was a popular jacket. I had a knock-off version. I remembered him not just because of his cool jacket but because of a particular habit we had in common. Terry repeatedly pulled and tugged at the waistline of his jacket the way people do when they are trying to smooth their shirt from clinging to their stomach and to keep it from riding up. I did this and so did my grandma.

I didn't judge him for this habit or for the couple extra pounds he carried. It was a strange point of connection.

Now in ninth grade and sitting next to one another, it wasn't long before Terry and I struck up a conversation that quickly became a friendship. He was hilarious, catty, sarcastic, and self-deprecating. He was not into sports but liked all of the same books, movies, and music that I liked. We both struggled with self-esteem and had suffered a lot of teasing around weight, appearance, and for looking or acting gay.

Pretty soon other kids started to assume we were a couple since we were always talking and laughing together. We went with it since we had such a great friendship anyway.

Our relationship was a safe space and a lot of fun but not a romance. Sex was a non-issue because my Catholic upbringing said it was a sin to have sex before marriage and Terry never pushed for it anyway. He wasn't Catholic but had a very similar moral up-bringing.

Being a couple meant that we walked to classes together, held hands in the hallway, and went to the movies on weekends or spent a few hours at his house or mine. And now we each had a significant other. We could check off that social requirement.

CHAPTER NINE

At the back-to-school dance sophomore year, Terry and I stayed on the dance floor all evening. During a slow song he went to find something to drink and cool off. I noticed a couple of boys standing against the wall watching everyone dance. They had been there all night in the same spot. One was short and stocky, a quiet ginger kid named Dave who was in my first period gym class. The other guy was tall with big feet, long skinny legs, a bowl style haircut and lots of freckles. His name was Lou, and he was in my homeroom and health class. I noticed them in much the same way that I'd noticed Terry: recognizing a particular awkwardness that we all shared. None of us fit easily into the stereotypical social groups. We weren't attractive, popular, rich, athletic, nerdy, super smart, or in band or theater. We didn't get into fights and didn't do drugs or break the law. Each of us existed somewhere on the periphery, a social purgatory of sorts.

With the night coming to an end, I felt bad for these two guys who stood for two hours and watched all the fun instead of participating. I walked over and asked the tall guy, Lou, if he wanted to dance. He seemed a little surprised but said yes. We made small talk, and it turned out his family recently moved into my neighborhood. We rode the same bus, but I hadn't noticed him in the back seat. The song ended and we parted ways with a "see ya around."

It was very different dancing with Lou although I couldn't quite put my finger on it. In my head all I could come up with was that he seemed like a guy. It didn't make sense to me because Terry was a guy too. There was a very distinct difference between the two, but I couldn't home in on it.

Over the next few days, I started to talk to Lou and his friends on the bus, then in homeroom or health class. He sat two seats behind me and would sometimes stick his long leg out across the aisle and pretend to trip me. A couple of weeks later Lou asked me to meet him at a school football game. I'd never gone to the games because I didn't like football. I said yes with the understanding that it was not a date, just friends. But deep down I knew I was headed in a direction that was going to end my ten-month relationship and possibly even my friendship with Terry.

Accepting the invitation to the football game was self-serving on my part. Even though I didn't find Lou attractive, something drew me to him. I didn't know what it was except that it was the opposite of what drew me to Terry. Lou was not the kind of guy that anyone would ever call *gay*; he was macho to the point of homophobic, which he made known in his snide remarks about Terry. Had I been a stronger person, a better person, with healthy self-esteem and integrity, I would have defended Terry and told Lou to fuck off with his mean comments. But I didn't. It was intimidating, and I feared conflict.

On the other hand, Lou gave off a little bit of a bad-boy vibe and something about that appealed to me. Terry was my best friend, and I loved him like a best friend, but I was tired of people looking at us like the queer couple. I wasn't comfortable feeling more masculine than he was; selfishly, I was trying my damnedest to just blend into the crowd and not draw attention to myself.

I had no idea that I was changing the course of my life forever.

Once I took on the girlfriend role with Lou it was a blur of red flags. He lived exactly a mile away from me across the subdivided neighborhood and insisted we hang out at his house every day and not mine, mostly because my parents had rules and his did not. He refused to walk with me or even meet me halfway, which required me to lie to my parents, who didn't allow me to walk across the neighborhood alone. I quickly convinced them that he always met me up the street, a spot not visible from the window.

Lou's parents were older than mine, his stepdad considerably older than his mom. She was quiet and reserved but still friendly and warm. I watched in horror the first time Lou yelled at her and made demands. It didn't take long to realize this was the status quo; he told her what he wanted, be it money, a ride, some material possession, beer (we were both fifteen), or pizza. If she hesitated or attempted to say no, he became loud, obnoxious, and rude, talking down to her as if *he* were the parent.

One of the first nights I visited his house he told his mom he was ordering pizza. He didn't ask me what I liked or what I wanted, he simply called and ordered a medium pizza with extra cheese and mushrooms. I told him I didn't like mushrooms, and his response was to say, "Oh well" and laugh. That was the first of an average of three pizza orders a week, always with extra cheese and mushrooms. He never asked if I wanted something different. I never brought it up again and relegated myself to picking out all of the little pieces of chopped mushrooms that were under the cheese, in the cheese, and on the cheese. It was impossible. Eventually I learned to like mushrooms. I never told my parents or friends how he acted because this level of selfish spoiled brat was so foreign to me. It was shocking.

Seeing each other every day meant it was only a matter of time before the rage he directed at his family members was aimed at me, like the day I was invited to go with Lou's family to dinner at his aunt's house. I arrived at Lou's on time, but his parents weren't ready to leave yet; it was going to be a while longer. So, we went to the TV room downstairs to watch music videos. Madonna's

"True Blue" led into Aerosmith, Whitney Houston, Genesis, and then Winger. Lou turned the channel with no warning.

"Hey! I love that song, turn it back."

Lou scoffed. "Seriously? That guy's a faggot."

I laughed, "Why? Because he looks like a male model and gets tons of girls? You love Poison and they wear so much makeup they might actually *be* gay. Just turn it back, I really like that song."

"Whatever," he mumbled and complied with my request. Minutes later the video ended, and the stream continued.

"How many people will be at your aunt's house for dinner?" I asked. He didn't respond and was still staring at the TV. "Hey… did you hear me?" I chuckled, thinking he was lost in the music video. My dad did this same thing all the time; we'd usually have to yell because he got so into his shows. But Lou didn't even turn his head. He aggressively scooted further down the couch away from me. It was so odd that I laughed.

"Where are you going?" I scooted down next to him still grinning at this silly game he was playing. It was totally unlike him.

Without a word he shot up off the couch and moved to the chair. His eyes never left the TV, but I noticed his jaw was set and he looked furious.

"What's wrong? What are you doing?" I felt my stomach churn. He didn't answer, didn't look at me. Something was way off, but I had no idea what had happened. I waited several seconds for him to respond. Nothing. Just silence, his eyes glaring into the TV.

"What did I do? Just tell me, please." I blinked back tears and waited but he refused to speak or make eye contact. "Is it the Winger video? Are you mad because I wanted to watch it?"

More silence. I had no idea what was going on. Nothing like this had ever happened to me before, not with Lou, Terry, not even with my parents.

"I'm sorry. I… I don't know what I did to make you mad but I'm sorry. What did I do? Please tell me."

No response. Lou was a gargoyle hunched in the chair, eyes glaring straight ahead from beneath furrowed brows, one clenched fist against his temple, the other arm folded tightly across his chest.

It was too much to take in. I fixed my eyes on the blue shag carpet at my feet and watched it become a watery kaleidoscope. Like two statues we sat under a silence so heavy I feared the ceiling might collapse in on us. I needed to get out.

After a handful of false starts I felt my body rise on shaky legs and move toward the stairs. "I… I'm going home." The words were careful, slow, and avalanche-proof, or so I thought.

"If you walk out that door we're DONE!" Lou's booming voice pressed *pause* on my exit.

"But you don't want me here, I'm…"

"I SAID, if you walk out that door we're DONE!"

Rewind. I was back in my seat in silence. It would be several hours, an awkward family dinner, and a silent car ride back to Lou's house before he would look at or speak to me. There was no acknowledgement of the day-long silent treatment, no apology, and no explanation. He held my hand walking into the house, offered me a soda and then initiated a make-out session as if nothing happened.

I'm not sure why I continued to stay with Lou other than the fear response in my brain was overriding all logic. And I was fifteen. Maybe if I had been able to make a clean break, I might have tried but Lou was on my bus, lived in the same neighborhood, and we were in some classes together at school. Asking my parents for help was also out of the question. I knew they would want me to stay away from him which would only add to the problem. My dad was very protective of his family and had a volatile temper. I felt stuck.

At least Lou's behavior was predictably unpredictable. His cold-shoulder rages were guaranteed to happen, but I rarely knew the when or why. There was never an apology or explanation when it was over: He'd simply flip a switch, act normal, and want to make out.

Over time I adapted to the dysfunction in the way someone adapts to another person's bratty toddler. But I learned quickly not to let my guard down and express my irritation.

I made that mistake one night when he yelled at me for hanging out with my friend Darcy at a party. Even though he had been preoccupied playing with fireworks, he suddenly berated me for being "stuck up her ass all night" instead of hanging out with him.

"She came home from school with me to hang out; of course I'm going to talk to her." I lowered my voice, hoping Lou would do the same but knowing with certainty that he wouldn't. The emotions I'd been stuffing for months ignited my words: "You're fucking embarrassing me!"

Lou lunged forward, gripped the front of my shirt with both hands and slammed me up against the house, pinning me there as he shouted in my face. With an extra shove he released his hold, slinging his hands free of my shirt as if he'd heaved a trash bag into a dumpster. He stomped off into the dark leaving me physically shaking and in tears.

When he approached a few minutes later, my first thought was to run until I saw the anguished look on his face.

"I'm so sorry. I don't know what happened." His voice shook and I was shocked to see tears rolling down his cheeks. He brushed his sleeve over his face, sniffling, and looked at me with desperation. "I just love you so much and I can't imagine losing you, and I don't know why I did that but I'm so sorry."

He pulled me close, wrapping me into a bear hug. The crook of my neck filled with his tears, hot breath, and a litany of *I'm sorrys*. I was still crying. I relaxed into his embrace and rested there for a minute, trying to get my bearings.

"It's… okay. It's okay." I said, unsure if my words were for Lou or myself. "It's okay."

That was the largest display of regret I ever witnessed, and I soaked it in. He had never apologized for anything before, so he must really mean it. And he was crying. Guys never cry so this must be a remorse so painful that I needed to comfort him. So, I did. I hugged him, I comforted him, I held him. I told him it was okay and that I loved him too, that he didn't have to keep apologizing. He confessed his sin, and I forgave with love. That's what Jesus said to do.

There were plenty of reasons to feel sorry for him in general. Maybe that's how I justified his horrible behavior. I'd heard stories about his rough childhood: how much his stepdad hated him and how much he missed his grandpa who had helped raise him but was now in a nursing home with Alzheimer's. He struggled in school and wasn't very academically inclined. Yet at the end of the day, he loved me, or so I believed.

And he was a macho guy, one whose sexuality was never questioned, which meant that my sexuality was never questioned. He was simultaneously the most dangerous person in my life and somehow the safest.

CHAPTER TEN

On a cold November weeknight, I arrived at Lou's house. Our routine had been the same for the entire six weeks since becoming a couple: I walked to his house at 5:30, greeted his parents, and went to his room. He placed an order for a medium, thin crust pizza with extra cheese and mushrooms and we watched the little thirteen-inch TV in his room until it arrived. After the pizza we headed downstairs to the basement family room and took over the big TV as his parents said goodnight and went to their bedroom upstairs. They were much older than most other parents and rather unsuspecting. They didn't police our activity and seemed unconcerned with two hormonal teens left unsupervised behind closed doors. I attributed a good deal of his parents' attitude to the spoiled-brat nature of my boyfriend. I'd never met anyone who would bully their own mother and talk down to her.

Once we made it to the family room, Lou switched the channel to MTV for an endless string of music videos. He loved the hair bands of the 80s and I hated them. The make-out session always started without delay. Though I hated my body and had never had my clothes off in front of anyone before, my fear of Lou's rage and silent treatment had settled us into a routine: I'd push his hands away, trying to cover parts of my body that he uncovered, and he continued to do the opposite until I sensed he was getting irritated. Then I gave in.

Nothing in my fifteen-year-old mind understood how fucked up this was. I truly thought that agreeing to be his girlfriend obligated me to whatever physical demands he made. I thought that was how relationships worked: Men were in charge. I saw it in movies and on television. In some ways I saw it in real life. My mom, grandmas, and aunts all deferred to their husbands. Everyone went out of their way to keep the men happy. Complaints about a husband's behavior or attitude were always whispered between females.

Throughout our relationship, I had made sure to remind Lou multiple times that I needed to remain a virgin until marriage. He didn't really respond to those comments and seemed to carry on like they were never spoken. Without fail in the heat of the moment he would push and push the boundaries. I did what I could to placate him even when it wasn't what I wanted to do. It seemed that if I could keep him satisfied in any other way possible without sacrificing my virginity, things would be okay.

Lou was quite persistent, and the end goal always seemed to be a shameless groping of my girl parts and his hand shoving mine into his pants. I'd learned that a hand job was my ticket out of the basement and meant I could go home. If my good Catholic up-bringing taught me anything it was *don't question authority*. Stand, sit, kneel, and respond at the appropriate times and keep quiet until the service is over.

But on this particular night on the blue shag carpet of the family room things were going too far. Our clothes were unbuttoned, unzipped, and he was on top of me. I thought he was going to try to have sex with me and I panicked. "No, I can't…" I said several times before adding, "and I don't want to get pregnant." That seemed like a good way to kill the mood.

He responded with a very irritated, "Fine!" rolled off of me and onto his side, propped on his elbow, pouting and glaring at the TV. He didn't fix his open jeans, but angrily flipped the hem of his T-shirt down to cover himself. In the short time we'd been a couple there were two constants: the unpredictability of his anger and the expectation that he was never left sexually frustrated. I stayed perfectly still on my back so as not to provoke him more than I already had. After a few awkward moments I felt very exposed and self-conscious, my pants and shirt still undone and disheveled. I slowly started to roll away from him until he reached out with one arm and stopped me, pulling me back so that we were in a spooning position.

For a minute I was surprised that he had not angrily shoved me away. Maybe he was trying to cool off and we could just watch TV. Those thoughts barely had time to register before I was face down on my stomach and he was on top of me.

He was nearly six feet tall, 185 pounds to my five feet three inches, 135 pounds which made it easy for him to keep me pinned to the floor and eventually pull my jeans down despite my attempts to prevent him. "Wait... stop... STOP."

He ignored my protests. I felt skin against skin.

In my fifteen-year-old virgin-naivety I thought being face down prevented access to the parts of my body he wanted. This hope was shattered by a forceful, searing pain that reflexively launched my chest up off the floor. I cried out and told him he was hurting me and tried to reach back with my hands to push his hips away, but he didn't stop.

It was over quickly. I don't remember him getting up. I don't remember if we exchanged words, and I don't remember fixing my clothes and leaving. My memory picks up midway through the mile-long walk home. *Curfew. Don't be late. Don't get in trouble.* It was cold, dark, and suburban quiet. I passed house after house in our subdivided neighborhood, all full of families in front of TVs, completely oblivious to what I'd just experienced.

When my house came into view, I felt a brief sense of relief and an urge to run the rest of the distance to the front door. But the thought of my parents finding out what had happened brought me to a full stop. *Fuck! Don't cry, don't cry.* I choked back tears and checked my watch. Sometimes my dad would be waiting at the door if I was even two minutes late. "You should have left two minutes earlier!" he would say.

I entered the house and went straight to the bathroom to see what was happening with my body. I was terrified and unsure if I'd been permanently damaged or injured. My gut instinct was telling me I needed to go to the hospital but to do that I'd have to tell my parents.

I can't tell them. How would I even say it? I can't say it. I can't go to the hospital. But… what if I do nothing and get some sort of infection or something bad happens?

They would take me if I told them what had happened, but I felt that eventually I'd be punished for lying to them and putting myself in that situation. I'd been letting them believe that Lou's parents supervised my visits and had the same house rules as theirs.

I imagined their words and their anger, particularly how angry my dad would be at Lou: not just furious but dangerous, and he'd surely go directly to his house in a rage. I could easily see him in an altercation with Lou's dad or even with Lou himself. I wasn't sure if he'd take a gun with him either. What if he did something and got arrested? My mom didn't have a job or a driver's license, and we lived paycheck to paycheck. What the hell would happen to us if my dad went to jail?

"Hurry up, I gotta go!" My brother banged on the bathroom door. I took a quick shower and went straight to bed, having as little interaction with my family as possible. Once alone in the privacy of my dark bedroom, I begged God's forgiveness. What was I supposed to do for the rest of my life if I was already going to be sent to hell?

CHAPTER ELEVEN

When you're fifteen and trying to fit in with your peers, there are two things that will put you on the map: having a boyfriend or girlfriend and having sex. I now had both. The next day at school, word got around in our social circle that we were no longer virgins. I hadn't expected the high-fives, shocked faces, and whispers asking for details. My fragile ego soaked it all up. For the first time in my life, I felt like one of the cool kids. It made me feel like an adult, and that was way better than feeling like I was going to hell. I embraced it fully.

Besides, I never understood the rule about saving sex for marriage. I figured it was about loving the person you were with and staying monogamous. In that sense it still seemed that being married was more of a technicality or a means of making the whole thing official in the church, like announcing it to the world and celebrating with God or something.

Lou said he loved me and wanted to be together forever. Surely sex outside of marriage couldn't be all that sinful if it was just with one person who loved me, right?

There wasn't much choice in the matter anyway. The excuse of "saving myself for marriage" was gone. Sex was now a free-for-all daily occurrence. Lou managed to get some condoms but quickly decided that it felt better for him without them. I brought up the pregnancy thing again in an effort to snap him back to reality, but he was unconcerned. I knew from health class that pulling out was not safe sex, but I could only argue my point so far before setting off a fight.

So, I turned to something I learned in catechism class. Instead of asking God for things, it's better to say prayers of thanks in advance, *knowing* with unwavering faith that God will fulfill your need. I changed my desperate nightly prayers to "Thank you God for not letting me get pregnant."

Within a span of a few short months our relationship became very streamlined and simple. We were either having sex or fighting. Any other activity between us was guaranteed to end in sex or a fight or both.

I'd learned how to navigate the majority of Lou's trigger points by then but much of what pissed him off was out of my control. He was incredibly jealous. It wasn't just guys on TV or guys at school, he was also jealous of the girls I talked to. If I was invited to stay over at someone's house, he got angry because that meant I wouldn't be at *his* house. If I invited someone to stay at my house, I had to bring her to his house with me, and she would have to leave the room when he wanted to have sex. If one of his friends was over, he would tell the guy to sit in the closet and shut the door while we had sex. Whatever I did and whomever I did it with had to be cleared by Lou first; another set of nonsensical rules to follow. Life was full of them it seemed.

Deep down I knew the relationship was unhealthy. In addition to the skewed power dynamic between us, we had nothing in common, no shared interests. Yet breaking up was a lifeboat I was too scared to jump into. As weeks turned into months it drifted further and further away until it was a dot on the horizon, impossible to reach.

Oh well. Things would be way worse if I broke up with him anyway, I reasoned. I'd still have to see Lou at school every day and on the bus. He'd hate me, glare at me, and call me things I'd heard him call other girls: fat bitch, whore, slut, fat ass, ugly skank. I'd lose most of my friends too since they were Lou's friends first.

There were no good options. Even if I garnered the courage to break it off, I'd be in a lifeboat with no oars.

So, I stayed onboard a slowly sinking ship and pretended it was a party yacht. That's kinda how life was on *General Hospital*. I'd been watching that soap opera with my mom since I was ten. The relationships were dramatic and volatile. Happiness was *always* short-lived.

At one point, my parents became concerned about my obsession with the show. "Do you understand this is not real life?" they asked me. "Yeah, of course!" I told them, annoyed that they asked. *Duh, it's impossible to find that many beautiful people in the same town.*

There was nothing fictional about the drama and scheming I was experiencing. Lou had minimal to no parental oversight and as a result, fewer hangups about breaking rules. Late one night close to my curfew Lou decided he would drive me home. At fifteen, neither of us had a driver's license or a learner's permit. I was shocked at the suggestion and thought he was joking until he put on his shoes, grabbed his mom's keys, and opened his bedroom window.

"We're going out this way, so they don't hear the front door," he whispered as he motioned me over to the windowsill.

"But… won't they hear the car start up?" I asked.

"That's why we're rolling it out of the driveway in neutral. I know what I'm doing, just come on!"

He unlocked the driver's door of his mom's old gray Chevy Nova and slid into its brick red interior. "I'm going to steer. You go to the front of the car and when it starts to roll, push me out of the driveway."

"Push?! By myself?" I was so out of my element.

"Yes!" he hissed, "The driveway slopes down a little, it will roll, and I'll be pushing off with one leg while I steer."

Clearly, he'd done this before. I watched him sit on the edge of the driver's seat, door open with one long leg of his six-foot frame outside the car. He put it in neutral and we pushed. It rolled relatively easily. I watched as he cut the wheel hard, backing it close to the curb, leaving room for oncoming cars to pass. He motioned for me to get in.

"Shut the door just enough for it to latch; we'll shut it harder when we get going," he instructed.

I looked at the house. "Won't they still hear the engine start?"

"That's why we're going to wait until another car drives by, then I'll start it. I know what I'm doing; don't worry about it."

I said a silent prayer that we wouldn't get caught and that a passing car would appear soon. I had fifteen minutes before curfew. We sat quietly until headlights beamed on the houses up the street. A car was approaching from around the corner.

"Okay, here we go..." Lou said. The oncoming car made its way toward us. As it was passing, he turned the key, and the engine started.

"Holy shit!" I blurted out in disbelief. Lou looked at me and we laughed. He drove through the neighborhood like a pro making his way along the familiar mile-long route to my house.

We were more than halfway there when I started to panic about getting caught. I lived on a corner lot with clear views of approaching traffic in all directions. "Shit, you can't pull into my driveway. My mom will hear the car and look out the window. Just drop me off now, and I'll walk the rest of the way."

"I know, I know..." Lou said, "we still have a few minutes, I'm going to drive around."

Lou drove past the house, continued up the hill and turned onto a cross street with a cul-de-sac. He put the car in park and cut the engine. "Okay, scoot over here. You're driving."

"WHAT?" I stared in disbelief, unmoving. I watched him walk through the headlight beams, around to my side. He opened my door.

"Scoot! You're going to learn how to drive."

More intrigued than scared, I slid across the seat and waited for the next instruction.

"Reach down below the seat and pull that lever." In unison we nudged the bench seat forward so I could reach the pedals.

"Okay, put your foot on the brake and then turn the key—not your left foot, numb nuts! You only drive with your right foot unless it's a stick shift." I made the correction, turned the key, and the engine came alive. My heart felt like it rattled in unison.

"Alright. Keep your foot on the brake and put it in drive."

"Got it." I answered through shallow breaths.

"Now let off the brake and give it some gas." Lou said.

The car began to move very slowly despite my foot barely touching the accelerator. The familiarity I knew as a passenger in the Chevy Nova was gone. The hood seemed to have doubled in width. It was a giant machine now, rolling mostly of its own accord. I gripped the wheel as if I were sitting atop a bull about to be released from its enclosure.

Sensing my fear, Lou offered encouragement. "You're doing okay; you're fine. Give it a little more gas."

I pressed my foot down just a little and the car lurched forward. "Shit!" I let off again.

Lou laughed, "You're okay! I'm not going to let you run off the road; you're fine!"

As we approached the cul-de-sac, I pressed the brake and brought the car to a stop. Without making eye contact I admitted defeat. "I don't think I can steer this thing around the circle."

"Yes, you can!" Lou said, amused. "It's just a circle. Come on, I'll help you steer if you get stuck." He scooted to the middle of the bench seat next to me, his long legs still in the passenger floorboard, and coached me around the circle. It was a choppy drive, but I did it and we laughed our way back to where we started.

In moments like these Lou genuinely enjoyed breaking me out of my fearful, rule-following shell. His vocal disdain for my parents' rules matched my own unspoken opinions. It was easy to lean into his bold ability to break them.

It's no surprise that my first experiences with alcohol were with Lou. His parents supplied it on special occasions with the condition that no one left the house on foot or behind the wheel. I didn't like the taste of beer, so he got his mom to buy wine coolers. The first time I had some was on New Year's Eve. He cut me off after I became tipsy and coached me on how to handle myself when my dad arrived to pick me up. "Don't try to have a conversation, just get in the back seat and say you're really tired. Then go straight to bed when you get home, and you'll be fine by morning." He was right. I was quickly learning how much fun could be had when I was brave enough to lie to my parents.

But some lies were just too risky. Like the day we were off school, and Lou's mom took the bus to work. Lou decided to take the Chevy Nova and go to the mall, thirteen miles away. (He still wasn't old enough for a driver's license.) I held my ground on that one and stayed home. He took his best friend Dave instead.

Later that summer when Dave got his license and an old Ford LTD, I found myself lying regularly. My parents didn't allow me to go joy riding. I had to have a specific destination, a time of arrival, and a time of return. So, I just lied and told them what they wanted to hear. I'd ride in the front seat of Dave's car between the two guys without a seat belt as we flew up and down old country roads. "Hill-hopping" they called it: trying to go airborne over small hills and dips in the road. I'd watch the speedometer climb with a mix of terror and excitement. It was another high, another moment to feel cool, to feel normal with no demands on my body or my salvation, aside from the lie I told my parents in order to go.

CHAPTER TWELVE

How many times could I thank God for preventing an unwanted pregnancy? A lot. My luck or my faith ran out by spring break of my junior year. I lied to my parents about Lou's mom being off work that week so I could spend nearly every day at his house, having sex and fighting as usual. There were only a few short weeks until junior prom and all of the stress that comes with it: the most obvious being the pink monstrosity of a gown I had to wear. An equally large problem that was hidden to everyone except me was that my period was due to start a day or two before prom.

I kept a small pocket calendar to track my cycle, as instructed by mom years earlier. I had so much shame around this monthly event that I couldn't bear to write any words or abbreviations for it. Putting a big circle around the date was too obvious. I feared anyone who happened to flip through this little calendar would immediately guess what it meant. So, I opted for a much more subtle mark: a small thin circle around the numbers, in black fine point ink. If you flipped the pages, you'd never notice it.

But prom night came and went without blood. I'd been late before and had the usual panic but pushed it out of my head and replaced it with holy begging and pleading.

The school year was nearly over, and my period was still late, three weeks and counting. I didn't say anything to Lou, having learned my lesson early on about pregnancy scares. He was always a total jerk yet still refused to use condoms. He said it didn't feel as good for him despite knowing I couldn't go on the pill or get an IUD without the involvement of my parents.

One morning during those final days of school we had one of our typical fights. We parted ways to our first period class with an "I'm done, it's over." This happened so regularly that I knew to just show up at our normal meeting spots after each class and stand next to him until he was ready to speak to me.

The day wore on and I stood by while he talked to other people and ignored me entirely. I tried holding his hand and he jerked away from me without a word. It was like I didn't exist, but it was also the norm for these situations. I was used to it.

At the end of the school day he left, still in silence. I started to panic a little because usually things were resolved by lunch time. There were never words of apology or asking to reunite. I'd just wait for him to start acting like nothing ever happened but this time he didn't.

All evening, I waited for him to call but he never did. It was a Friday, and he had to work so I couldn't call him. I knew he would be out all night and sleeping until Saturday afternoon.

Lou had started a part-time job at a pizza place in order to afford gas and insurance on the old blue Cutlass his parents bought him. A lot of teens worked at Big Jon's Pizza.

Lou made new friends there and was falling into a routine of going out drinking and partying after the Friday and Saturday closing shifts. The shop closed a full hour after my midnight curfew so we both knew I'd never be part of his weekend plans. On Saturday I caught him by phone long enough to ask if we were back together and he said no. I was shocked. Actually, I was more than shocked. I was frantic and nearly hysterical at the rejection. The fight we had that set off this chain of events was petty as were most of our fights. It was nothing of importance to our relationship that would be a reason to break up.

I did all of the things a teenager knows to do in this situation: I called my friends and cried, I had my friends call his friends and ask why and what was wrong. I think I even called some of his friends myself. Somewhere in all of the calls, someone told me, "He just wants his own space." That was all I needed to hear to understand that his own "space" was drinking and partying all night on the weekends with his new coworkers. I was devastated.

I had a friend named Sharon who was a year ahead of me, a senior. She was graduating that week and had a baby girl named Amy who was three months old. I talked to her a lot about the breakup because she had a volatile relationship with her baby's daddy. I also confided to her that I might be pregnant.

There were a lot of long-distance calls to Samantha too. I cried a lot and slept all the time when I wasn't working my fast-food job.

****

Weeks went by. Lou rarely spoke to me, but every few days I'd usually hear from him in a brief phone call. He would ask me to come over to his house. He was no longer living in the same neighborhood; his parents had moved to an apartment about ten minutes away.

I would get my hopes up thinking he wanted to get back together. He'd pick me up or my dad would let me borrow the car and I'd drive over. He wouldn't really say anything to me, but after a few minutes he would initiate sex. I took this as a sign that he wanted to be with me, evidence of us getting back together. But when the sex was over, he would go cold again and stop talking to me. If I asked if we were going to get back together, he would get mad at me for bringing it up. He would either tell me to leave or grab his car keys and storm out of the room: my cue to follow him because he was taking me home in angry silence.

I never gave up on this scenario and fell for it time and time and time again. He would tell me to come over, we would have sex, and then I'd be told to leave. I guess I figured he must still love me if he kept inviting me over. The alternative was too traumatic to think about: being dumped, fat, ugly, unwanted. And probably pregnant.

My last period was March 27, and it was now the end of June. It wasn't looking good. I kept ignoring my intuition. I was tired, and no matter how much I slept it wasn't enough. I felt sick from the stress of the breakup and the push/pull game Lou was playing. It was easier to sleep than to be awake and depressed.

By the second week of July, I agreed to get a pregnancy test at the urging of both Sharon and Samantha, who I'd been calling regularly now that I had a job and could pay the long-distance charges each month. According to Sharon's calculations, I was nearing the end of my first trimester and would probably start showing soon. She told me about the health clinic where she had her pregnancy test done and offered to drive me.

It was a quick visit, only the few minutes it took to pee on a stick and be told it was positive. The nurse consulted a calendar and said my due date was January 3, 1989, right in the middle of my senior year of high school. She handed me a piece of paper with the test result on it and the date. I folded it up and stuck it in the back pocket of my jeans.

I braced for the tears, panic, and fear I'd been carrying to explode from my head like a mushroom cloud. Oddly it didn't. It faded to complete silence.

On autopilot, I slept, ate canned tomato soup—the only food that sounded palatable—and showed up at work when scheduled. I felt separated from the rest of the world as if I were watching my life from behind glass, like a TV show. Nothing was funny, amusing, or even sad anymore.

But the pain was still there; it didn't go away. It no longer manifested as tears, words, and sobs. It was a brick in my stomach and a knot in the back of my throat. When I moved, it hurt and when I would lie perfectly still, it hurt. Relief was only possible when I was sleeping.

My brain refused to play out a scenario of my telling Lou I was pregnant. It refused to play out the scenario of telling my parents, too—also unbearable. But dying would fix everything. Dying would end the pain and end the consequences.

Maybe I could just go to purgatory and beg God for mercy. Jesus was all about mercy; surely, he would be kind to me. That was my best option for sure. I waited until everyone went to bed before quietly going upstairs to the kitchen and looking through all the prescription medicine bottles I could find. My mom took blood pressure pills and thyroid pills. I didn't know which were which but figured it didn't matter.

I grabbed the bottle with the most pills, plus a brand-new 250-count bottle of ibuprofen, a glass of water, and locked myself in the bathroom. I dumped the prescription pills out into my hand. Those were smaller and would go down easier than the big chalky ibuprofen tablets.

"God, please let me go to purgatory," I whispered, grabbing my water glass. I caught a quick glimpse of my reflection in the mirror. The sight of my body instantly reminded me that there was a baby in there.

Since getting the positive pregnancy test, I'd had a strong intuitive certainty it was a boy. In that moment in front of the mirror I heard one sentence in my head. Maybe it was me, maybe it was God, the universe, spirit guides? It doesn't matter. I didn't attribute it to anyone but clearly heard the words: "If you kill yourself, you're going to kill this innocent baby, and he has done nothing to deserve to die."

I don't know how long I stood there. I can't recall any thoughts after that. I still didn't want to be alive but was left with an inarguable sense that it wasn't fair to the baby. He didn't ask to be conceived; it wasn't his fault. And he already had a piece of shit for a dad. I could debate the sin of premarital sex all day, but this was different, it was blatantly unfair. If it was that obvious to me, then surely God felt the same way.

Through tear-blurred vision, I put my mother's pills back into the bottle and replaced the childproof cap with clumsy, trembling hands. I poked the cotton back down into the ibuprofen bottle and closed the lid. I quietly made my way back into the kitchen, returned the bottles to their spots in the cabinet, and placed my water glass in the sink. I crawled into bed and cried myself to sleep.

CHAPTER THIRTEEN

I organized a plan to get out of town for a few weeks by asking my parents if I could visit Samantha in West Virginia. My dad agreed to drive me there on a Saturday, drop me off, spend the night at his parents' house and drive back to Kentucky the next day. Two weeks later the rest of my family would be returning for their annual week-long summer visit, and I'd go home with them. This meant I'd have three entire weeks away from my fast-food job and away from Lou's bullshit.

I talked to Samantha on the phone several times during the week leading up to my trip. Each time she encouraged me to tell my parents about the pregnancy and get it over with, but I'd hang up the phone and immediately lose my nerve. With only three days left in the week, I made another late-night call for her support. We talked about the possibility of being visibly pregnant by the time my trip ended and that it would be best to tell my parents now before they figured it out on their own. Then I'd have the added benefit of getting out of town and out of the hot seat for a while.

It was 1:30 a.m. and everyone was in bed asleep. "Just go up there, wake up your mom, and tell her. Get it over with now while you have the nerve. You can do it," Samantha encouraged. One more wish of good luck and the promise of prayers and I hung up the phone. I quickly headed up the stairs to my parents' bedroom before I could change my mind. I knocked softly and opened the bedroom door. My mom was always a light sleeper, and she woke immediately.

"What do you want?" she mumbled and sat up.

"Can you come downstairs? I need to talk to you."

"Now?"

"Yes." My voice was shaky, and I turned and went back downstairs to my room to wait for her. I picked up the folded paper with the clinic pregnancy test results, unfolded it, and sat on the edge of my bed.

She came in, looking more than a little irritated at having her sleep disrupted, and sat next to me. "What's going on?"

I had no words, so I simply handed her the paper.

"You're pregnant? That's just great. I can't believe this. How could you let this happen? I can't believe this!"

She was looking at me, looking at the paper, looking at me. I couldn't face her. I looked at the ground, choked down tears, and managed an "I'm sorry. I know."

The air was heavy with her disappointment, making it difficult to breathe. She was saying other things now and perhaps I was answering her questions, I'm not sure. The alarm had already sounded in my brain and things were powering down. She was trying not to cry; she gave me a quick hug and told me she loved me, took the paper, and went back upstairs.

I wanted to call Samantha again to hear a comforting voice, but I couldn't move. I wanted to teleport myself to her room and make all of this go away. I cried and prayed for sleep to come and never leave.

A few hours later I woke to the familiar sounds of my dad preparing to leave the house for work, which meant that it was 5:15 a.m. The clatter of his keys, metal coffee thermos; the rustle of shoes on the carpeted steps, the low hum of my mom's whispered voice.

The sounds became louder as they made their way down the steps of our bi-level entryway. My dad's solid footsteps and my mom's staggered steps as she moved one step at a time, the sleeve of her nightgown swishing against the wall as she braced for balance.

I waited for the sound of the door being unlocked and the garage door raising but it didn't come. Instead, I was startled by the opening of my bedroom door. I kept my eyes closed and pretended to be asleep as my dad approached my bed, leaned down, and put a kiss on my forehead. He walked out and closed the door behind him.

This was most definitely NEVER part of the routine. Ever. I heard the rattle of the lock, the lifting of the garage door, the engine of my dad's car, and then the sound of my mom closing the garage. She shuffled back inside, locked the door, and creaked back up the stairs to her room.

She had to have told him; that's the only explanation. But why did he give me a kiss goodbye? Did he want me to know he's not mad at me? How's that possible? I drifted back to sleep thinking, *Maybe this won't be so bad after all.*

I woke up around noon, having had such a restless night. I went upstairs and grabbed some food and returned to my room, deciding to keep a low profile. My dad would be home at three, and I really had no idea what to expect.

On a trip back upstairs to use the bathroom, my mom said, "I told him but you're going to talk to him tonight."

I didn't know what that meant exactly and I didn't question it, I simply went back to my room and waited it out. It was Wednesday and I was leaving for West Virginia on Saturday morning. Surely, I could survive the next seventy-two hours.

They seemed to be handling the news pretty well so far. My mom had hugged me after I broke the news and told me she loved me, and my dad had kissed my forehead on his way out the door that morning. How bad could it be?

Like clockwork, dad returned home at 3 p.m., made a snack and went to the couch in the family room. As was part of his daily routine, he turned on the TV, finished his snack, and stretched out for a nap that would last until he was called for dinner. It seemed like a typical afternoon in our household.

But after dinner, the routine took a twist; my dad went to his room instead of the couch. I assumed he was going to nap in there rather than watch TV in the family room like he normally did and thought maybe this whole pregnancy thing was no big deal. But before I could get comfortable with that thought, my mom called me into their bedroom to talk.

My dad was stretched out on the bed and my mom was standing on the other side of the room, near the door. I walked in, cautiously, and sat gingerly on the edge of the bed near my dad's feet. "How do you think you're going to support this baby?" he jumped sternly and immediately into conversation.

I wasn't expecting such a direct and unfriendly line of questioning. "Well, I... I... can put the baby up for adoption."

My mom jumped in to quickly counter my response: "You think you're going to carry a baby for nine months and just hand it over? Yeah right."

I didn't know what she meant and before I could ask, my dad told me this had happened to his sister, my Aunt Linda. He said my grandparents took care of it. He said I had no idea what kind of responsibility comes with raising a child, what limitations it imposes.

"I'll just put it up for adoption, then," I answered.

My mom came back louder, with the disgust and disdain that was often so evident in her voice when she was angry at me: "Oh, yeah right. You're really going to just hand that baby over. No, you won't! You won't be able to do it!"

Why was she so hateful all of a sudden? Why did she not say these things to me earlier in the day? Why did she hug me and tell me she loved me last night when she clearly hates me?

Before I could respond, my dad spoke up in a low, even tone. "You're getting an abortion and that's how it's going to be."

I thought for sure I must have imagined those words coming out of his mouth. "What?"

"YOU HEARD ME, YOU'RE GETTING AN ABORTION."

I quickly reminded him that we were Catholic and didn't believe in abortion, but this seemed to make him angrier.

"You have no idea how a baby will limit your life! How are you going to go to college? Get a job? Your entire life will be altered, you'll struggle for the next eighteen years! I saw this with your Aunt Linda—do you have any idea how hard it is to raise a child on your own? Grandma and Pappaw have had to do most of it; Linda never had it easy and never will."

My aunt had one child, my cousin Dee. She had one abortion before that. My dad was speaking to both of those circumstances now, informing me that my life would be ruined with a child and that abortion was the only answer.

"I'm not getting an abortion."

"The hell you aren't! It's settled."

I looked at my mom for help. "Mom! We don't believe in this; the church says it's a grave sin, please tell him!"

"I'm not getting in the middle of this. This is your battle, not mine."

Her words hit me like a slap across the face. I stared at her in disbelief, in betrayal. "But... you're Catholic! You raised me Catholic, you've taken me to church my entire life... this is what you want for me, to be a Catholic! You know we don't believe in this; I'm not killing this baby!"

"I'm not getting in the middle. I'm not causing problems in my marriage. This is your fight." She turned and walked out of the room.

Sixteen years of mass every Sunday, catechism every Wednesday, silence from noon to 3 p.m. every Good Friday, stations of the cross, confessions, confirmations, communions, rosaries, bedtime prayers, and a ban on using God's name in vain... all stamped *invalid* in that one moment.

I turned and faced my dad, angrily swallowing the tears that were starting to flow. "I'm not killing this baby. I don't believe in abortion."

"Don't tell me what you're going to do; I'll physically put your ass in that car!" he sneered.

"Then you better tie me down, drag me in there, and knock me out... and pray to God I don't get loose because I will *not* stay on that table."

CHAPTER FOURTEEN

The next day I knew I had to talk to Lou. He didn't know about the pregnancy or that I was leaving in a couple days and would be gone for three weeks. After several phone calls and a lot of pleading, I was able to convince him to pick me up so we could talk. He was still having me over for sex a couple times a week but that was only when HE wanted it; and he certainly wasn't interested in talking.

It was early afternoon, a couple of hours before his scheduled shift at the pizza place. The light blue Cutlass whipped into my driveway with '80s hair band music blaring.

I got into the car and without a greeting or a glance, he quickly backed out and floored it. The recklessness of his driving had always been an indicator of his anger level, so I knew immediately what I was up against. I stayed quiet but not out of fear. I was annoyed by his attitude. He knew my parents got angry when he sped off with me in the car and that I'd get yelled at when I returned.

Within minutes we were sitting in the empty portion of the shopping center parking lot where he worked. Still in silence, Lou shut off the car and stared straight ahead, his jaw tight and his brow furrowed. He folded his arms and postured like a spoiled brat.

"Why are you pissed?" I asked flatly. Several seconds passed with no response. He sat unmoving, still staring straight ahead. Same old bullshit silent treatment.

"Aren't you going to talk to me?" I asked, my voice slightly louder.

"You're the one who wanted to fucking talk, so talk!" He snapped back.

A familiar weight on my chest began to bear down. My mouth went completely dry within seconds. "Why are you so mad at me? What did I do?"

He stared straight ahead, glaring out the windshield. An actual conversation was not going to happen, it was pointless. But I had to tell him.

"Well, I'm pregnant."

His head whipped around, a fiery hate-filled glare locked onto my eyes like a laser, obliterating the little bit of confidence I had displayed seconds earlier. The tears were instant as I lowered my eyes and mumbled an "I'm sorry" into my lap.

"FUCK!" He banged both hands on the steering wheel, punctuating his words. "FUCK! FUCK! FUCK!" In a sudden fury of motion he started the car, slammed it into drive and smashed the accelerator, the tires screaming in response. He turned the wheel sharply, causing the car to careen sideways. This violent explosion ripped through what had been icy silence seconds before.

"LET ME OUT OF THE CAR!" I screamed. He was speeding through the parking lot. "LET ME OUT! NOW!" I screamed for my life.

He made a squealing sharp turn into another empty section of the lot and hit the brakes hard, the force throwing my small, pregnant frame against the dashboard like a rag doll. By sheer luck or divine intervention, I hit sideways, facing the passenger door, one hand coming to rest near the chrome handle.

Without hesitation I shoved open the long, heavy door of the car to make my escape but only one foot had landed when Lou stomped on the accelerator. The movement sent me flying to the pavement tumbling toward the back tires. I heard myself scream and had a keen awareness of my head hitting the ground with a single bounce. A spinning black tire filled my view, passing far too close to my face. It must have been my scream that made him slam the brake, stopping the back wheel inches from my head.

I heard hysterical sobs which confused me for a split second until I understood they were my own. It was as if I had left my body and watched this play out but then was quickly slammed back into it.

Lou was suddenly standing over me. "Get in the fucking car, now!" he ordered.

My body was on some sort of delay because it wasn't moving as quickly as I needed it to. I felt the back of my head, expecting to find blood, but it was dry. He grabbed my upper arm and yanked me to my feet. Still sobbing, I got in the car. He slammed my door shut and jumped in the driver's seat with noticeable irritation.

I couldn't stop crying. I scooted close to my door and turned away from him, curled into myself, and choked out three words: "Take me home."

He flew out of the parking lot and headed back up the hill toward my neighborhood. We rode in silence as I tried to get my bearings and stop crying. It was only a five-minute drive to my house.

He didn't pull into the driveway, but instead parked on the street. "I guess you're going to go in there and tell your parents I almost ran over you," he angrily accused.

"No!" I shot back. "Why would I? So, they can just get madder at me? I'm not saying anything." I wiped the tears off my face and tried to will myself to calmness and normalcy so that my parents wouldn't ask questions when I walked in. He remained silent.

I flipped open the little mirror on the visor and looked at my face, red from crying, eyes swollen and watery. I wondered if I would have a miscarriage now but immediately removed the thought from my mind when it prompted more tears. My focus switched to making myself not look like I'd had a brush with death.

I methodically examined each arm and leg, brushing off dirt and tiny crumbs of gravel. My head hurt and I checked again for blood, finding only a tender knot.

I replayed the fall, checking my memory. Yes, my head bounced once. I didn't understand how I wasn't bleeding but maybe I was confusing human skulls with eggshells. I noticed a scrape near my elbow that was radiating dull pain. It would probably develop into a considerable bruise in a couple days.

Lou's emotionless voice broke the silence: "I don't want it."

I looked at him, waiting to hear what my mouth was going to respond. I still felt a little out of it, removed from the gravity of this moment.

"I. Don't. Want. It." He impatiently enunciated each word for sarcastic emphasis. "Get rid of it."

Was he actually telling me what to do with this baby in *my* body? I felt a jolt of irritation. "I'm not having an abortion. I don't believe in it. I'm Catholic."

"Well, I don't want it." He was glaring directly into my eyes. But it didn't inflict the pain it did earlier in the parking lot before he turned into a psycho.

The fear that normally plagued me in these situations was completely gone. I felt annoyed and sick of his shit. "I don't want or need anything from you and I'm not having an abortion. Period. It's not happening." He had no idea I'd been through this argument with my dad already.

"Oh sure, so then you can take me to court and screw me over for child support? Then I won't have shit to live off of and have to send YOU half my paycheck? That's fucking bullshit!"

"I DON'T WANT YOUR GODDAMN MONEY!" I screamed in his face, a surge of adrenaline practically lifting my body off the seat.

"Yeah right! We'll see. I'm fucked now. You're totally going to fuck me over for the next eighteen years! This is unbelievable!"

The sight of this tantrum—his body language, facial expressions, the words spitting from his mouth—was repulsive. I was done with this interaction and felt a sense of satisfaction in delivering my last piece of news. "I'm going to West Virginia Saturday. I'll be gone for three weeks."

A look of surprise flashed on his face. "Sure. Go have fun; fuck all of your old boyfriends while you're there."

"What the hell are you even talking about? I'm staying with Samantha and then with my grandparents."

"I'm sure she will fix you up with someone, so have fun being a whore."

These last two comments were so bizarre, unfounded, and ridiculous that I had no response. He was out of his mind. I opened the door without saying a word and started toward my driveway. The engine revved as he squealed the tires and drove away like a maniac.

CHAPTER FIFTEEN

I half expected my parents to cancel my trip to West Virginia, perhaps as a punishment for getting pregnant. But they didn't. After the blowup with Lou, I tried to spend my remaining hours in my room away from everyone.

Everything felt tangled and confused. I was so angry with Lou and felt brave enough to finally walk away and tell him to fuck off; but now this baby meant we were connected for the long term. The baby… I couldn't even wrap my brain around that part.

If anything felt certain it was my decision to keep him. When I told my parents I'd put him up for adoption, I knew I didn't mean it. I knew it as the words were coming out of my mouth. I suppose my mom knew it too, having carried three of her own pregnancies.

Still, I couldn't understand why she didn't stick up for me. I felt blindsided by both of them. Why did they want me to break one of the biggest rules in the church? I'd struggled to understand so many things about Catholicism. I rationalized that the ban on premarital sex was a technicality. I doubted the whole communion wafer turning into the literal flesh of Jesus, but I went with it. And I gave up trying to understand the crucifixion and accepted that too.

But the rule about abortion seemed logical to my sixteen-year-old brain. In fact, it seemed more straightforward than anything else the church taught. The sixth commandment was "Thou shalt not kill." I'd been taught that an abortion kills the fetus and ends the pregnancy. What's not to understand? It wasn't up for interpretation. Although, I'd heard people question it in terms of rape and internally I agreed with them. Even though the church didn't make an exception for it, I felt certain that Jesus would. I never spoke that aloud of course. But I surely didn't get pregnant as a result of rape so how could abortion even be considered in my case?

If anything, I felt bad for my baby. He didn't ask to be brought into this shitty world with two irresponsible, shitty parents. I didn't care about Lou, but I was going to do what I could for this baby. I was the only person he had and at the moment, the only person who wanted him.

At 7 a.m. on Saturday morning, I loaded my bag into the car and started for West Virginia with my dad. Under any other circumstance I would have relished a road trip with just the two of us. It was rare to have one-on-one time with him since I had two siblings. He was truly my idol in every sense; I thought he was possibly the smartest man alive. He was funny, protective, and affectionate. This was the first time in all of my sixteen years that he stopped talking to me. And there we were in a car together for five and a half hours of silence. It was the longest ride of my life.

At least he was dropping me off *before* going to his parents' house. The last thing I wanted to do was face my grandparents. I tried to imagine their reaction to the news of the pregnancy but felt immense shame.

I'd been a little nervous about what Samantha's parents might think but my mind was set at ease the day before we left. On a quick phone call to confirm my arrival time Samantha relayed a message from her mom, Beth: "Tell her that we love her, and she is *always* welcome here; this is her second home and always will be."

Just after 12:30 p.m. we pulled into the shopping center meeting spot. "There they are!" I felt my cheeks lift into a smile for what felt like the first time in months. Samantha was smiling too. I gave my dad a quick obligatory hug goodbye and hurried to the welcoming arms of my best friend. "Make sure she eats; she hasn't been eating much at home," he said to Beth as they chatted through his open car window. I didn't look back but heard the car pull away, taking the weight of the world with it.

As I settled into the back seat of Beth's car, she caught my eye in the rearview mirror and said, "Well, you need to eat! Let's get some lunch before we head home."

Home. I blinked back tears of relief and took a deep breath of fresh mountain air. My shoulders relaxed. Lou's rage and my parents' disappointment were 300 miles away. I walked into Samantha's log house feeling as if I'd never moved to Kentucky.

"Can you believe my room is finally finished?" I followed Samantha up the stairs to the former attic space. It was freshly painted and free from the dust, boxes, and *Hustler* magazines that had been there years earlier.

"This is awesome!" We flopped onto her queen-sized bed. I brought her up to speed on the happenings of the last few days: the fight with Lou and my brush with death, the uncomfortably silent drive with my dad. She was equally surprised and confused about the abortion argument with my parents.

"So… what's going to happen? Are they really going to take you in for an abortion when you get home?" Samantha asked.

"I have no idea. I hope not because I'll fight them every step of the way."

My words hung in silence for a few moments; the scenario began to play out in my brain like a scary movie. I changed the subject.

"Man, I'm so freaking happy to finally be here. Thanks for putting up with all of my late-night phone calls."

Samantha shook her head and said, "Good grief, you don't have to thank me for that. You're my best friend! I felt bad being so far away while you're over there going through hell. I can't imagine."

We heard the stairs creaking and the sound of her mom's voice as she entered the door-less attic opening. "Girls? Sorry to interrupt..." She made her way over to the bed and perched on the corner. "We're going to 7:00 mass this evening so you all can sleep late tomorrow. How's that sound?"

I felt a tiny twinge of panic. I wasn't showing yet so no one would know I was pregnant, but the idea of walking into my old church was more than a little intimidating. The thought must have been written on my face. Samantha looked at me for confirmation as she answered, "Sure…"

"We don't have to tell anyone about my situation, right?" I asked her mom.

"No. That's no one's business but yours," she assured me. I nodded. Another beat and she continued, "Now listen… you're not the first teenage girl to get pregnant and you certainly won't be the last. God loves you; we love you, and your parents love you even if it doesn't feel that way right now."

She stood up and made her way back to the stairs. "Now be ready to go by 6:15. We'll eat dinner after mass but you all can come down and find a snack if you get hungry before then. There's cheese and crackers… and I think we have Pringles. You want me to come up and do the Pringles jingle?" She laughed at her own joke, a reference to an old potato chip commercial we hated.

"Nooooo! We're good!" we answered in unison. She continued down the stairs giggling.

Samantha rolled her eyes and shook her head. It was her standard reaction to her mom's silly jokes.

"Remember when she did that at your seventh-grade birthday party?" I reminded her.

"Yes, right in front of the boys too. That was SO embarrassing, oh my God." We both relaxed into giggles, washing away the heavy conversation of earlier and replacing it with shared memories of being embarrassed by our parents.

On Monday Beth drove us into town to look at used cars for Samantha. After a few hours of negotiations and paperwork, Samantha was handed a set of keys and just like that, we were no longer kids being chauffeured around by parents. We were independent and free. I was overjoyed to be there for this memorable event and living vicariously of course. Our first stop was the car wash where I helped her scrub down the inside and outside until it sparkled like new.

The next day we started to make big plans until we realized we had no gas money. I was ready to give up. But Samantha was much more resourceful, assuring me her dad would never miss the big bag of spare change that had been collecting dust under a small end table for years.

"Well, she's pissed." Samantha laughed as we watched an irritated bank teller hoist the bag of change from the drive-up window and carry it off to a coin counter. We waited a very long time, still trying to guess what the total was going to be.

"Man, if we are lucky maybe it will be $30!" I said.

"Oh, I bet there's every bit of $35 in there."

The teller eventually returned with a bank envelope of bills and passed it through the window. Samantha looked at the figure written in pen on the outside of the envelope.

"Holy fucking shit."

"How much?" I asked.

"$78.32."

We stared at the number in disbelief as she slowly and carefully pulled out the stack of bills. Our open jaws curved into wide grins. Grins turned into laughter, which turned into squeals and shouts of "WE'RE RICH!" as we pulled out of the bank parking lot.

"We are eating steak for dinner!" Samantha proclaimed and made a direct route to the Western Steer Steakhouse in the middle of town. We walked into the restaurant and settled into an oversized booth near the salad bar.

"Wow, I'm actually hungry," I said, having nearly forgotten the feeling of hunger.

"Good!" Samantha said, passing me a menu. "Order anything you want, I'm buying." She laughed.

"Thank you, by the way. Sorry I'm so broke." I felt bad for not suggesting a cheaper meal, which would've at least been the polite thing to do.

"Oh stop; we're celebrating. And I'm glad I get to treat us! Well, I suppose my dad is treating us although he doesn't know it." She cracked up.

We placed our orders and talked comfortably. Every so often my mind would drift back to the reality of what awaited me in Kentucky. In those moments I'd feel a knot in my throat, a wave of distant fear. I never acknowledged it but somehow Samantha could sense it. It was an unspoken exchange between us—each time it happened she'd find just the right unrelated thing to say, reeling me back to safety.

Our dinner was delicious. We ate until we could barely move from our seats.

"Good lord, I feel like Templeton the rat in *Charlotte's Web*," I admitted with a laugh. "You know, when he went to the fair and got all fat?"

Samantha nodded. "Yes! I'm right there with you. We'll roll each other to the car, don't worry."

I'd forgotten what it felt like to laugh like this; to be with someone who never said a cross word or gave me the silent treatment—someone generous and kind who was going to treat me to a steak dinner with the expectation of nothing in return, save for my presence and conversation.

CHAPTER SIXTEEN

By partway through my senior year, I was happy to not be dating Lou. Most of my teachers and classmates didn't make a big deal out of my pregnancy—aside from moments like when the Home Economics teacher announced Kentucky's high teen pregnancy rate, and the class turned to look at me. My former Marriage and Family teacher saw me and said, "Well, I see you didn't listen to a damn thing I said last year."

I was grateful that my parents were being supportive, and we were planning for me to commute to college the following year. We added a crib to my tiny bedroom, and I drew Disney characters to hang on the wall above it.

But as soon as I detached from Lou, he suddenly had renewed interest in me and the baby, showing affection at school and asking about my pregnancy. When he bought a onesie with the words "I love my daddy" on it and insisted that the baby wear it home from the hospital, and when he insisted that he attend the baby shower, in spite of my mom's resistance, I felt steamrolled by this sudden intrusion and solo decision-making. Nevertheless, he managed to hook me in just before I pulled away.

We chose a name for the baby: Randall, and we planned to call him Randy. I was still certain it was a boy even though there was no ultrasound to confirm.

January 3rd came and went with no labor pains. None. At three days past due I saw my doctor and he said the baby had dropped into position, but nothing was even starting to happen. He told me to come back in a week and we'd talk about inducing.

It was one of the longest weeks of my life.

I couldn't sleep comfortably, my ankles were swollen, and I felt like a whale. I was doing a great job of *not* thinking about the process of labor and delivery. The baby was so huge and heavy, each time he moved it was extremely uncomfortable. From across the room, you could see my stomach undulating and contorting as if it were housing an alien.

I woke up on Friday the 13th at 6 a.m., as I did every single weekday morning, to call Lou and wake him up for school. He refused to use an alarm clock, and I was tasked with setting my own alarm, getting out of bed, walking to the phone, and dialing over and over until he picked up. Sometimes it took multiple calls before he'd answer, grunt, and hang up. Since I was upright, my bladder would decide to sound its own alarm, and I'd make my way up the stairs of our bi-level house to the bathroom. If my dad happened to be getting ready for work or my brother for school, I'd have to wait my turn.

On this particular morning, I was extra tired because my back had been hurting most of the night. But I made the required wake-up call, trekked to the bathroom, and found a spot of blood on my underwear indicating labor had started. Shit was about to get real, and my baby was going to have a Friday the 13th birthday.

Despite my protests my mom had decided months earlier that she was going to be in the delivery room to witness the birth of her first grandchild. I was mortified. It was already the most embarrassing and uncomfortable situation I could imagine. I'd come to that conclusion years earlier when I learned how babies come into the world. Still, I had no say in it; she had laid down the law.

Lou had also claimed his spot in the delivery room, which was more about being territorial than being a support. As it turned out, *he* was the primary source of my humiliation when it was time to start pushing.

I was barely seventeen years old, severely at odds with my body, and had no idea what I was doing. My brain couldn't handle embarrassment and exposure of this magnitude. There were people around the foot of my bed, bright lights aimed on the parts of my body I hated the most. I didn't know how to "push" or "bear down." My stomach was so big, any move I made felt like all I was doing was straining my neck forward, yet I kept getting the same directives over and over. A nurse said, "Push down like you're having a bowel movement." I did... and soon after, I had a bowel movement. I was totally unaware until Lou flipped out and made a scene, letting everyone know how disgusting it was.

Given the choice, I would've rather been laboring in a packed football stadium, spread eagle on the jumbotron—or dead; that was a good option.

Both the nurse and my mom tried to assure me that bowel movements were a normal part of childbirth sometimes. It wasn't helping. I really wanted everyone to stop talking to me and make this whole nightmare end already.

Pushing was going nowhere. Then some part of my epidural tubing came undone, but no one noticed until I started to experience a great deal of pain. It was late afternoon at this point, and I was exhausted.

My doctor had been there in the morning to check on me but had to go back to the office for afternoon appointments. He was a very kind man, in his fifties, who, on my very first visit with him, did my exam and then invited me and my mom into his office. I nervously waited, expecting him to chastise me for being pregnant at sixteen but he did the opposite. In the most sincere and gentle way possible he explained that I had no obligation to jump into a marriage with the baby's father, that college was still very much an option if that's what I wanted, and all I needed to worry about was taking care of myself and my baby.

Out of the four doctors in the practice, he earned his spot as my favorite and I'd hoped all along that my delivery would be on his shift, but that was not the case. I almost cried when he left my room. When I found out which doctor was on duty, I fought all the harder to keep from sobbing. It was the only one of the four I really didn't like. He was much older than the rest, probably seventy-ish, and he was not friendly to me at all when I saw him in the office months earlier.

My epidural tubing was repaired and by 5:30 p.m., I was pushing again. The cranky old doctor was trying to get the baby out with forceps. He was in danger of bruising the baby's head and made the announcement that a C-section was necessary. None of this info was explained to me, and I barely knew what a C-section was. They wasted no time wheeling me into the operating room. I'd never had surgery before, not even a broken bone or stitches.

A nice male nurse was hooking me up to things and explained that they could do the surgery while I was awake as long as I was still numb enough.

"I'm going to use the tip of these surgical tweezers and gently poke at your belly. If you feel anything at all, tell me."

In a matter of seconds, I felt the tip of the tweezers lightly poking a couple inches below my belly button. "I can feel that."

The nurse's concerned face came back into view above me before poking again. "How about that?"

"Yes."

He smiled and patted my hand before moving toward the foot of the bed. I heard him speaking to the old doctor. "The epidural has worn off; she can feel the poke test."

When the doctor responded with, "Let's try the knife…" I wondered if I had misheard his words until a searing pain moved down my stomach.

"OWWW!"

My nurse reacted immediately: "Stop! She can feel that!"

There was a scramble of movement and another calm male voice from behind my head said, "I'm going to put this mask on you, and I want you to count backwards from ten for me." A black object came into view and rested over my mouth and nose. "Ten… nine…"

CHAPTER SEVENTEEN

I heard voices but my eyelids wouldn't budge. It felt as if I'd been asleep for days, and I was fading in and out, unable to fully wake myself. Two people were talking, one voice very familiar. Their conversation was lighthearted, there were polite laughs, and something in the tone and inflections that was playful, one voice more prominent than the other. If I could only wake up…

My eyelids lifted enough to catch bright light, and I continued my effort to force them open. A female voice spoke close to my head, "Well there she is!" and a blurry face hovered over me. She smelled of perfume and dark hair framed her face. "You did good, sweetie. You have a little boy." I suddenly remembered where I was and tried to speak but had no voice. My throat felt like there was a piece of cotton stuck to the back of it. My eyes were still so heavy I could only keep them open for a second or two at a time before they slammed shut again. However, my ears were now fully online and shifted back to the conversation. A familiar laugh registered immediately. It was Lou.

He was the one talking with the nurse. I knew that tone, it was the fake one he used with adults he was trying to win over. It was interspersed with a laugh that was too forceful to be genuine. I felt a wave of nausea.

He was trying to flirt with the damn nurse. *Is this seriously my life right now?* With a renewed effort, I forced my eyes open.

He paused mid-fake-laugh, looked at me, and said, "It's about time you wake up!" Then went back to rambling at the nurse. She was laughing at times, obviously not flirting back because she was an adult, but her attention was on her job and me. She appeared next to me again, more in focus than before and I could see she was indeed beautiful. "Here's some ice chips, darlin'."

As I grew more alert and slowly ate the ice chips, the nurse told me about Randy. He was nine pounds eight ounces, with a little knot on his head from the forceps, and without "a hair one on his little old head!"

Oddly, there was nothing cuter to me than a baby with chubby cheeks and a little bald head. I couldn't help but smile.

As they wheeled me to my room, we paused outside of the nursery and the nurse held Randy just close enough for me to put the softest kiss on his bald head before my bed was in motion again.

Later, a nurse brought him to my room, and I held him for the first time. He was sound asleep as I studied his little face and kissed his forehead. I listened to him breathing and couldn't believe he had been in my belly only hours earlier. I examined his little feet, knees, and elbows, recalling the way it looked and felt when they had been moving under my skin.

Randy wasn't able to stay in my room because I was not allowed to get out of bed until the next day. Even though it was typical to have a horizontal bikini line incision with C-sections at that time, the hateful old doctor cut me vertically from belly button to pubic area. My stomach looked like it had one long zipper: twenty-five surgical staples, making it difficult to sit upright without pain or pressure on the wound.

Since I had to be put under general anesthesia and spend additional time in the recovery room, Randy had his first bottle in the nursery. I had zero interest in breastfeeding, which we all knew from the start. I hated having breasts and the idea of using them to feed a small human, despite how natural it was, sounded like a horror movie to me.

During our hospital stay, I watched family members meet the baby for the first time, snapping photos and carefully passing him around. My grandparents drove through snow and some spots of freezing rain to see us. My parents shared messages of love from family members far away, including Samantha, and shared my brother's suggestion that I name the baby Jason since he was born on Friday the 13th at 6 p.m. My dad laughed when I said that his poor little head made him look like Uncle Fester from the *Addams Family* and my mom went on about how irritated she was with the doctor: "He kept messing with those damn forceps, I wanted to hit him! That baby wasn't coming out! He was too big! And now the poor thing is all puffy."

It was a huge relief to have my parents there with me. Despite being a little shell shocked, I knew things were going to be okay.

They also helped prepare for my transition back home, setting up a bassinet and all of the baby items in my sister's room to be a temporary nursery for me and Randy. The plan was for me to take her room while I recovered since it was on the same floor as the bathroom, kitchen, and living room, and she would sleep in my bed downstairs. It felt a little like Christmas with all the excitement and last-minute preparations.

Also, part of the plan was Lou sleeping over, which was not a big deal; he stayed with us often even though we were never allowed to sleep together, even after I became pregnant. My parents reasoned it would not set a good example for my younger siblings; therefore, Lou was always relegated to the upstairs couch or my brother's room.

That night at the hospital I called Lou and happily relayed all of the details my parents had arranged and how excited I was to go home. He seemed underwhelmed and then out of nowhere proclaimed, "Well I'm sleeping in the room with you and the baby."

I thought he was joking until I recognized the all too familiar shittiness in his tone. Every ounce of energy and joy disappeared like a popped balloon. I reminded him that the idea would never fly since the rules had been in place forever. It was nonnegotiable. But this only made him angrier, and he demanded I hang up, call my mom and tell her he wasn't sleeping on the couch anymore because it was his baby, and he had a right to share a room with me. I choked back tears, and felt the room begin to slowly spin.

And just like that, my life was instantly back to status quo: placating a seventeen-year-old narcissist, stuck in the middle of him and my parents, trying my best to keep them from finding out what he was.

He was asking me to do something that was the norm in his house; he always bullied his mom and made demands. But he also knew my parents very well, so well that he'd never be bold enough to challenge them directly.

I couldn't convince him it was a bad idea, and I couldn't tolerate his angry voice on the other end of the phone. My mom was not the tyrannical spoiled brat that Lou was, nor was she cruel and threatening like him. It came down to survival, the path of lesser resistance. I hung up and tried to compose myself before dialing my own number.

It went just as poorly as expected. My mom was pissed and offended that I even asked. Unable to contain my tears, I cried and begged her for several minutes. If she'd only known that I wasn't actually begging for this asshole to be in my room, I was begging to not have to call him back with the answer. She informed me she was hanging up; her answer was final.

By the time the next phone call and round of tears ended, I was dazed and dizzy. My stomach hurt. I looked at the clock. It was close to 11 p.m. I prayed the night shift nurse would bring pain killers when she came in to return Randy to the nursery. He had slept peacefully through the three horrendous phone calls. I looked up from the wad of tissues in my hands to see two dark brown tiny orbs looking at me through the clear plastic bassinet. It was quiet and he was totally calm, just staring into my soul.

You're mine, I thought. My eyes started to well up again. *And I'm... a mess.* I winced and slowly, painfully, worked myself up from the bedside chair to peer down into the bassinet. He continued to look at me, unbothered by my appearance, so I reached in to rub his belly and his chubby face. I was too unsteady to pick him up, but we were content in that moment, silently comforting one another.

Part Two

I Am Mom

CHAPTER EIGHTEEN

I spent the second half of my senior year settling into mother-hood. My mom was a huge help, teaching me how to sterilize bottles, how to change a baby boy's diaper quickly to avoid getting peed on, and so many other little important details. It was exhausting but I was fortunate that Randy was a happy baby and was sleeping through the night by the time he was a month old.

I fell madly in love with this little human and couldn't wait to get home from school to see him. He was the center of our household. My parents and siblings showered him with love and affection twenty-four-seven. More than anything, he was the center of my world, a beaming source of love and wonder. I was his number one person. He reached for me. He laughed for me. And he slept next to me.

This was an entirely new existence, opposite of the misery and hopelessness I'd come to accept as normal over the past three years. I rarely had time to worry about what others thought of me, not at school, not even with Lou, who eventually decided we were officially boyfriend and girlfriend again. I took Randy to mass with us on Sundays, and I didn't care if people judged me. My parents weren't ashamed of me and would have quickly come to my defense had anyone made comments. The focus of my world was on this amazing little boy, and I'd go to any lengths to protect him and give him the best life possible.

We still had a bookcase full of story books that had been passed down from me to my siblings, so I read to Randy every day. Sometimes I'd just talk to him, his little face fixated on mine despite having no comprehension of the topic. Just like my dad had done for me, I made up little games and songs to make him laugh. I'd give voices to stuffed animals or make silly faces and sounds. His giggles and smiles brought me to life.

I didn't go back to my fast-food job after he was born. Lou was still working at the pizza shop and bought diapers every week and helped with clothing and other necessities. I applied for public assistance at the local social services office and received vouchers that covered the cost of baby formula, baby food, and later, whole milk. My parents and I agreed that I would find a job in the summer and start college full time in the fall. They did not want me to lose that opportunity. I'd always been torn between majoring in something health care related or in art. Since I was responsible for another little human, the obvious choice was to declare a nursing major.

The same week I started college, I also started a part-time job as a receptionist at a nursing home. I would work a few hours on Friday evenings and eight-hour shifts on Saturdays and Sundays.

My primary source of anxiety, aside from being away from Randy so many hours a week, was that the nursing home was run by an order of nuns. Being raised Catholic I knew that nuns existed but there weren't any that attended our church. I'd never interacted with a nun. In fact, all I knew of them were the scary stories my mom told from her years at Catholic school. They hit her hands with rulers and said some really mean things. The stereotypical nuns I'd occasionally see on TV or in movies seemed much the same: old, cranky, strict, and judgy. I was concerned with how these women might view me as a teen mom.

The nursing home employed about ten or twelve nuns in various positions: nurses, a physical therapist, a cook, and nurse aides. I would be working under the direction of the facility administrator,

Sister Mary. Sister Mary explained the duties of my new job and that she would be training me on the switchboard since I was working weekends, and her administrative assistant was off. When the subject switched to balancing my work schedule with the demands of college, I explained that I had a seven-month-old son. I figured I may as well get that piece of info out in the open.

I was very proud of Randy and if she was going to say anything judgmental, I'd just quit on the spot and look for another job. Much to my surprise, she didn't even flinch when I broke the news. She smiled and asked his name and wanted to see a photo, which I quickly retrieved from my wallet. She gushed over his cuteness and showed the photos to other people in the office. No one looked at me judgmentally or made any rude comments; they were all quite friendly and agreed Randy was adorable.

Over the next few weeks, I settled into my new routine of a full load of college classes and working at the nursing home on the weekends. It was a lot, particularly since we only had one car in the family. I'd drive my dad to work then head to campus until it was time to pick him up in the afternoon. Evenings were busy with Randy, homework, and driving my mom to the grocery or any other errands she needed.

The twenty hours of each weekend at the nursing home was something quite different. I was still adjusting to being around the nuns, reconciling reality with stereotypes. I was fascinated by Sister Mary. She was not at all what I expected. For starters, she wasn't old and cranky. She looked at least a decade younger than her actual age of forty-nine. She had big blue eyes, a warm smile, and was very personable. Her sense of humor and genuine interest in others was very relatable, yet she was professional and business-minded which was all new to me. She was a model of hard work and high expectations. She had a bachelor's degree and a master's degree. I really didn't know any women who had graduated from college. Two of my aunts and one cousin had recently started taking night classes in addition to their day jobs but their respective degrees would be years in the making at that pace.

It was my first experience in a professional work setting and although it was 1989 and not the '50s, witnessing a woman in her position was all new to me. It didn't stop with Sister Mary either. The entire facility as well as the adjacent senior living complex was managed and administered entirely by women.

Despite being the youngest, least experienced employee in the office I developed a good rapport with everyone. No one ever treated me differently for being a young unwed mother.

One Friday evening after I went over my typing assignments with Sister Mary, the conversation turned to things more personal, which was not unusual. She really did feel like an aunt as well as a role model. She regularly asked how my classes were going, how Randy was doing, and so forth. I proudly showed her the most recent photographs of my little boy and detailed his latest milestones and cute behaviors.

"He's adorable," she laughed as she looked through the photos. "God sure is good, isn't he?" I nodded an acknowledgment despite feeling a wave of anxiety. For months my mind had been wrestling with that concept: an all-loving, forgiving God, and the sin of sex before marriage. It wasn't like it happened once and I got pregnant. My entire relationship with Lou was based on sex from the very beginning. There was the obligation of sex, sex as a marker of being "normal" (as opposed to gay, as I'd been taught), the drug-like thrill of physical pleasure, sex as a means of making amends, sex as a teenage bragging right, and sex as a measure of love and self-worth.

"What's wrong?" Sister Mary's question snapped me back to our conversation. I apologized and said I was fine, but she gave a gentle and genuine push for more. "What's on your mind?" she nudged.

There was a watery sensation in the back of my throat as it tightened. A wave of fragility washed over my body, silence filling the space where my answer should have been. I worked to override these familiar warning signs.

Sister Mary stayed silent but connected, the way my grandpa was whenever we unexpectedly encountered a deer on a walk through the woods. He'd place a firm hand on my forearm signaling me to freeze and we'd stay like that indefinitely. Later he'd explain that's what you do when you intrude on the deer's space, you wait and let it lead.

"If sex before marriage is a sin, why is Randy the best thing in my life? Why does he make me so happy? When am I going to be punished?" I blurted all of these questions out in one breath. She winced and opened her arms wide, engulfing me in a hug. "Oh honey…" she whispered and squeezed me tight, holding onto me for several seconds.

When she pulled back and looked at me, I noticed tears in her eyes. "Honey, the minute that egg was fertilized that was a child of God just like you. God doesn't punish, he's a God of love." She went on to explain that too often people put human qualities on God and even though we call him our father, it's not the same as our literal birth fathers. She assured me that he doesn't sit in the sky waiting to punish us; that's not how it works.

"God is not a *man* even though we say *he* and *father*. God is *infinite love*, beyond our understanding." She smiled and playfully added, "I don't know why we have to use *he* to refer to God anyway; he could be a woman for all we know. That would make more sense." She laughed.

I took a deep breath. My lungs seemed to expand fuller than they ever had. My body felt light as if my limbs could move more freely than before. Sister Mary hugged me again before grabbing a box of tissues off the desk, pulling several for herself before passing it to me. The next few seconds were full of sniffling, our bodies releasing emotion through spontaneous chuckles.

We closed up the office for the night and made our way to the employee parking lot. I thanked her for talking to me. "Don't you *ever* doubt how much God loves you or that baby. Or that baby's daddy," she said as we parted ways. Our conversation replayed in my head for days. The concept of a God who doesn't punish provided a level of closure to the shame I'd been carrying for being a teen mom. Sister Mary's unofficial absolution of sorts marked the beginning of a new direction in my life.

CHAPTER NINETEEN

I worked at the nursing home for almost four years. During that time there were just two priorities in my life: Randy was number one, of course. Second priority was being a good Catholic, and I had plenty of support from the nuns I came to know at work.

I grew closer to Sister Mary, and we had many talks about the tenets of Catholicism, God, and just about any other topic. We formed a unique familial bond during those four years. I wouldn't describe her as being like a second mom to me, although I craved her approval and attention as much as my actual mom's. The two women even share the same birthday ten years apart with my mom being the younger. But I suppose Sister Mary was more like a cool aunt or a much older big sister. She gave herself the title of *Aunt* for Randy. I often brought him with me to pick up my paycheck and all of the nuns came to know and love him. Aunt Mary even gave him his first haircut in the convent kitchen.

The other nuns at the nursing home were all very friendly to me and a few were instrumental in furthering my growth as a Catholic. Two nuns taught classes for adults who wanted to become Catholic and asked if I'd like to sponsor a woman in the class. I'd never heard of this before but agreed. My role as sponsor was to attend all of the weekly classes with her from September to April and then witness her official consecration into the church during Easter Saturday Mass. I looked forward to class every Monday evening, my one night of socializing without Lou or Randy. The people were friendly, and I loved learning the faith through an adult lens. I did a lot of self-study on my own too, reading philosophical books by prominent Catholic authors and clergy members. I had subscriptions to Catholic magazines and devotionals, and I attended one-day retreats or any speaker events that came through town.

When one of my nun friends, who was a reliable and focused lab partner in anatomy and physiology, moved to Nashville, she invited me to visit her Dominican convent, and I took my first trip on my own.

Nashville was only four hours south, an easy drive, so I made the trip. It was the first time I had traveled somewhere alone, and my only expense was gas money. Besides, how many opportunities does a person get to stay in a 150-year-old convent? I was curious to see firsthand what this was all about.

It was an enjoyable few days of quiet, prayer, and some visiting time with my friend although the entire experience felt as if I'd walked into a parallel universe. There were fewer comforts and a strict daily schedule for prayer times, work, silence, and personal time. Their clothing or *habit* as it's called was also more traditional and covered each woman head to toe except for the face. Visitors followed the same schedule and rules regarding silence during meals and prayer times. On a phone call home to check on Randy, I sensed a panic in my mom's voice as if she worried I'd sign on as a novice and never come back. But the thought never once crossed my mind. It was difficult enough being away from Randy, and I couldn't wait to get back to him.

At the same time there was something about the Dominican life that was very appealing to me. I couldn't quite put my finger on it. *Maybe in another lifetime?* I wondered. Perhaps it was a combination of things. Most obvious was the silence, peacefulness, simplicity, and being "right" with God as I saw it. They seemed to live by a very clear-cut set of rules.

They never had to think about money or car payments. There were no boyfriends, which meant no fights, no possessiveness, no cheating, no power struggles. Best of all there was zero clothing hassle. Sure, the long habit and head covering were probably unbearable in the hot summer months, but the trade-off was totally worth it: no miserable shopping trips! They didn't have to deal with finding the right outfit or sizes that differ from store to store making it absolutely necessary to try on ANY and EVERY article of clothing before buying. They didn't have to spend hours in front of dressing room mirrors agonizing over whether something made them look fat or if it would need to be hemmed or altered and how much more that would cost. The Dominicans didn't need to find matching shoes, purses or jewelry; there were no panty hose, shapewear, underwire bras, attractive underwear, or period underwear. Their hair was completely hidden by the veil and that must be the best thing ever: wash it, brush it, cover it up. Wow. No ridiculous styling routines, hair products, or expensive haircuts. Going gray? No one will ever see so who cares!

I imagined with sheer joy the ability to wake up, shower, get dressed, and be out the door in ten minutes. No makeup, no hair spray, no misery, and no one to impress. My body would exist simply as a means of getting my soul, my personality, from point A to point B and that seemed heavenly.

I returned home to the real world. At twenty years old I was still living with my parents, sharing my tiny bedroom with my three-year-old. My twin-sized bed was on one wall and his twin-sized sports car bed on the other. I'd quit college after three semesters, unable to keep up the pace of school, work, and family duties. At the nursing home I had advanced from receptionist to administrative assistant and managed to pick up a few more hours, although it wasn't enough income to move out on my own. A large chunk of my money went to car payments on my very first car, thanks to my grandpa who cosigned the loan.

While I had hoped to move into a subsidized apartment where other teen parents I knew lived, that option would put Lou in the child support system until Randy was eighteen. No part of me wanted to put him in a completely unpredictable, uncontrollable, long-term financial obligation.

My relationship with Lou, while always difficult, was becoming more uncomfortable for me. He loved Randy every bit as much as I did, that was never the issue. I was beginning to see that we were two totally different people who never really should have been together in the first place. A clean break was not going to be possible because we now shared a child. Our relationship dynamic had not changed; our interactions were still either fights or sex but now interspersed with coparenting.

I accepted that I was stuck living at home for a while longer. However, that didn't solve my moral dilemma with the relationship. It had always been volatile and dysfunctional but now it was impacting my belief system. I felt like a fraud going to mass every week, sponsoring new members, going on retreats and so forth but still having sex outside of marriage in a relationship that I knew was not healthy. On the surface it looked very black and white: Sinful behavior was outlined very clearly. I'd learned that confession was not a get-out-of-jail-free card. Everyone makes mistakes and can have their sins forgiven but confessing a sin or behavior that you know you're going to repeat is not okay.

I didn't know how to tell Lou that sex was off limits. He'd never accept that. So, I did the next closest thing. I stopped taking birth control pills. That too was a sin for Catholics, and it would at least give me good cause to turn him away as much as possible. Plus, he hated condoms so maybe that would be another deterrent.

Go figure, neither of those things worked the way I'd hoped. It just caused more stress and more fighting. Finally, I did the one thing I'd always been too fearful to do: I broke up with him. I tried my best to explain how fighting all the time was not normal and that even though *he* dated other people when I was pregnant, I did not. I needed time and space. If we were meant to be then it would somehow work out, and we'd get back together, but for now I needed to be single. It was difficult, particularly when sharing a child and trying not to disrupt his little world either.

For the first time ever, I started to think about what I wanted in life, besides being Randy's mom and being a good Catholic. I was completely stumped. Friends, even Sister Mary, encouraged me to start dating since I'd never actually done that before. It sounded exciting in a general sense but when I thought about meeting men it turned my stomach. Sure, I could recognize a good-looking guy who had great dating potential (there was one in my adult catechism class) but the minute I tried to imagine having some interaction, it felt completely weird and unappealing. I felt like I was shopping for a car that I didn't want or need but was obligated to have.

A friend at church wanted to introduce me to someone, the brother of one of her other friends. She said he was single, my age, and also liked art. "Just call him!" she kept saying. Eventually I agreed to let her pass along my number. It was awkward but we had a couple of phone conversations that were okay and then he asked if I wanted to get dinner and see a movie.

I was completely disinterested. No part of me wanted to say yes but no part of me knew how to say no. It was like being back in fifth grade, afraid to hurt someone's feelings. I'd also have to explain my answer to the friend who set us up. So, I gave up and said yes. Everyone was invested in my dating: my mom, grandma, friends, coworkers, and even Sister Mary. Everyone but me, of course.

CHAPTER TWENTY

Soooo, what happened?" my friend asked with a nervous laugh as if I'd shoved the guy down a flight of stairs or something. It was the day after my date with her friend's brother. Confused, I scanned my memory for something awful.

The worst part of the date for me happened before it started: clothes shopping. I still hated my body, which three years after Randy's birth was still twenty pounds heavier than my overweight pre-pregnancy weight. I would rather have my fingernails ripped off with a pair of rusty pliers than shop. But I did it and settled on a ridiculous outfit that included some jacket monstrosity with flowy sleeves. It looked like it came from Bea Arthur's *Golden Girls* wardrobe.

The guy picked me up and dinner was unremarkable. I didn't feel any attraction towards him at all. He seemed to feel a bit awkward like I did, or at least that's what I picked up from his body language and the lulls in conversation. But we were in it, so we continued to the movie theater. That's where I really put the nail in the coffin, although I wasn't even aware of it.

"Well, it was okay," I told my friend. "He's a nice guy but I don't think it's a match for either of us."

Another nervous laugh as she responded, "Righhhht. But what happened with the movie? He said you left an empty seat between the two of you."

Oh damn. Somehow after the fact that did sound like odd behavior. Very odd. Rude even. *Oh my God, I really did leave a seat between us. WHY did I think that was okay?*

"Oh shit. I did. It made sense in the moment, I mean he went into the aisle first and I started to sit in the seat next to him, but it was weird and seemed too close, so I moved over one seat and was like 'Ohhh yeah I won't crowd you, let's spread out.' Shit that must have looked strange."

My friend sighed and forced a laugh, "Yeah, that's not usually what people do on dates for sure."

I did my best to laugh off my blunder but internally it was kind of alarming. What the hell was wrong with me? Even Sister Mary knew it wasn't normal dating behavior.

"Oh honey..." She shook her head and said, "What were you thinking?" Her tone was compassionate and kind.

"I don't know, it made sense in the moment." I shrugged my shoulders. "I wish I could fast-forward to age forty and not have to deal with any of this."

Her eyes widened. "What? Why? You're only twenty, your life is just getting started. What's going to happen at forty?"

"I don't know. It just feels like forty will be better. I don't want to deal with relationships and dating and figuring out everything. I want to skip all of this mess and be done."

She seemed taken aback by this admission and unsure how to respond. After a few seconds of silence, she opened her arms for a hug. "Trust in the heavenly father. He always has a plan."

"Thanks. I wish He'd just *tell* me what to do—you know, *speak* to me like he did to Moses in the Old Testament."

She laughed. "Well, that would be too easy. And no fun. God speaks to our hearts; we just have to listen."

I was grateful for her kindness and loving nature but still felt discouraged. *To hell with dating, who cares. I can't even succeed at breaking up with someone.*

Lou was unyielding. He kept showing up at my parents' house, calling me nonstop, telling me how heartbroken he was. "Please, I need space" I would tell him over and over. Lou's parents had moved to a town farther south, a solid twenty-minute drive each way and I did not want to let Randy go visit without me, definitely not for an overnight. I trusted Lou to take care of him, but I did not fully trust his parents and there were too many scenarios in which things could go wrong. Lou slept late on weekends, Randy did not. Lou liked to play video games for long periods of time, or he might run to the store for something, or decide to go out with friends. The only way to ease those fears in my mind was to either take Randy down there to visit myself or to let Lou stay at my parents' house with us. Many times, Lou would just drop in after work anyway, at which point I didn't have the heart to force him to leave. That would have been hurtful to both him and Randy. It felt impossible to balance.

The situation dragged on like this for the better part of six months. Lou tried desperately to get back together, even going so far as to find Samantha's phone number and call her for advice. He talked to Sister Mary, he talked to anyone he could think of in hopes of getting some support. They all told him the same thing, "give her space," but he refused to listen.

Eventually I ignored my own advice too. I simply gave up. Neither of us were happy living with our parents and neither of us made enough money to be independent. I had zero career prospects since I'd quit school. I had zero interest in men and the whole idea of dating had become ludicrous to me. Even if by some miraculous shift in my brain I suddenly wanted to date men, what kind of nightmare would that be? Lou would probably never give us a moment's peace. What if the guy was not a good stepdad to Randy? How could I possibly send Randy to Lou every other weekend?

The only things I knew with any amount of certainty were that Lou was a good dad, Randy loved him, and Lou wanted to be with me. Maybe it would get better, maybe we'd make it work and find a way to get along. I wanted to do the right thing for Randy and the moral thing for me, so I told Lou I'd get back together with him, but we had to get married. He agreed and we set a date for a small Catholic wedding mass, the minimum of six months in advance. In the interim we put our money together and found an affordable two-bedroom apartment down the street from the church.

Over the next few months, I regularly thought about the vows I was scheduled to take. I'd learned in my Catholic studies that a marriage vow is unbreakable because it's not just a promise to your spouse it's also a promise to God. This was a lifetime commitment. I also spent a great deal of time in prayer, believing in earnest I was doing the right thing and that all of those dead ends of career, dating, and independence were God's way of leading me to this decision. How could it possibly be wrong?

CHAPTER TWENTY-ONE

With all of my focus on choosing readings and songs for the wedding mass, it was easy to avoid thinking about what I'd have to wear. My grandma would regularly call and ask my mom, "Did she get a dress yet?" The answer was continually no. Anytime I thought about it or was asked, my brain shut down and immediately changed the topic. I did not want a wedding dress and the thought of it was unbearable.

One week before the wedding I had no alternative but to go shopping. Money was also an issue because there was so little. With literal *days* to spare I found an ivory ensemble that was sold as a set: a skirt, blouse, and jacket. The jacket had some fancy adornments and overall, it looked like something appropriate for a civil ceremony, not necessarily a church wedding. I bought it anyway. I needed the shopping trip to be done.

When it came time to actually walk down the aisle, I was completely embarrassed. That morning I'd gone to a hairdresser who convinced me that a "body wave" would look good. I had no idea what that was, but it turned out to be a half-baked perm. The curls were supposed to be loose and more like waves, but it was a much shorter style than I'd ever worn. By the time I added makeup and put on the ivory outfit, I looked like a twenty-one-year-old grandma. I wanted to cry. As I made my way down the aisle with my dad I tried to focus all of my attention on four-year-old Randy, standing proudly in a little tux holding a ring bearer's pillow. He was absolutely adorable, the brightest being in the entire church that day.

Our honeymoon was one single night in a hotel thirty minutes away. It was all we could afford and was completely devoid of romance, passion, or fun. We checked in at 4:30 p.m. Lou immediately initiated a few clumsy minutes of unremarkable sex and was flipping channels on the TV by 4:45. There was an ice storm predicted to start around 5 so instead of leaving the hotel for dinner we ordered room service, something we had both seen in movies but never actually experienced. The only thing we could afford on the menu was an overpriced cold turkey sandwich with soggy french fries, which we ate unceremoniously in front of the TV.

By 6 p.m. Lou was lost in sitcom reruns and I realized this was going to be the rest of the night. And my life. I thought I might lose my mind. I missed Randy and considered leaving to go pick him up until I looked out the window and saw my car encased in freezing rain like a giant ice cube with wheels. I opted for a hot shower with hopes it would help me fall asleep quickly and put an end to the entire day but even that got derailed by the start of my period and an embarrassing trek to the front desk to purchase tampons.

I suppose our disaster of a honeymoon set the tone for married life. Four days into it we had a huge fight that ended with Lou throwing his wedding band at me. His demeanor changed almost immediately after the wedding. He was no longer the same guy who spent months trying to convince me of his undying love and devotion. In addition, neither of us had lived out on our own before so there was a rough adjustment period as we tried to establish a routine, pay the bills on time, and divide up chores and responsibilities.

Randy was struggling with the adjustment as well. The only home he had known was at my parents' house where my mom helped raise him and still watched him when I worked. He liked our apartment but by evening he would ask, "Can we go home now?"

Every night before bed I dialed my mom's number and handed him the phone so he could talk to them and say goodnight.

Being a season of major change for all of us, I left my job at the nursing home in search of something full time, something different. I was tired of sitting at a desk and my weight kept on climbing so I started working warehouse jobs through a temp service. I could wear my comfortable jeans and T-shirts, no more business casual clothing. The work was easy, and I enjoyed going to different places and seeing how each one operated. It felt good to move my body despite the soreness at the end of the day.

With my growing list of job skills, it didn't take long to find a permanent job that paid more than anything I'd been able to earn up until that point. It was a greeting card distribution center not far from my parents' house, which made it easy to drop off Randy on my way. The work was absolutely grueling and the pace they required was nearly impossible to maintain. My feet hurt so bad that it was often difficult to stand up the next morning.

One of the managers was an attractive redhead, probably in her late twenties. She had a warm smile and wasn't loud and bossy like some of the others. I started to look forward to seeing her at the short meetings required at the start of each shift. Throughout the day she moved around the huge building checking in on each employee's production pace. I pushed myself to meet the numbers in an effort to impress her and I saved any questions I had for her daily check-in rather than ask another employee. At some point I became aware of how my heart would beat a little faster and I'd get a sudden jolt of energy whenever I saw her. After our interactions, I'd walk away trying to contain a smile.

Sometimes she would pop into my thoughts when I wasn't at work. I started to wonder what she was like. *What were her hobbies, what kind of music did she like, what was her favorite show, did she have a boyfriend? A boyfriend. Why did that question hit differently in my psyche than the others? What was I feeling and why?*

I wrestled with understanding these emotions as they intensified over several weeks. While I hustled throughout the warehouse filling orders, my brain churned, searching for answers.

I like her; I have a crush on her. Does that mean I'm gay? No, that's not possible because I'm married to a man. Although I really don't like men at all… but I'm technically married to one. A person can't be gay AND be in a straight marriage. We have sex so that means I'm straight. But… I think about women during sex. What does that mean?

Each new question and answer in my head began to coalesce, like the individual greeting cards I picked and added to the cardboard box that would become a single order.

Wait, there's a word for this. It's bisexual. That's what bisexual means, you like both. Well, women and only Lou I guess because I'm actively in a relationship with him. But bisexual is the word. That's what it is. That must be what I am.

And there it was. The giant light bulb. The answer was instantly so obvious and right in front of my nose the whole time. I couldn't believe it took so long to figure it out. I laughed at the silliness of it all. I laughed as a release of emotion, the long exhale and relaxation that comes after taking a test or completing a large task. *Finally.*

I don't remember how long this period of mental relief lasted but it was definitely short-lived. The thoughts that had made so much sense moments before circled back around for a cold reality check.

I'm bisexual. I'm married to a man. Married. For life. A vow to God. An unbreakable vow to God I made just months ago.

I was furious and internally raged at God. *Why? Why now? If I was supposed to figure this out, why couldn't it have happened BEFORE I took those vows? WHY?*

I felt tricked, like I promised something without being given all of the information. I thought of the times my dad complained about "bait and switch" marketing tactics and suddenly understood his outrage. I was trapped now, for life. Some part of my brain argued back, *Yeah but gay sex is still a sin so you couldn't have acted on it anyway.* That too was bullshit. At least I could have called off the marriage and not made a fucking lifetime VOW if this information had come to me a few months ago. MONTHS! My life was forever altered by a difference of a few months.

I was devastated and entirely on my own to deal with the fallout. This was not a conversation I would share with Sister Mary or any of my Catholic friends. I couldn't talk to Samantha about it because I'd never mentioned my attractions to girls or crushes on teachers. It certainly wasn't something I wanted to put in writing, in a letter. Besides, our lives were so busy now there was no time to write and no time for long and expensive phone calls. Even if a call was possible, where would I call from? I had no privacy. The last person I needed to find out any of this was Lou.

CHAPTER TWENTY-TWO

Despite acknowledging and naming my attraction to women I gave no thought to divorce or breaking my vow. I'd just have to do my time and try not to think about it. However, the resentment I felt toward God grew, making it easier to choose sleep instead of mass on Sunday mornings.

We were as mismatched as we'd always been, but the one thing Lou and I had in common was our love and devotion to Randy. If we weren't at work, we were with him, laughing and playing. We'd spend hours playing video games, setting up action figures, firing Nerf darts, or watching cartoons and movies. Every Monday night Randy and Lou watched *WWF Monday Night Raw* wrestling and then wrestled each other during the commercials. I wasn't a fan of the show but loved seeing them have so much fun.

We settled into a routine. Lou had become quite the capable house painter but still had no health insurance benefits, no retirement, no paid time off, and a ceiling on the hourly wage he could earn. We lived paycheck to paycheck, but I figured this was what it meant to be an adult: marry someone, raise kids, go to work, struggle financially, repeat.

I left my job at the greeting card warehouse and went to work at a call center for an office supply chain. I felt trapped taking back-to-back phone calls in my cubicle all day but being an anonymous voice on the phone meant I didn't have to contend with being judged for my physical appearance. It wasn't so bad at first, but I burned out quickly and realized what a mistake it was to drop out of college years earlier. With no better options, I stayed put.

Our rent was going up each year, creating pressure to buy a house. Friends and family members repeatedly told us we were throwing our money away, that the mortgage on a small house would be nearly the same if not less. I believed they were right, but we had no savings and no money for a downpayment.

So, we made an arrangement with my parents and moved in with them temporarily, saving as much as we could for the minimal 3 percent downpayment required by FHA loans. We were there for about a year and a half when we managed to find a very small ranch house—barely 900 square feet—in the same neighborhood.

To offset the forty-hour-a-week misery at the call center, I reenrolled in college part time and registered for an evening class. Drawing 1 was my very first formal art class, aside from taking general art in high school. All of my excitement disappeared when I was handed the syllabus. Each week's homework assignment was a specific type of self-portrait to be completed in front of a mirror. These weren't sketchbook drawings, they were full size (2ft x 3ft) detailed *studies*, each one taking several hours to complete. Several hours of looking at my face in a mirror, drawing it with detailed accuracy, and then hanging it on the wall of the drawing studio for formal critique with the entire class. *Well, I guess this is my punishment for only attending mass on holidays.*

At least the in-class assignments were fun things like drawing a still life or a live model and learning technical skills. I saw immediate improvement in my abilities, which helped me push through the weekly homework. I was so angry at having to look at my face and draw it that I became hyperfocused and completed each portrait in one multi-hour sitting. When I finally stepped back and looked at my work, I was shocked. *Holy shit, I didn't know I could draw like that. How did that happen?*

Lou was nearly speechless. "How the hell do you even do that?" I took the drawing over to my parents' house. They too were impressed. After their initial "wow" comments my mom asked, "Why did you draw your face so fat?"

"Because that's what I look like, mom."

She immediately disagreed and we volleyed back and forth for several minutes. I was adamant it was an accurate representation, having stared at the mirror for hours. Over the course of the semester all of my self-portraits produced the same responses from family and friends: "Wow that's amazing!" followed by, "But why did you draw your face so fat?"

I thought I might lose my mind. Eventually I came to the conclusion that perhaps people assume an overweight person would take creative license and draw themselves thinner or more attractive. Not me. I had no desire to be delusional. Besides, if I did, it would be glaringly obvious to the viewers. They'd probably feel sorry for me, thinking I had no clue how fat I actually was.

At the end of sixteen weeks my suffering paid off and I earned an A in the class. I'd learned so much and desperately wanted more. So, I took one class a semester for two years while continuing to work full time at the call center, a job that became increasingly miserable every day. Eventually I was able to convince Lou to let me quit and go back to school full time for a bachelor's degree. I'd major in graphic design since it could provide a decent income and had paths for advancement.

I'd have to max my student loans all four years and use the overage to pay a portion of our bills. It wasn't ideal but the alternative of completing a bachelor's degree over the course of ten years wasn't ideal either. There were no long-term career opportunities at the call center aside from management, and I was too much of a people-pleaser to even consider it.

With nothing to lose and everything to gain, I enrolled full time at Northern Kentucky University in August of 1997. It was a dream come true. Something lit a tiny flame inside me, and I felt alive in a way that was completely new. There was an immense freedom, not just from the forty-hour workweek stuffed in a cubicle, but freedom to move through each day as I saw fit. There was also the freedom to think and learn… to consider a world outside of my tiny, repetitive, boring existence in Kentucky.

I walked around campus smiling from ear to ear, feeling euphoric, which was a completely new feeling. The closest thing I could compare it to was the love I felt for Randy and the time we spent together.

I loved my classes, not just the art ones but anthropology, literature, geography, art history. My brain was more awake than it had ever been, and I reveled in the information. I learned about other cultures and people in far off places. Hell, I even learned where those far off places were on a map. It was like waking up from years of sleep and eating your first meal, but not just any meal, the favorite meal your grandma cooks from scratch.

With all this new information came new perspectives and new insights which allowed me to view the world and its people in a different light. Through art history classes I learned about other religions like Hinduism and Buddhism. It was fascinating to see similarities across various belief systems. I recognized elements of Jesus and his teachings in Krishna, Buddha, Osiris, and many more.

This broadened viewpoint made me feel more connected to the rest of humanity. It also helped me resolve an internal conflict I'd always had around Catholicism's claim as "the one true church." I'd been led to believe that Catholicism was the only legitimate form of Christianity. Yet everything I understood about Jesus, according to the gospels, made it very difficult to accept that only Catholics were going to heaven and everyone else needs to convert if they want in. Most people are born into whatever faith their parents follow so how can someone go to hell for not knowing what they don't know?

I let go of that conundrum. There were Christians and non-Christians all striving for a common good, perhaps all going toward the same destination but by different routes. Maybe Catholicism is the one true church *for Catholics*.

New perspectives weren't limited to religion and the world around me. I was learning new things about myself too, particularly my academic ability. My grades were surprisingly excellent. I'd never been a straight A student in high school but suddenly, at this higher level of education, I was pulling in A's with ease. I couldn't believe it. Even more shocking was the fact that I was getting A's on written assignments, something that had always been difficult and frustrating in high school. I'd know what I wanted to say but sit frozen in front of the paper, unable to string together words. That problem was gone, and ideas flowed freely out of my head and onto the page. For the first time in my life, I felt intelligent and not so lost.

I was older than nearly all of my classmates by close to a decade in most cases. I didn't mind though. The age gap helped ease my awkwardness a bit by creating clear and comfortable boundaries. There is no pressure to fit in when you have a kid, a spouse, and a mortgage. I still felt awkward, ugly, and embarrassed by my physical appearance, but my work spoke for itself and that's where I gained respect from the people around me.

Sometimes other students asked for my help or my input on their projects, particularly in critique sessions where the entire class displayed their work for group feedback. While critique is arguably the most fearful part of college art classes it was definitely my favorite. I was proud of what I created and proud that it was finished on time. As a perfectionist, nothing was more valuable to me than feedback and suggestions on how to improve my work.

It was my enjoyment of the critique sessions and working with my peers that led me to consider teaching. I was too far into my program and too far in debt to change majors, so I'd have to push pause on that dream for a while.

But for now, I was happily immersed in a world I never knew existed. I'd always thought of art as a technical skill: an ability to draw or paint or sculpt. I thought one's success and worth as an artist were based entirely on how realistic their work was, how accurate to real life, and whether someone would want to hang it on their wall. I couldn't have been more wrong.

I was discovering that art is vast and multidimensional. It's a historical record of our existence. More importantly, I discovered that art is a *language*: a vehicle for expressing an idea, experience, an emotion, and so much more.

This changed everything. I tried to loosen up my work in an effort to find my voice and my message. It was difficult if not impossible. But I wanted to grow in that direction, to learn the "language." My ability to draw and paint from a photo with great accuracy felt like reading someone else's writing. Sure, I could "read" it in an interesting and entertaining way, but I longed to create—to speak—something that was *me*. Who was I? What did I have to say?

CHAPTER TWENTY-THREE

I don't recall a conscious decision to lose weight or workout per say, although I'd hit my all-time high on the scales a few months before returning to school: 240 pounds on my five-three frame. It was humiliating and embarrassing to be around so many people on campus and in the classrooms. I really didn't fit in at all in terms of looks or age. Luckily, my mind was too caught up in the euphoria of learning and freedom. But I was no longer sitting in a call center full time, instead walking long distances every day just getting around campus. The full schedule of twelve to fifteen credit hours, along with my duties at home—all of the grocery runs, errands, finances, cooking, and spending quality time with Randy—left little time for mindless eating.

The university had a workout facility with an indoor track, some cardio equipment, weight room, basketball and racquetball courts, and an indoor pool. The first few times I made use of it was taking Randy over to play basketball on the indoor courts. Spending time just the two of us was always a real treat and gave us something fun and free to do together no matter the weather. Eventually we even tried out the racquetball courts, which was always good for a laugh.

Randy had played rec league basketball for several years of elementary school. When he tried out for the school team and didn't make the cut, he was crushed. But I promised a lot of practice time on campus and that I'd help him improve. I was sure he would make the team the following year. As it turned out, the extra practice time worked to my benefit as well. I loved basketball and was always glued to the TV during March Madness. I hadn't physically picked up a ball and played since the street games played with my brother when we were growing up. It felt good to help my son and to help myself in the process. We made a lot of memories and even started attending the university's women's basketball games, watching them win a national championship.

The weight came off slow but steady. Around year two or three, I took it up a notch by adding in my own solo workouts a few times a week. I'd walk the indoor track and daydream about what it would be like to jog instead of walk. Over time, as I got a little lighter and a little more confident, I started to jog a few yards in the middle of my walking.

Going into my final year, I had worked up to a regular routine several days a week that alternated two laps of jogging and two laps of walking over the course of two miles. My daydreams of jogging around the track could be retired and were quickly replaced with much bigger dreams of a new life. I wanted to travel, see the world, meet new people, visit all of the beautiful works of art I'd studied in textbooks and lecture slides. It was strange and exhilarating to suddenly—in my late twenties—realize it wasn't a waste of time to desire those experiences. They were things that felt possible, even if not immediately.

In the new daydream that filled my workout hours I was divorced and free of the misery, possessiveness, and fighting that I'd experienced since age fifteen; it was me and my son taking off together to make a new life in a city far away. Finally coming to terms with my attraction to women, the daydream also included living happily ever after with a beautiful, intelligent woman.

In this scenario I could never imagine telling my family members I was a lesbian. It felt impossible. The word itself didn't quite feel right although the definition technically fit. But getting divorced and taking a design job in another city? That was something I could tell them while my personal life could remain personal.

For an hour in the gym several times a week, this dream energetically fueled my body lap after lap around the track. I thought about the kind of living environment I'd have, one totally different from my current situation. Lou liked new things, expensive things. He liked to keep up with others, always needing a bigger and better version of some material object, never buying pre-owned. We had completely different tastes. The dream of my future life was a comfy little house with worn wooden floors, lots of books, and an eclectic mix of art and furniture items that were anything but mainstream.

Yet the most powerful, tangible part of this recurring daydream was the woman in my future. I couldn't "see" her visually in my mind's eye, but I could feel the warmth of our connection; a profound love that held both passion and deep friendship, a literal partnership of two souls building a life together, encouraging and supporting each other to become the best versions of themselves. It was mysterious but I decided to not get caught up in figuring it all out. After all, it was the *future* and in the present moment all I knew was that this dream kept me putting one foot in front of the other. Outside the gym, my reality was quite the opposite.

On more than one occasion, I was invited along as part of an unofficial class road trip to the Chicago Art Institute. It wasn't a university-sanctioned trip; it was basically the students and a professor or two coordinating a caravan to the museum, five hours away. It was never an overnight stay but rather a "leave at 5 a.m., view the artwork all day, drive home" marathon. Many students carpooled but the main point was for everyone to get up there at the same time and have the experience together.

I'd never been to Chicago and there were many well-known pieces in their collection that I was dying to see in person. Most of the students going on the trip were ahead of me in the program but in the same studio class with me. They were familiar faces, but I didn't know anyone on a personal level. In my gut I knew it was useless to tell Lou I wanted to go, since he would never say yes. However, I went over it again and again in my head and didn't see anything shady or dangerous or inherently wrong with my going. It wouldn't even be a full twenty-four hours away from home. I could drive my own car, alone, and just follow everyone there, walk through with the group, follow everyone back.

So, I braced myself and asked him, getting the details out quickly to avoid a hasty decision. His face answered a split second before his mouth. It wasn't a simple "no" but an incredulous "no" coupled with the laugh that said I was insane for asking.

In a futile effort to understand why I couldn't go; I tried a different angle. "It's basically as if I'm going alone but with the benefit of following a group up and back, and through the exhibit; so it's actually safer than going totally alone. I can pack some pb&j sandwiches and snacks so the only cost will be gas." I got it out all in one breath that time.

He paused his video game and looked directly at me. "So you're just going to take off with a bunch of guys and I'm supposed to be okay with that? I don't think so."

Tension struck my chest like a gavel, my signal to exit the room.

It didn't matter which words I chose or the speed with which they were delivered. There was never a combination that could override his default belief: I was always trying to screw him over.

This was the typical ending to nearly anything I asked to do, whether it was going out for happy hour with coworkers or going to dinner with a female friend. It didn't matter, his *no* always came down to a trust issue.

On a few occasions, like the second opportunity for a Chicago trip with the drawing class, my frustration got the best of me, and I blew up. "Look at me! I'm fat, ugly, married, and older than these people! They are my *classmates*; I don't even have conversations with them! I don't want to sleep with any of them and it wouldn't matter if I did because NOT A SINGLE ONE OF THEM WOULD EVER TOUCH ME, LET ALONE FUCK ME!"

Even that crass, self-deprecating but blatantly true statement was futile.

"Oh, so what's that say about me? And trust me, if you offered any one of them a blow job, they'd say yes, no matter how fat you are; guys don't care if they can get something for free."

Again, this was the point where I knew to shut up and give up. You can't reason with crazy or stupid and in that moment, he was both.

The Chicago trips weren't even the hardest losses to take. Standing in a long line at the bookstore at the start of the academic year, I saw a flyer on the wall for something called study abroad. It detailed a trip to Europe over winter break, three weeks, worth three credit hours in one of four different areas of study. The next paragraph detailed a spring break trip to Peru and three other trips to take place the following summer. It was pretty pricey, but the flyer said financial aid was available.

I was mesmerized by this study abroad concept. It sounded amazing, except for the idea of being away from Randy for an extended period of time. I'd never been away from him for more than two consecutive days/nights. But perhaps one of the shorter trips wouldn't be so bad. I knew better than to even consider bringing up such an outrageous proposal, but again my logical mind said, "You are not doing anything wrong, you could earn credit hours, it's an incredible opportunity."

He looked at me with confused shock and then laughed as if I'd told a joke. "What? I don't think so."

This was clearly so outlandish that he wasn't even mad, he went right on about his work and didn't even notice me leave the room. I worked to swallow the knot in my throat while waiting for the sick feeling in my stomach to subside. I felt foolish. And betrayed by my own absence of tears that, like Lou, refused to waste energy on this topic.

In spite of all this, Lou appreciated my artwork and was genuinely impressed. One time he was comparing my painting of a zebra to the magazine photo I used as reference. "I don't even know how you do that; how do you see all of those colors in the black stripes? I just see black." I gave an explanation, and we talked about color and light. Rare moments like these were a welcome break from our typical interactions.

To his credit if he didn't understand a piece of art, he would readily admit it, ask questions, and be open to the response. He too was a creative person, an amateur woodworker. He learned some basic techniques at his construction job and would figure out other things by trial and error.

So it was no surprise that he took great care in building a workspace for me when I returned to college full time. My "studio" space was one end of what used to be the narrow, single car attached garage. The previous owners of our house had converted it to living space.

I described the kind of shelves and desk area I needed, and Lou made it happen. The space was great. I could leave in-progress pieces pinned to the wall and there was plenty of storage for all of my supplies.

He was supportive of all things that kept me close to home. But I was imagining a completely different home.

CHAPTER TWENTY-FOUR

While I was busy with my return to undergrad studies, Samantha had finished her degree and was settling into her role as a new mom. Though we didn't have much time to write letters anymore and only fit in a long-distance call every now and then, we began instant messaging on our desktops weekly. We decided to start a "moms only" weekend once a year. The midpoint between her house and mine was Athens, a small college town in southeast Ohio. There wasn't much to do there, but we weren't looking for entertainment, rather a couple days to hang out and catch up without the demands of parenting and spousing.

While her husband was happy to give her a break for a weekend, mine was less enthused. But I was not about to take no for an answer. She was my family. She'd visited many times over the years and Lou knew well enough that all of our visits were the same: talk marathons, laughing, and good food. I stood my ground and went forward with my plans.

That first year we picked the cheapest hotel we could find, The Budget Coach Inn. After checking in we nicknamed it The Budget Roach because it was so incredibly outdated and old. It was still a fantastic weekend. We sat on the ratty old room chairs and uncomfortable double beds eating the cheapest fast food, laughing and talking until we could no longer hold our eyes open.

It had been a few years since our last visit and there was so much more to talk about now. She was the ideal person to appreciate and understand what I was experiencing in my second chance go-round with higher education; and I could appreciate all of the challenges and joys she was experiencing in motherhood.

On this particular trip Samantha brought a large clasp envelope full of prose poetry she had written during her years as an English major with a creative writing concentration. It was a side of my friend that I'd never seen before, and I was impressed. She taught me some basics about different types of poetry and categorized her own work as "Appalachian realism." She'd even had some pieces published.

I read through each of her poems, recognizing some of the characters and places. It felt like home to me. We had been best friends for nearly our entire lives, her family was my family and vice versa. I still called West Virginia home because all my grandparents and other extended family were there. It was still the place I visited at least once a year.

My connection to Samantha's writing was so strong that I summoned the courage to ask if I could create some illustrations for the poems, perhaps assemble them into an art book. She gave me a resounding YES and sent me back to Kentucky with the whole packet. I was excited and determined to put my newfound art skills to work and produce something to showcase her writing.

I'd just finished my third year of undergrad and had recently been introduced to bookmaking and letterpress printing. One of my professors cleaned up and restored the university's old Vandercook Letterpress machine and was incorporating it into her Book Arts class and other projects. Letterpress printing came about at the height of the Renaissance, however the Vandercook presses were made in the early 1900s. Individual letters (metal or wood) are arranged to spell out and "set" the text you want to print. It gets locked into place on the press, then rolled with oil-based printing ink. A piece of paper is attached to the machine's roller mechanism and gets pressed on the type to create a printed page.

The whole process requires precision and attention to detail, which happened to be two of my strengths. I was completely obsessed. However, doing an entire book of prose one letter at a time was not feasible with the amount of time I had available. My design professor had some ideas to help me streamline the process and suggested I make the book my senior project. I'd do an independent study in the fall to print the type and one in the spring to create and print the illustrations.

The book was completely handmade. I carefully measured and hand-cut book board, covered each piece with book cloth, assembled the pages, then bound the whole thing with leather cord. It was a great deal to take on but a labor of love that would leave me with a tangible reminder of my senior undergrad year.

More importantly, it was an artistic collaboration with Samantha. (It had been twenty years since our construction paper catalogs.) I sent her samples of different types of book cloth and printing paper; I showed her a mockup of the type of binding technique I'd use. She determined which pieces of writing were best for the project and sequenced them accordingly. We talked about imagery for each, and I sent proofs of each illustration as it was created.

The finished product was called *Sunday's Supper*, the title of one of the poems in the collection. I'd used the press to print an edition of sixty books. With a little research and ingenuity, I was able to sell a few copies to rare book collections in libraries and universities around the country, as well as a couple copies to a rare book dealer in San Francisco.

The boost to my self-confidence was priceless. Samantha was over the moon; she loved everything about the book. She was equally impressed with my ability to sell some to collectors. But unbeknownst to her, Samantha's approval carried a lot of weight. I'd felt imposter syndrome since high school. She'd made good grades, was active in band, and in the school musicals. After graduation she was accepted at West Virginia University and lived on campus, having the full college experience. She was successful in her studies, dated different guys, and had the opportunity to make a month-long cross-country road trip with some classmates. She'd even traveled to Europe with her aunt and sister.

Throughout those years it was easy to compare my experiences (having a baby in the middle of senior year, quitting college after three semesters, marrying Lou, working dead-end jobs) and feel like a bit of a screw up, not as smart. But now I was about to finish college and had discovered a passion for learning, not just about art but about everything.

To her credit, Samantha never said or did anything to warrant my insecurities. She wasn't even that kind of person. I supposed that's why I kept my fears hidden. Maybe now I could let it all go. The book was just one of several good things happening those days.

CHAPTER TWENTY-FIVE

In May of 2001, I walked across the stage and received a Bachelor of Fine Arts degree in graphic design, one of the first in my family to complete a four-year degree. I was three months shy of my thirtieth birthday. My parents, in-laws, grandparents, and siblings were all in attendance. Even Samantha, her son, and husband made the drive to celebrate with us.

I'd officially conquered the label of "just another dumb teenager who got knocked up in high school and dropped out of college." I wanted Randy to be proud of me, to see that he could grow up and do anything, be anything, even when the odds are stacked against you.

Now I just needed to find a job. I'd been coasting along all four years totally focused on creating the best work, the strongest portfolio. Whether the grade was an A or not, I would tweak projects after they were graded, following up on any suggestions the instructor made. Ironically, I failed to apply my keen understanding of branding and packaging to myself as a potential employee.

My design professor gave me a lead on a job opportunity with one of the large firms in Cincinnati. She felt I was a shoo-in for the position, although I had my reservations. I'd visited a few big firms on class trips, and we had plenty of designers come into our classrooms as guest speakers and guest teachers. They were mostly males, twenties to thirties, many dressed primarily in black, carrying an air of being too cool and too hip for words. The few women I encountered were much the same: young, attractive, and hip. I was none of those things.

I was still significantly overweight despite having dropped thirty-five pounds. In terms of feminine body shape, I had a flat ass and small chest which is the opposite of what our culture defines as the standard for femininity. Every aspect of my body, top to bottom, disgusted me to a degree that even I recognized as extreme.

Finding a suitable outfit for an interview was a real challenge. I was too fat for petite sizes and too petite (short) for plus sizes, meaning nothing ever fit properly. The shortest length of pants I could find were still too long and often covered my shoes to drag the floor. My body was largest around my hips and lower abdomen so if a shirt fit comfortably around that area it was guaranteed to be too large in the shoulders and too long in the sleeves.

Clothing sizes for women are a total mind fuck.

Alterations are a luxury when you can barely afford the clothing to begin with, especially if *every* item you own needs altering. I tried using the iron-on sewing alternative called Stitch Witchery to create a half-assed hem job on dress slacks. Sometimes I resorted to duct tape for jeans and thick material. The right shoes may have helped but I couldn't do heels. I just felt ridiculous and clunky.

Despite the inner reality check I was experiencing I went to the interview my professor arranged mostly because it would be rude and unprofessional to do otherwise. The art director was a hip looking guy, probably in his early forties. He seemed nice enough, having heard a lot of great things about me from my professor. I opened my portfolio to show the first piece, a *Time* magazine cover mockup, and explained the assignment. He whispered a "wow" under his breath, paused for a few seconds and then asked, "This is your design?"

It seemed like a strange question, but I answered, "Yes, it is," and flipped the page to a series of three different billboard designs for The National Coalition of Art Censorship. He studied each one carefully as I gave a simple explanation of the assignment and waited for him to comment or ask questions.

"These are all yours? Your designs?" he asked.

"Yes, all mine. This was not a group project." I paused before turning the page, waiting for him to ask a less obvious question. He studied the work a moment more and then silently signaled with his hand to turn the page.

The next set of pages showed a direct marketing campaign for an art supply retailer. "Nice. And is this part of their existing brand elements?" he asked, pointing to the hand-drawn mannequin interacting with the type and graphics.

"No, that's my original creation. I drew each one by hand, colored them with illustration markers, scanned to Photoshop, enhanced the color, and exported with clipping paths into individual files. I did the same with the background on the foldout postcard. The retailer has no existing brand elements aside from the name of the store in the typeface shown. I left that unchanged to maintain brand recognition."

"Hmmm" was his response.

Anticipating his next question, I added, "It's all my original concept and execution, it was not a group project." He looked at me, nodded, and gave the hand signal to turn the page. I felt more than uncomfortable by this point but confident in the next several pieces, as they were my strongest. It was a semester-long original brand creation for a product of my choice with full-scale marketing campaign: product research, logo, magazine ad, package design mockup, point of sale display, aisle placement mockup, and a ninety-second, animated commercial.

From his body language and limited comments, he seemed impressed. But the same questions were posed: *This is all your original work? Did anyone else collaborate on any part of it?*

I didn't get the job, and I wasn't surprised since the interview felt more like an inquisition. Copyright infringement is serious business, so part of me did understand the art director's need to question ownership of the work. Yet I couldn't help but wonder if the line of questioning would have been different had I been an attractive female or even an attractive male.

My professor, the one who recommended the position, was surprised and a bit irritated on my behalf when I gave her a recap of the interview. She assured me that he was questioning ownership of the designs because the work was so strong. "He's an idiot for not hiring you," she added.

Eventually I found some freelance work that was not exciting, but I could charge $25 an hour which was more than I'd made doing any other type of work up until that point. The best part was that I could do it from the comfort of my home without worrying about dress clothes and fitting into the office culture.

I continued freelancing and job hunting as summer turned into fall. My mind was still playing out possibilities of a new life for me and Randy somewhere far away. I continued to frequent the gym, and the pounds slowly continued to drop. I turned thirty that August and for the first time in my life I felt like maybe there were good things on the horizon. There was a whole world out there that I wanted to explore, places I wanted to travel, and amazing art to experience.

I felt guilty formulating this vague plan in my head, knowing that acting on it would be a shock to Lou and an absolute nightmare for everyone involved. But I could no longer stand the possess- iveness, the constant expectation of sex (and the tantrums when I resisted), the insults and name calling, the jokes about my weight; it was the same fights over and over. We were two very different people, which had always been the case, but I was ready to break away… someday. I didn't have the details figured out; I'd have to find a permanent design job with a real salary first. It was going to take years, but I could live with that for the time being.

Inside I was becoming more and more comfortable with the dream of a future *female partner*. My brain rarely used the word *lesbian*; it was too… scary? Final? Jolting? Sinful? I was barely a "Christmas Catholic" those days. I felt trapped by a religious vow taken in a church that I'd never fully belong to as long as I had an attraction to women.

I don't know. Everything was still getting tangled up in language and labels just as it had years earlier. I didn't like feeling locked into the category of *bisexual* based on what seemed a technicality (as ridiculous as it sounds), but the b-word was easier to digest for now.

Silently wrestling with those thoughts and trying to make sense of my life was exhausting. I'd never discussed it with anyone, not even Samantha. There were a couple of times I wanted to tell her but couldn't form the words. It's not that I feared her reaction, I knew she was a very accepting person in general and never homophobic. However, I did fear that it would somehow change our interactions and make her question my intentions. I never wanted her to be afraid that I'd make a pass at her or flirt. I didn't want her to be uncomfortable sharing a room or even a bed with me.

I got my chance soon enough. That September the planes hit the World Trade Center, and everything changed. The world felt very different, very uncertain. We talked on the phone regularly and shared our shock and fear. Her thirtieth birthday was the fifteenth, so we made plans to meet for a weekend at her aunt's house in Cleveland.

Her aunt and uncle had a gorgeous house on Lake Erie and over the years I'd visited her there many times. Her family was my family and Aunt Bobbie and Uncle Tom always welcomed me like one of their own.

This particular weekend was overshadowed by the rising death count crawling across the CNN news ticker twenty-four hours a day. "Welcome to thirty," we said. *Life is unpredictable, and tomorrow is never guaranteed. What kind of world will our sons have as adults?* We pondered. Randy was only twelve and her son was just five.

We shared one of her aunt's spare bedrooms that weekend. When our kids and spouses weren't with us, we always opted to sleep in the same bed so we could talk and laugh until sunrise. It was the last night of our visit, and we lay in the dark on our backs listening to the sounds of Lake Erie through the open window. I wanted to tell her my secret but each time I opened my mouth nothing came out. *This is your last chance, you idiot!* my brain screamed. I glanced at the alarm clock on the nightstand. It was nearly 3 a.m. The gaps of silence in our conversations had been growing longer as our bodies prepared for sleep.

"I have to tell you something." I heard the words tumble out of my mouth all on their own. "I…"

"Yeahhhhh?" she answered with amusement.

I had nothing. Not even a stutter. My voice box was an engine that my brain couldn't turn over. Click… click… nothing.

I continued to stare at the ceiling when she turned her head to make eye contact. "*What?*" she asked again.

"I'm thinking!" the engine started. A nervous half laugh escaped my lips. We both laughed.

"What… just say it!" Her words carried the same playful, feigned annoyance we had shared since elementary school.

For the next couple of minutes this exchange continued. I struggled in the purgatory of not having the words but knowing there was no turning back. Every passing second was building anticipation, increasing the magnitude of what I was trying to say.

Soon her tone shifted to concern. "You can tell me anything, I'm your best friend."

"I like… girls. Like, I guess… I'm bi. Or something." I thought my eardrums would split in the beat of silence before her response.

"Okay."

"Okay?" I waited for more.

"Wellllll, I *want* to say I'm surprised but…" she chuckled. "I mean… okay that sounds bad…" We laughed. "I'm not surprised, like I don't mean it in a bad way. I mean… I can see it. It makes sense."

She struggled a few moments longer, taking great care to not offend me in some way. Far from offended, I was relieved beyond measure. With her assurance of support and unwavering friendship I fell asleep feeling unburdened and no longer alone.

CHAPTER TWENTY-SIX

The beginning of 2002 brought big changes: Lou and I both found new jobs; my weight was down to 178 pounds from 240 four years earlier; and I was pregnant.

The plus sign on the test stick seemed almost sarcastic. *Positive? Positively awful.* All that weight loss screeching to a halt. I'd just had my wedding rings resized two and a half sizes smaller. And the dream of starting a new life some day? My brain couldn't even go there.

Just last Christmas, I had given a strong *hell no* to a family member's question of whether Lou and I would have more kids now that I was done with college. Lou and I fought about it later—we had always intended for Randy to *not* be an only child—but my hormones had been unbalanced since discarding my birth control pills at age nineteen. After we got married, I saw a doctor but all he could offer me was either birth control pills to regulate my hormones or fertility drugs to try for a pregnancy. We decided neither of those were good options. Nine years had passed with no pregnancies, which seemed like enough proof to me that it wasn't possible. Yet there I was.

But I didn't cry over it. This wasn't the first time I felt like God pulled the rug out from under me. I guess this was his plan to help me keep my wedding vows and stay straight. I felt robotic for the next few days until something shifted. I thought about the one good thing in my life: Randy. That pregnancy was unexpected too and came with its share of uncertainty and chaos. It all culminated into something beautiful and amazing so maybe I'd have that again, times two, now.

The due date was impossible to calculate since my cycles had always been irregular if not totally absent. The doctor ordered an ultrasound the following week. They determined I was fourteen weeks, which put the due date in late September. And they confirmed what my intuition had already told me: It was a girl. I had an idea for a name that Lou liked as well: Rylie. Her middle name would be Claire because that was Samantha's middle name.

Having missed the entire first trimester there was no time to think about the 180-degree turn my life had taken. The dreams of a new and improved future life were unplugged and packed away. In its place were reruns of the past, albeit some memories more pleasant than others: caring for a newborn, sleep deprivation, soft skin and chubby cheeks, weight gain, the first smiles, and love. So much love.

Randy was excited about having a little sister despite the thirteen-year age gap. My mom was thrilled as well and immediately offered to buy a crib and other items. Over the next four weeks we transformed our spare bedroom into a nursery. The crib was decked out with a pastel animal theme based on the drawings of John Lennon. I found the matching lamp on eBay and some other wall art. A handful of outfits hung on tiny hangers in the closet including a tiny pink basketball jersey. I had been coaching a basketball team of eight- and nine-year-old girls and wasted no time giving Rylie number ten in honor of my favorite professional player Sue Bird. It hung beside a plush basketball and the tiniest set of high-top sneaker booties.

I spent every minute of my downtime at work browsing baby gear and reading up on fetal development week by week. We were fully immersed in the excitement of what I could only call a miracle baby. It was hard to ignore the popular saying, "With God anything is possible."

I was exactly eighteen weeks pregnant the morning I woke up bleeding. It wasn't a lot, but it was definitely worth a call to my OBGYN's office. They told me to come in and the first doctor available would see me. This confirmed my initial thought that a little spotting of blood wasn't totally out of the ordinary. I figured if it was dangerous they would have told me to go to the ER or call 911. So I called Lou's pager and when he called back, I assured him that I was okay and there was no need to leave work, I'd keep him updated. Next, I called my boss and said I had to see my doctor but would be in right after.

The doctor did an exam and then sent me to the next room for an ultrasound. The technician was quiet as she moved the device every few seconds, stopping to hit a button on the console that takes photos of the screen. "There's baby's heartbeat," she said. I think it was her way of letting me know the baby was alive. The muscles in my shoulders released a tension I hadn't noticed was there.

While I waited for the doctor to read the results, I remembered being in that exact room just four weeks earlier to find out the baby's sex and due date. And only a week before *that* was the positive test result. This was a pregnancy in fast-forward; my body had been growing this baby long before I knew she existed.

The doctor was back. I had something called an incompetent cervix. I already knew the role of a cervix in pregnancy—it's a narrow gateway that opens up or dilates during labor so the baby can move into the birth canal—but I had no idea a cervix could be declared incompetent or defective.

To his credit, the doctor described what was happening in easy-to-understand language. My brain animated his words like a cartoon as he spoke:

Think of your cervix as the tiny opening of an upside-down bottle. Think of the fetus in its amniotic sac of fluid like a water balloon that slowly expands over nine months. Now picture the water balloon inside the bottle. If the cervix is defective, it can't support the weight of the water balloon, so it starts expanding. As it expands, the water balloon starts to slip through, like an hourglass.

"That's where you're at right now. The balloon, the amniotic sac, is beginning to slip through the cervix. If that continues the pressure will cause your water to break and you'll deliver."

No further explanation was needed. I nodded an acknowledgment, and he continued.

"I'm sending you next door to the hospital so give me a minute to make some phone calls and get the paperwork started. You can use the phone on the counter to call your husband if you'd like, just dial nine first," he instructed.

I'd have to call my mom and have her call Lou's pager to relay the info. "Do I go to the ER or through the main entrance?"

"One of our nurses will take you by wheelchair, over the skywalk." He scribbled notes on my chart.

"I could just drive over..." He turned to look at me. For a split second I thought he was irritated but his tone was gentle and direct, the way you deliver difficult news to a small child.

"You're four centimeters dilated. Gravity is not your friend right now; we need you off your feet."

CHAPTER TWENTY-SEVEN

When I was seven years old my parents took us to a big amusement park in Pennsylvania. I begged and begged my dad for my very first roller coaster ride. He gave in, as dads do, and we got in line for the Rebel Yell. I must have been barely tall enough to ride or maybe back then there were no height restrictions considering the primitive safety standards of a bench seat and one lap bar across both occupants.

I don't remember much, just my dad's big arm around me, pressing me into his rib cage. My dad, however, remembers it quite well: the terrifying drop over the first hill, the speed, his fear. He said he looked down at me and saw tears rolling down my silent face. "You know daddy would never put you on a ride that wasn't safe right? It's almost over." I nodded and held tight.

It's almost over. Even after seeing blood that morning and going to my doctor, I was unprepared for the terrifying drop. I'm not sure why I hadn't cried at all that day; maybe it was just happening too fast and was so unexpected. I didn't cry when I was transferred to a hospital in Cincinnati or when they tilted my hospital bed with my head below my body or when they told me that my only hope was to stitch my cervix closed for the remainder of the pregnancy, a procedure called a *cervical cerclage*. I didn't cry when they said the procedure failed and delivery was imminent, and Rylie would not survive. *Is God my father protecting me? He wouldn't give me something I couldn't handle, right?* It was seeing my mom's tears and Lou's that set off my own.

So, for the remainder of that very long day, we waited for the worst, and I cried with each family member who came to my bedside. Someone handed me the phone from the side table, and it was my grandma's voice on the other end of the line. I didn't recognize it at first because she was crying. Later the phone was passed to me again; this time it was Sister Mary. Her voice was shaky with emotion. She was never one to hide her tears and I liked that about her. The conversation was short; she never said the words miracle or faith as one might expect in this situation. Still, her words were impactful. "We don't determine someone's *lifetime.* A lifetime for some people is eighty-four years, for others it's fifty years or twenty-six years or five months in the womb. It's not up to us to define."

The hours crept by without anything progressing. Around midnight the doctors were a little surprised I hadn't delivered yet but assured me it would happen by morning... until the next morning came with no change. Rylie's heart was still strong, and her vitals were normal. There were no contractions. My cervix had decreased to about two-and-a-half centimeters. My doctor could offer no logical explanation as to why my body didn't deliver but he laid out the game plan. I'd be admitted and remain on bedrest for as long as the pregnancy would last. I was at eighteen weeks and a day. If we could somehow make it until week twenty-three, they could start steroid injections to speed the development of her lungs.

But it wasn't as simple as limiting my movements to buy time. In addition to the cervical issue, the slow leak of amniotic fluid was a deadly risk for both of us. A tiny pinhole exposed Rylie's water-filled environment to potential bacterial infection. If that happened, it would infect her first and then me if they didn't catch it in time. For this reason, they began taking my temperature every shift. A fever would mean infection and I'd be induced immediately. "But what if she is still alive?" I asked. The answer flashed in his eyes before I heard the words: "She can't survive outside the womb."

The hospital's high-risk unit was my new home. It was an entire floor of women on bed rest trying to maintain their pregnancies to a point of safety. There was nothing to do but watch TV and worry about my unborn child. Like most people in 2002, I didn't own a cell phone. Nokia phones were cool but expensive. My only connection to others was the landline on the bedside table, useful as long as the people I wanted to talk with were not at work or school.

More than anything else, I missed Randy. I'd never been away from him more than two or three days at a time and that was pretty rare. He couldn't visit me because he was only thirteen. Lou came to the hospital almost every day, either after work or on his lunch hour. It was little league season, and some nights Randy had practice or games, so I'd have to settle for a phone call.

Two weeks passed with no new developments. One afternoon I was transported, bed and all, to get an ultrasound. It was the routine twenty-week ultrasound that takes place in all pregnancies, high risk or not. The ultrasound tech printed screenshots for me to keep, each one highlighting different parts of Rylie's tiny body. When it was over the tech parked me in the hallway to wait for a transport back to my room. After a long while I began to wonder if the person forgot about me. I was somewhere deep inside the maze of badge-access-only hallways. There were no people in sight, no phone, practically no sounds. I felt my body preparing to cry. *I'm SO alone right now.* The thought was followed by one strong kick, the first one of the pregnancy. I knew instantly what she was saying: *Alone? Excuse me, I'm right here!* The message was so clear that a laugh of relief kicked off a wave of tears. I put my hand on the bump of my abdomen. *You're right,* I answered. *We are stuck in this together.*

That was our first bonding moment, the first time I truly connected with the soul whose tiny body lived inside my own. It was impossible to feel alone after that. I still had plenty of periods of loneliness, of wanting to see and interact with my family. But from that moment on, it was always the two of us passing the hours between visitors.

The days piled up. The ticking of the analog clock on the wall grated on my nerves and my favorite nurse had it removed from my room. I spent my first Mother's Day without Randy, but we talked on the phone and his teammates signed and sent me the game ball from their Mother's Day game. Three times each day I held my breath with a thermometer under my tongue and silently chanted, *Please, no fever. Please don't let me watch my baby die in my hands.* I listened to my baby's heartbeat. The sound always brought me out of my head and back into my body, our body.

On a Sunday evening twenty-two weeks into the pregnancy, I sat alone in my hospital room. My visitors had long gone. Lou was at home with Randy preparing for school and work the next day. I was mindlessly flipping channels when I stopped on a documentary about premature babies. For ninety minutes I had a peek into the experiences of a few families and their extreme preemies. The information was overwhelming. There were months-long hospital stays, birth defects, special needs. I shut it off and considered what we were praying for. *If Rylie made it one more week for the steroids, would she then make it another three in order to have a chance at survival? What would survival look like? Months of tubes and machines in an incubator? Blindness? Developmental delays? How would we afford specialized care? Like one of the families on TV, would she live just a couple of months and die anyway? Would we be faced with deciding whether or not to remove life support?*

I was so lost in these questions that I didn't realize I was sobbing until a nurse entered my room with a panicked look on her face. She did her best to help me pull it together and encouraged me to call Lou and ask him to come stay with me. She offered to bring in a rollaway bed, blankets, and pillows, and assured me he could use my shower in the morning before work. It was a good idea. I calmed down enough to talk despite a continuous stream of tears quietly rolling off my face. I made the call and asked him to come stay. We lived only a mile from my parents and Randy could easily stay with them.

But he said no.

I was so surprised by his answer that I asked again, certain that he must have misunderstood the question. *No,* he repeated. He wasn't rude about it or mean, he just said no he didn't want to take Randy to my mom's, he didn't want to drag his work clothes and toiletries to the hospital, and that he'd sleep like crap on a rollaway bed which would make his workday miserable. I didn't understand, yet I didn't have the strength to argue.

The next two nights were the same. I felt unconsolable and begged him through tears to please stay. I did not want to be alone in that fucking room. I'd been there for weeks, and he hadn't spent a single night in the room with me. It was always the same excuses plus some new ones like he had to help Randy with his homework, Randy had baseball practice, or he needed to wash his work clothes.

I didn't share a lot of this with my parents, but I talked to my mom on the phone. She knew I was having a string of very difficult days, so she offered to have my sister bring her over the next afternoon, Wednesday, and we'd watch movies and eat lunch together in my room.

Wednesday arrived and just before noon the nurse came in for the temperature check, normal. And we listened to Rylie's heartbeat, also normal. She offered a lunch tray, but I passed, instead asking for the VCR cart because my mom and sister were bringing food and movies.

Minutes later my sister knocked and entered my room with a bag of food and two movies, but no mom. "Her stomach was upset," she said. I was a little hurt that she didn't call to tell me this herself.

We ate the lunch my mom had prepared and put on *Runaway Bride* with Julia Roberts. After the movie ended, I got out of bed and walked the three short steps to my bathroom to pee. Since my condition had been stable with no contractions, I was permitted to get out of bed to use the toilet. When I reached between my legs to wipe, my hand snagged on something. I looked down and saw a loop of umbilical cord outside of my body. My throat tightened making it impossible to swallow. I rushed back to my bed yelling at my sister to get the nurse *NOW*.

It was a scene from a movie: nurses snapping into crisis mode and rolling me—bed and all—top speed down the hallway to labor and delivery. Immediately, a doctor was at my bedside with a portable ultrasound machine. The room went silent. "She's gone," he said softly. "There's no heartbeat… the cord prolapsed. It slipped through your open cervix and kinked." He put his hand on my forearm. "It wasn't your fault, there was nothing you could have done differently… I'm so sorry."

My sister became hysterical. The nurse took her out of the room. Someone had called Lou, but he wasn't there yet; it was a solid thirty-minute drive from his job to the hospital.

I replayed the last several moments over and over, combing my memory for any sign that I missed, any physical feeling I missed. There was nothing. It had only been a few hours ago that I had heard her heart beating.

She left without my noticing, just like she arrived.

Part Three
I Am Broken

CHAPTER TWENTY-EIGHT

I was still waiting for Lou when a nurse came in and tried to gently ask questions I was not prepared to hear nor answer: "Do you have a funeral home in mind? Do you want cremation?" She started to explain a default arrangement the hospital had with a crematorium across the road "should a family choose to do nothing." *What does that even mean?* "I know these are difficult questions…" she continued. *Yet you're still asking them.* I had no answers and told her to come back later.

I don't know why I assumed the doctors would take Rylie's body from me via C-section. She was gone but I still felt an urgency to get her out, to protect her somehow. From what? I didn't know but instinctively I needed to get to her.

But that's not how it works. Lou finally arrived. Our family members had been in and out of the room crying with us and I'd just calmed a bit. The tears had slowed to a pause, and we were catching our collective breath when a nurse asked if we were ready to start Pitocin, a drug given to induce labor. The slow realization that this nightmare was going to continue for hours and culminate in the delivery of my dead child was too much for words.

The rest of the evening was the same rotation of family members and tears. Another nurse arrived with difficult questions, more appropriately timed at least: "After you deliver, will you want to hold your baby? We can stamp her footprints if you like. Will you want photographs? Will you want any family visitors during that time? What is her name?"

We sorted it all out, deciding to forgo the photographs and family visitors with the exception of Sister Mary. She agreed to come in and pray with us, read something from scripture, and offer a final blessing.

Around 11 p.m. I was experiencing the intense late-stage contractions of labor for the first time in my life. It was like having a massive charley horse throughout my torso, over and over. Eventually I was given Demerol or some other heavy-duty med and the pain disappeared. Since I was in the fifth month of pregnancy, Rylie was very small and very easy to deliver. The nurse stamped her footprints, placed her in a tiny blanket and handed her over.

She was no more than seven or eight inches long, her head about the size of a golf ball. She was delicate like a baby bird, and everything was perfectly formed: the tiniest ears, hands, feet, fingernails, and toenails. Very carefully I placed the pad of my index finger beneath her hand and marveled at the scale. Her entire right hand rested on the tip of my finger. We sat like that for a while, sealing it all in my memory. I never wanted to forget that she was here, she was real.

At 6 a.m. one of my ob-gyns stopped to offer condolences as he started morning rounds. Unlike the daily visits of the previous four weeks, there was little to talk about. We stared at each other in silent acknowledgement of a shared pain. The patient was suffering, and the doctor was powerless to help. I asked him to discharge me as fast as humanly possible and he did. I was home by 8:30 a.m.

I'd never experienced the death of a close family member before. All four of my grandparents were still alive as were my aunts and uncles. I'd watched enough daytime talk shows to know that grieving is a process with stages and cycles and each person moves through it differently. Yet I had no idea there was a physical component to grief. Sure, I'd lost my appetite during a heartbreak or felt nauseous when Lou and I had huge fights, but it seemed more like a stress response than grief.

Rylie's death left me with two distinct tracks of grieving that converged in a level of pain I'd never imagined. My body was on its own track, physiologically adapting to the sudden loss of the tiny human it had been growing for more than five months. Somewhere inside me was a womb gauge with the needle on *empty* as if I didn't know. *Empty... I feel empty.* This sentiment flashed into my awareness repeatedly, a dashboard warning light that never shut off. It was the answer I never gave to the question everyone asked, "How are you?"

After the first two days of literal emptiness, my body switched on breast milk production. Was it confused? In denial? There was no warning, just the sensation of wetness and a large damp circle forming on the front of my T-shirt. *Are you fucking kidding me right now?* My knees buckled in defeat. Surely this was some kind of cruel joke from God, right? The milk, the entire month-long hospitalization, all of it.

My muscles were jello. I'd gone from working out several times a week to lying in a hospital bed for a month. I needed more fuel to move regularly and avoid exhaustion, but I had no appetite and usually felt too sick to eat.

The second track of grief was psychological, emotional. It was heavier by far and in many ways, it had begun the first day of my hospitalization. But the worst-case scenario had happened, and I was home … yet there was no closure. The whole experience had become a haphazard pile of fragments, of images, words, emotions. My brain spent every waking moment sifting through each piece, examining it from every angle.

I fought against it, tried to distract myself or at least reduce the flow of memories to something manageable. The pain was too damn big. It refused to be contained or ignored. It originated directly behind my breastbone, practically tangible, as if a surgeon could crack open my sternum and lift it right out. But at the same time, it felt miles below the surface, solid, black, and heavy like an oncoming train.

Every day was the same. Distract, distract, distract. I'd fight its approach until it collapsed me physically, until I could no longer keep my body upright, and then I'd drop like a rag doll. The pain barreled through me. It rattled my limbs and roared through my vocal cords.

Alcohol my brain said over and over, *just drive down to the corner store and buy a big bottle. You can come home, put away your car keys, and wash it all away.* I wasn't a regular drinker and didn't drink alone. But when I did drink it was always to excess so I knew exactly where the idea was coming from.

But Randy... I argued silently. Rhythmic thumps of his stereo system carried through the common wall separating our bedrooms. I knew the alcohol option would take me away from him for more than just a day. The intuition was so clear, so strong that I felt resentful it was summer break. I wanted to believe that if he were still in school all day, I'd somehow be able to drink myself numb after he caught the bus and then be functional by the time he got home. But it was June. Summer was just getting started and I'd already been away from him for so long. Alcohol would have to wait.

CHAPTER TWENTY-NINE

I did all the things people do after a major loss. I slowly and cautiously went about the business of picking up where life left off. With a full-time job and a family, I had plenty of routine to at least go through the motions. I knew it would take time but figured eventually I'd get there, and things would go back to some kind of normal.

I moved my body through each day's tasks and responsibilities. It was familiar and comfortable, but I had become unrecognizable to myself. My sensitivities were different than before like someone snuck in and rewired my brain. I couldn't predict my own emotional reactions to anything. Tears would start out of nowhere with no trigger at all. It sounded trite but I felt *broken*. There was no other word to describe it.

Rylie died on a Wednesday and somehow that became the first day of the week for me. My internal calendar marked the passage of time by how many weeks it had been since May 22nd. My brain was able to do lightning-fast calculations between any two points on a timeline. At random moments I'd have a bizarre thought like: *This time eleven weeks ago I was in the hospital watching* Food Network, *totally unaware that Rylie had only four days left to live. Or If Rylie had made it to twenty-seven weeks and was born a preemie, she'd now be eight weeks old.*

Strangely, the more time that passed the more difficult it became to be around other people. After weeks of condolences, cards, and phone calls I became an outside observer watching others go on with their lives as normal. My emotional thermostat was not working. I felt everything with an unbearable intensity. *Was I a cold person before this? Had I been indifferent and judgmental and didn't know it?*

Rylie's September due date came and passed. Somehow, I thought maybe I'd start to feel better after that date, that the grief would shift to something bearable. But it didn't. I'd never been to counseling or had a therapist before but desperately needed help. I told Lou I wanted to see someone. He said I didn't need a therapist; I'd be fine, and it was normal to feel that way. I tried to explain my struggles and the feeling of being totally miswired, but he wouldn't concede.

I hadn't prayed because I wasn't sure of God's role in this. Maybe he took Rylie away because of my attraction to women and my dreams of taking Randy and moving far away. After all, divorce meant breaking my vow to both Lou and God. The thought tortured me so badly I eventually went to see Sister Mary.

I pulled into an empty space in front of the familiar brick building just after evening prayer time. Through lamp-lit windows I could see three figures settled in the living room, two appeared to be crocheting or knitting and one was reading. To my relief Sister Mary answered the door, sparing me a condolence conversation with the others.

"It's a little chilly but can we talk outside, in private?" I asked.

"Sure, let me grab my coat. Let's sit in your car."

I started the car and turned the heat on low. Sister Mary climbed into the passenger seat and grabbed my hand and squeezed. "How are you, sweetie?"

That's all it took for the tears to start. "Not good."

She pulled a little packet of tissues from her coat pocket and offered one. "Talk to me. What's on your mind?" she said.

I hated these situations. It was the crushing task of confessing something, the fight to form words, and the fear of releasing them. The tears were steady now, making it even harder to speak. She gently tried to help.

"You miss your baby… it's okay, the grieving process is a process…"

"It's not that," I interrupted, choking out the words. "It's, maybe it's my fault—"

"Don't even go there," she said sternly.

I fought to pull myself together, desperate to interrupt her admonishment. "No! There's stuff you don't know." She looked at me and waited. I resisted the urge to bang my head against the steering wheel.

Her tone softened, "What don't I know? Tell me."

It was impossible to look at her. I leaned against my door, dropping my head into my palm. "Something's wrong with me… I like women."

In a pause of silence, she connected the dots. "And you think God took this baby away from you." I nodded a yes. "That's not how it works, you *know* that's not how he works. You're putting human qualities on God again; he doesn't give us things just to rip them away in vengeance."

I stayed silent, still unable to make eye contact. She continued. "Is there someone else, did you cheat on Lou?"

"No! Neither. But before the pregnancy I'd been thinking a lot about leaving some day. And dating women."

"He loves you; he's a good man," she said quietly.

I felt a jolt of irritation. "Yeah, I know…" was all I could offer. It was my own fault. I'd painted myself into this corner by always protecting Lou and never telling anyone about the fights, the teasing, the jealousy, the tantrums. I couldn't argue with what others saw outside our relationship: a man who worked hard, loved his family, was friendly, and liked to help others.

Sister Mary continued, "Do you still want to leave?" I shook my head no, which was true at the moment. I felt like a stranger in my own body these days. Leaving was the furthest thing from my mind.

"Then it doesn't matter that you're attracted to women. You're married. It's no different than if you were attracted to men, you see? So don't worry about it, let that go. God loves you; he's grieving with you. And he loves Rylie. Her life, *every* life, has a purpose, and we aren't the ones who define a lifetime."

Our talk didn't magically lessen the pain or change the grieving process, but it made me feel loved by God again. I wasn't going to hell for my attraction, I was "good" again, safe. She told me about a beautiful old church fifteen minutes away and said if I wanted to go to mass there some Sunday she would go with me. The very next weekend we went, and I instantly felt connected. I went back the following weekend alone only to find there was a baby being baptized during mass, a little girl. I tried to pull myself together. I fought against the familiar thought that this was another sick joke from God. *It's not a joke, it's the promise of the future, the babies you will have and baptize here someday.*

I joined that parish and was back to mass regularly. In my downtime at work, I began reading different books on topics of Catholicism, studying the faith in earnest. I was no longer planning how to get out of the marriage and start a new life, and I wasn't interested in dating women. The attraction was still there; it didn't go anywhere. I just relegated it to the back corner of my brain. The Catholic rules say it's okay for it to be there, you just can't act on it or think about it.

Despite having a bit of spiritual peace and the familiar rituals of Catholicism, I still didn't recognize who I was. But I was open to learning. For the first time in our entire relationship, I was interacting with Lou with less drama. We were getting along, and I was attached to his side. In my mind I thought, *I'm cured! I can continue to honor my vow to my husband and to God and I won't go to hell.*

CHAPTER THIRTY

W ell, the bad news is that yes, you *do* have a UTI. The good news, at least I hope it's good news, is… you're pregnant." The doctor waited for my reaction.

It was November 22, 2002, exactly six months since Rylie's death. It was a bit of a surprise, but it *was* good news. At a follow-up visit after the stillbirth I was told that any future pregnancy had an 80 percent chance of carrying to full term. There were preventative measures they could put in place.

As it turned out, those were good odds. On July 10th my healthy full-term baby girl Violet was born by scheduled C-section. I was in love. Randy was a big brother at age fourteen and adapted quickly. He held her for the first time a few hours after she was born, and I thought my heart would explode with happiness. Randy had never been around newborns before, so this was all new territory. "Her head looks like a tiny little melon," he laughed. For the next year or more that would be his nickname for her, Melon.

Violet was a very happy baby. She rarely cried and she smiled constantly. For all of the pain we'd been through, it seemed we had been given an equal measure of pure joy. I almost felt guilty for feeling such bliss after months of grieving. In the back of my mind, I questioned myself: *You know this is not Rylie; they are two different babies, right?* Two months later that doubt and fear was put to rest with a single piece of mail. It was a large postcard from a photography studio that read:

Happy first birthday! We would like to give
your baby a free photo session to celebrate this
milestone.

It was September 2003. Had I carried Rylie to term it would in fact be the month of her first birthday. The postcard was an immediate gut punch. Yet in that moment I understood joy and pain can coexist and it was okay.

Lou seemed happy as well and for the first time in our seventeen-year-long relationship, we rarely fought. Sometimes he even went to mass with me and the kids, although he wasn't Catholic. Violet was in fact baptized in the new church I'd been attending.

Life revolved around Violet and Randy. We took her to all of Randy's high school football games, then his basketball games. He enjoyed being a big brother and I enjoyed seeing the two of them bond. Things seemed good in general, a fairy tale almost.

Two months before Violet's first birthday I found out I was pregnant *again,* this baby due on Valentine's Day. It was clear that whatever caused years of infertility was no longer an issue. With the same high-risk specialists and same protocol, I was hopeful. Financially it was going to stretch us pretty thin, but I was happy for Violet to have a sibling so close to her age, just eighteen months apart.

There were no problems with the pregnancy other than the baby, a boy, was bigger than average. By the time I hit the five-month mark, I was incredibly uncomfortable and couldn't imagine how I'd carry to term without him splitting out of my stomach like an alien. My C-section was scheduled twelve days early and Max was born on Groundhog Day, February 2, 2005. "Congratulations, you have a kindergartner!" the doctor joked as he lifted the ten-pound baby out of my stomach and held him high above the partition for me to see.

Life got exponentially busier. Randy was sixteen, learning to drive and starting his first job at the same Catholic-run nursing home where I'd worked and met Sister Mary. He played football and basketball, and we attended nearly every game with the two babies in tow. It drew lots of attention with strangers, who often commented, "Wow, you started over!" referring to the age difference between Randy and the little ones.

With growing expenses, I went back to working five days instead of four. There were hours of downtime each day between clients; it was just the nature of the work. So, I spent all of it studying my faith. Some days I'd go to mass on my lunch hour. I felt like I was finally doing everything *right*; that I was finally *normal* as long as I left my attraction to women safely stored away in a tiny corner of my mind and pretended it didn't exist.

****

The other obstacle to my perfect Catholic family was that Lou was not Catholic. He had never belonged to any church and had never been baptized. It wasn't against the rules to marry a non-Catholic, according to the church, as long as the children of that marriage were baptized and raised Catholic.

A very basic, selfish part of me wanted him to get out of bed every Sunday morning and help me get two toddlers to mass on time. A less selfish part of me wanted him to experience the sense of peace and community that comes with belonging to a church. In general, he was more socially inclined than I was anyway, so I knew he would enjoy the fellowship.

Things were going south again. I wondered if all the problems in our relationship would be eased if we worshiped God together, as a couple. Would he find an inner peace that calmed his short-temper and jealous nature? Would I be able to completely dissolve my attraction to women and never revisit my dream of a different life?

I couldn't escape the reality that he and I were still very different people, as we'd always been. The peace we settled into after Rylie's death five years earlier was short-lived. I was fully engrossed in the joys of raising my teenager and babies. I had no time, energy, or desire for anything more in life. Things had returned to what had always been abnormally normal for us: frequent arguments, distrust, and general incompatibility. We still had very different interests, different tastes in everything from music and entertainment to clothing and household decor. We fought about money, sex, household responsibilities, and everything in between.

I'd also grown tired of mean-spirited teasing and name-calling. He had nicknames for me like chubby, fatty, and other words or phrases that referred to my weight or some aspect of my physical appearance. If I complained or asked him to stop, he got irritated. He claimed that he was just teasing, saying, "I love you AND your fat rolls. You should be glad you have someone like me." Unable to make it stop I began insulting him back. It never seemed to him. It just became some sort of funny game. But I was sick of all of it, his jokes and mine. I'd grown up around family members who always created nicknames and made fun of other people whether it was strangers or neighbors or even other family members. I did it too, thinking it was normal and harmless because the jokes were always made behind someone's back. Now it just felt totally screwed up and not okay.

I wasn't happy but I truly believed all marriages were like ours and if a couple claimed to be blissful it was probably because they hadn't been together very long. Or they were lying. Still, I'd made a vow to Lou and to God so there was no out. This must be why vows mention "for better or worse."

Our relationship issues had become a daily source of stress until driving to work one morning I got an idea that I thought must be a message from God. On the local Catholic radio station someone was talking about the miraculous power of praying a novena. I had heard of novenas before but didn't know the specifics.

The voice on the radio said that a novena is a method of praying or asking for something urgent and/or very specific. You recite the same prayer every day for nine days (the Latin word *novem* is the number nine) and if your devotion and desires are in earnest then God will answer your need.

I hadn't planned out the specific wording of what I was asking for, but I thought it would be something about Lou finding God. The next morning, I got out the booklet and began reading the prayer. When I got to the last line, the fill-in-the-blank portion for my intention, the request that tumbled out of my mouth was not at all what I expected. I asked God to "purify my marriage." I wasn't sure where that came from but since the novena is the same prayer every day, I accepted it and didn't question. For the next nine days I prayed it word for word, ending with "purify my marriage."

A few months later Lou transferred jobs and was paired with an older man who was a devout Catholic. They were having regular conversations about God and religion and soon Lou told me he had decided to begin the adult catechism classes to join the church. His coworker would be his sponsor. I was happy for him and for us. I was also a bit shocked considering that was my initial prayer intent (for him to find God) but the actual words I used were different.

It didn't take long for me to find out that "purify my marriage" was going to rest squarely on my shoulders, not Lou's.

CHAPTER THIRTY-ONE

About a month after Lou began his catechism classes, I aggravated an old lower back injury and ended up in bed on a heating pad, mindlessly changing channels on the TV. It was my third or fourth loop through the lineup when I stopped on a scene of two young women having a conversation. One blonde, one brunette, both attractive. In a matter of moments, I understood they were friends but there was an undercurrent of attraction between them. Both women seemed cautious and uneasy, slowly noticing their friendship changing. I continued to watch this for ten more minutes until the show ended. Another episode of the series came on and I watched it too.

The next day I returned to work and spent my downtime looking up the TV show, the plot synopsis, and episode descriptions. Obsessively I watched short clips of scenes and interviews with cast members. The main storyline of the series was the friendship that turned romantic. It did not have sex scenes or anything graphic, it was primarily about each woman's struggle to come to terms with the attraction, labels, stereotypes, and acceptance by family and friends.

I was trying to make sense of my own feelings around the story. I was anxious and couldn't focus on my work. Something from my past was awake now and it made me very uneasy, although I couldn't quite put my finger on it.

Over the next several days I could think of nothing else. On breaks at work, I was watching past episodes and when there were no more to watch I didn't know how I'd manage to wait for the next season. Sprinkled throughout this obsession were moments of panic and confusion and an increasing undercurrent of fear. *What the hell is going on? What am I feeling?*

Eventually I stumbled upon a fan forum—message boards and conversation threads—about anything and everything related to the show. I created a username and began to read what other people had to say about the series. It was all very anonymous and interesting. Sometimes I posted my own comments and ideas about storylines or characters.

I quickly became familiar with several regular fans like me even though no one used their actual name as their username. It was primarily females from all over the world and most were gay. A few were straight or bi. I liked the anonymity and the fact that no one questioned my interest in a show about two young women coming to terms with their sexual orientation.

There was a section of the forum called Fan Fics. It seemed a strange concept at first. People wrote stories about the fictional characters from the show. But then I recalled the stories Terry used to write in ninth grade about a different popular TV drama. I'd not heard the term *fan fiction* back then, but it was obviously the same thing. I'd been impressed with Terry's writing and the creative scenarios he concocted so I decided to check it out.

The fan forum was a daily habit. I accessed it from my computer or my phone, wherever and whenever. Most of the fan fiction expanded the main characters' romantic connection far beyond what the show implied. Many times, the stories crossed into the genre of erotica. I was morally conflicted at first, but my curiosity was stronger. I rationalized my actions because it wasn't pornography (there were no images) and it was written tastefully like romance novels. And it was fiction of course. Stories, not real people.

It was also quite educational. I'd long had my own fantasies about women, but they were very benign considering I had no real-life experiences to draw from. Again, I rationalized. I was only reading; it wasn't any worse than reading a spicy novel about a man and a woman.

After a few months Lou noticed I was spending a great deal of time on the computer or my phone. He confronted me, asking point-blank if I were having some kind of affair. The question was laughable considering I didn't even know the real names of most of the women I interacted with in the message boards. But I also felt bad that my secrecy made him think I had a boyfriend somewhere. So I told him about the show, the site, and my embarrassment at being so sucked into something fictional. He didn't care much about the show itself but didn't like that I was chatting with "a bunch of lesbians."

"What if I were secretly chatting with a bunch of gay dudes about a show with a gay guy couple?" he asked. "Wouldn't that seem odd to you?"

He had a point. In that scenario I'd wonder if he were gay or leaning in that direction. I felt overwhelmed with shame. To make matters worse, there he was going to catechism classes every week to become a Catholic while I'm reading lesbian fan fiction in my spare time. *What the hell is wrong with me?*

Wracked with guilt and humiliation, I managed to work up enough courage to talk with Sister Mary. She was the only person aside from Samantha who knew I was attracted to women. It was an uncomfortable conversation, far more difficult than the last one we had. She suggested I see a therapist to get some professional help and gave me the number to a small group practice that operated on a sliding scale. Lou trusted Sister Mary's advice on the situation so he let me make an appointment for my very first therapy session.

I was also struggling with depression and anxiety. My primary care physician had been prescribing anti-depressants and we had yet to find one that worked. Sometimes the side effects were bad, or the medication increased my appetite, so I'd immediately stop taking it.

There was no reprieve from the fear and panic I felt. And it was impossible to get the TV show out of my head. I prayed about it, begging God to help me, to change me. I started going to mass and confession twice a week on my lunch hour. Instead of feeling more connected to God, he felt further and further away.

My therapist, Carol, was a petite woman I'd guess to be in her late fifties. She struck me as a teacher, specifically the type who enjoys their job and cares about their students. She was welcoming and kind while maintaining clear professional boundaries. Every Monday I spent my lunch hour in Carol's office talking, sometimes crying. Our first several sessions were mostly history-gathering, recounting major events that had happened over the course of my thirty-five years.

She seemed to be far less panicked about my connection to the show and its fan site. One afternoon we spent an entire session trying to pinpoint the source of my distress and fear.

"Why are you scared? What will happen?" Carol asked me.

"It's going to fuck up my entire life. I don't want it here."

"What is *it*? Can you elaborate, be more specific?"

Good question. It was such a powerful, clear, and intuitive feeling, a "knowing," that I hadn't considered how to define it.

"I don't know. It's hard to describe. I guess it's like some past version of me? I know that doesn't make much sense."

"What does it look like, how do you know it's you?"

"There's no question that it's me. But in appearance… it's more of a shadow. It reminds me of a photograph someone took of me when I was thirteen, but in silhouette."

"When did you first notice it? Does it speak to you?"

"I noticed it soon after I first stumbled upon the TV show. It just… showed up…" I was suddenly aware of how wacko this sounded but Carol didn't seem alarmed or panicked so I kept going:

"kind of like someone you knew a million years ago, you've long forgotten they existed, and boom they just walk through your front door unannounced."

She nodded and leaned slightly forward in her chair. "What do you fear it will do? How will it fuck up your life?"

I had to think about that for a minute. I didn't question the reality of my fear, in fact I knew with every bit of my being that this presence was going to wreck everything. I just hadn't considered *how*.

"I don't know. Maybe that's why it's so terrifying. But from the minute it showed up, I knew it was bad news. Things are going to go wrong; I know it like I know the sky is blue."

Things began to unravel pretty quickly over the next few months. My thoughts were so strange at times. Once at a gas station I was standing outside the car filling the tank and realized that I was three different versions of myself: There was the present me who was at the gas pump, the menacing me from the past who showed up when I started watching the TV show, and there must be a third me having this thought and observing the other two.

In the moment it seemed a very lucid and logical realization, so benign that I went home and shared it with Lou and later with my mom. Their reactions were not what I expected. They seemed very concerned and a little freaked out. I thought about it again, but it still felt logical to me, just an observation.

I was getting increasingly frustrated with God though. He wasn't listening at all. I told him all I wanted was to be a good, normal Catholic. I found that TV show by accident. It wasn't like I got on the internet and started searching for something about lesbians. I told God I didn't want to break my vow and that I was willing to stay in my marriage and be a good mom, that's all I wanted. I didn't want to think about women, I didn't want to date women, I didn't want to be attracted to women on TV or in stories.

Why did you make me this way? I screamed that question to him over and over.

Months went by and nothing improved. My prayers became more frantic and more useless. I'd go to confession at noon and within hours I'd be reading lesbian fiction, or I'd notice a pretty woman in the grocery store or in a TV commercial. I was starting to feel like the only way to stop this whole thing was to be dead. It was a thought that brought a wave of relief but in the next instant I'd think of the kids and start to cry. *I can't do that to them. I can't leave them.* I was trapped.

Soon Carol recommended a psychiatrist. She said it wasn't good to keep switching medications and that I could still see her for therapy every week. The psychiatrist could manage the meds. I was hesitant, believing a psychiatrist was for people who are *really* not okay. "If you had a knee injury, you'd probably see a knee specialist rather than your primary care doctor, right?" Carol reasoned. "A family physician only gets a six-month rotation in psychiatry, it's not their specialty," she continued.

It made sense. I took the referral and made an appointment with Dr. Nicole Black. Her office was in an upscale neighborhood in an old house that had been converted to a doctor's office. It had dark walnut wood floors, high ceilings, and very little natural light. It was eerily quiet in the empty waiting area. I heard a door open and the sound of high heeled shoes. An attractive woman dressed in a light blue blouse and ivory pencil skirt appeared in the doorway. She softly spoke my name as a question. I nodded and followed her into an office that reminded me of an old book-filled library room in a rich person's home. I wasn't sure if she was the doctor or the office manager until she shut the door and took a seat in the wingback chair across from me. She crossed her legs and scribbled something on a yellow legal pad. Her sandy-blonde hair was not quite shoulder-length, and I guessed her age to be around thirty.

I looked around the room while she wrote. My eyes scanned three walls of books and framed university degrees before meeting her intense stare. She wasn't frowning but she wasn't smiling. This was uncomfortable. After a few more painful seconds of awkward staring and silence she spoke. "Tell me why you are here."

I recounted my medication history: names, dosages, and length of time I took each one before trying the next. Her fingers flew, writing it all down on the yellow legal pad. When we were done, she looked at the list for a few moments in silence. Again, with practically no emotion and a neutral face she spoke, "There's so much here, it's going to take a while to determine a diagnosis. Your brain chemistry is too muddled from so much switching. See me again in two weeks."

CHAPTER THIRTY-TWO

That damn TV show. Almost two years had passed since the night I was channel surfing and found it. And then there was the terrifying version of myself that came with it, a shadowy figure I could see in my mind that was there to fuck up the normal, Catholic life I'd created.

I couldn't figure out where God was in all this. Seemed like he ditched me for sure but why? I knew I'd been living a good life up until the TV show. I was being a great mom, a decent wife (or at least doing my best), and I was being a good Catholic. I listened to Christian music, I prayed daily, I studied the faith, educated myself on papal encyclicals, read the Bible, and baptized my kids, taught them prayers, and took them to mass every Sunday. At Christmas, I refused to buy Santa decorations and instead focused entirely on the birth of Jesus. I asked God to purify my marriage and then things went to hell. Why?

It was practically impossible to not think about women and to not notice women anywhere I went. How did it go back to this? *Okay. So I'm human. Fine.* Humans are sinful by nature, but God forgives sin. "Ask and it is given unto you" is a quote I remembered from scripture. The problem was that I was asking—begging daily—for help and it didn't come. Instead, I was on multiple heavy-duty meds: lithium, Lamictal, Topamax. At one point Dr. Black gave me Klonopin for crisis moments when I felt detached from reality and unable to stop crying. She cautioned me against taking it when drinking because it could kill me, so I took that to heart. I was careful to only drink on days when I didn't have a crisis episode, which luckily was most days. After work I'd go to my mom's to pick up the kids and then go home to start dinner. But before dinner prep, I'd mix a drink.

Just one.

It filled a reusable 32-ounce plastic cup from 7-Eleven but in my mind, it was *just one drink.*

Food was on the table, kids were corralled, and I'd take my evening meds with my meal and my *one* drink. Then I could manage the last two hours of my day: play with the kids, argue with Lou, go to bed, and prepare to do it all again the next day.

I stopped watching the TV show when the series ended. I was still reading fan fiction though and had even tried my hand at writing some—secretly of course. That prompted another accusation from Lou. I told him what I was writing and said he could read it if he didn't believe me. He didn't react with anger, which was unusual, but it probably would have been easier for me to handle than his unexpected kindness. I broke down and started to cry. I was so overwhelmed with the mess that was my life and the lack of control I had over any of it, not to mention the lack of help from God.

My emotional breakdown in that moment became a confession. I told Lou that I had been attracted to women from the time I was a little kid and had had crushes on my teachers and on women in movies and TV. He looked somewhat panicked and asked if I was going to leave him. It was a fair question. "I don't *want* to leave. I don't *want* to feel any of this. It's making me crazy. I'm praying and begging God, I go to confession two and sometimes three times a week. I can't make it stop, but I just want to be *normal.*"

At that moment it was all true. I didn't *want* to leave despite being miserable and having dreamed of leaving years earlier. What

I wanted more than anything was for all of it to disappear so I could go on being a good Catholic and a good mom and fulfill the stupid vow I made.

Lou's demeanor changed. He seemed totally fine, which took me completely by surprise. "Well, we just need to get you laid by a woman. Get it out of your system."

What in the actual fuck was he talking about? I glanced down at my 32-ounce cup expecting that it must be empty and that I'd misheard his words. The cup was still filled to the midpoint and Lou was laughing.

Some part of me felt a little lighter having shared that heavy secret with another person. Now three people knew. Unfortunately, it didn't make my situation any easier. Hell, it complicated things exponentially. Lou wanted to know what types of women I found attractive, which movie star or entertainer I'd sleep with if I could pick anyone. It became a continual topic of conversation. If we were watching TV together he'd ask, "What about her; do you think she's hot?" I'd never been asked these questions before or had those conversations. I answered honestly and felt a sense of relief that he wasn't acting angry or jealous. It was a topic that didn't provoke arguments, which was rare for us. It also gave me a free pass to ponder these things without shame or guilt. It was fun.

Until it wasn't… The fun ended when those conversations morphed into sexual fantasies. Sure, I'd had plenty of fantasies in the past, but in the past, they were *my* fantasies; thoughts of my own creation that I could choose to indulge or block out and none of them ever included men.

In sharing a secret about myself with Lou I'd unknowingly opened a door that could never be closed. He barged through at will, inserting his own narratives and editing mine. I was angry but I also knew I had no one to blame but myself. It was my own actions that prompted the initial conversation.

Gradually my relationship with Lou felt less like a marriage and more like we were frat brothers. We frequented strip clubs, which was more to my benefit than his. Most strippers enjoy female customers and will forgo the no-touch rule, something I found out quickly during a lap dance. The dancer placed both of my hands on her bare breasts and said, "Nearly every girl who works here is at least bisexual."

****

We saved a little money and planned a four-day trip to escape the cold gray February weather. As was typical, we had different interests and had to make some compromises. I agreed to a gambling budget so he could piss away money in the slot machines; he tolerated the desert heat forty-five minutes south to watch me zipline across a canyon. We both agreed to spend an evening checking out a Vegas strip club.

It was huge, at least six or seven times the size of the clubs back home. The girls were considerably more glamorous than what we were used to and there were a lot of them. We agreed to a budget of one private dance each. A gorgeous brunette stopped by our table and took a seat next to me. She struck up a conversation with both of us, asking where we were from and so on. After a few minutes she asked if I would like a private dance. Feeling a little awestruck and intimidated I asked her to check back with me later. We watched a steady stream of performers on the main stage. Lou set his sights on someone and left momentarily for a dance. I watched the dancer who had talked with us earlier and hoped she would come back to our table.

An hour later she did, and I was ready. She took my hand and led me off to a dimly lit side of the club with two long rows of partitioned cubicles. When we entered one, I expected to see a chair or a booth but instead there was a padded table, similar to a medical exam table. It was reclined completely flat with wide steps on either side and mirrors on the ceiling above. The dancer pointed to a small table in the corner that held neatly folded towels and spray bottles. "These are cleaned after each dance, don't worry" she leaned in close to my ear so that I could hear her over the music. She smelled good.

I handed her my cash, and she ushered me onto the table. The next six minutes permanently altered my brain chemistry.

When it was over she walked me back to where Lou sat waiting. We left the club and started the long walk back to our hotel. He was talking but I had no idea what he was saying until he grabbed my arm.

"I said *are you okay*?" he laughed at me. "What happened back there?"

I nodded my head but needed a few moments to form sentences. I felt completely dazed and intoxicated even though I'd only had one drink. Lou was talking again. I struggled to make sense of it.

"Well, are you going to tell me what happened?" He was in my face now, still amused, but I recognized a hint of concern.

Stammering and more or less coherent, I recounted what had happened. It had been the closest thing I'd ever had to a sexual experience with a woman. And she ended it with a kiss. A real one, my first one.

Lou's reaction was the typical frat brother reaction: surprise, high five, feigned jealousy, and complaints about how women get to have all the fun in a strip club. We continued our walk back down the strip, stopping to drink and people watch. I was still dazed and trying to process whatever was going on in my brain or my energy field or any other part of my body for that matter. From time to time our conversation went quiet and he would again ask if I was okay but with less amusement each time. There was an uncertainty and doubt in his eyes that made me wonder if he felt what I was feeling. Had we had carelessly ventured into something that couldn't be undone?

I stopped going to weekday mass and confession. It wasn't making a difference, and my sins were becoming increasingly too humiliating to verbalize. I was angry too. My patience had worn thin with a bullshit God who was nowhere to be found. From where I stood this was already hell so I may as well make the best of it. *Fuck you God, you made me this way. What's the point?*

CHAPTER THIRTY-THREE

Have you had any more thoughts of harming yourself?" Dr. Black's emotionless tone matched nicely with her deadpan stare and stiff posture. It used to make me nervous but that was several appointments ago. Now it was just annoying.

"Well yeah. There's still no other solution. I still like women. I'm still married."

I watched her writing this info on her notepad, like she always did, and wondered why she didn't have a better memory.

"How often do you have these thoughts?" she asked.

"They're not random thoughts, it's just the way things are. The only fix to my situation is to be dead. But I can't do that to my kids; I don't want to do that to them. So, I'm trapped. I have to wait to die naturally and then go to hell for eternity. It's stupid."

She scribbled more notes and then put the notepad down. "I can't let you leave the office. I'm going to call your husband to come get you and I'd like him to take you directly to an inpatient facility."

"A what?"

"It's a brand-new facility, it's only been open for a couple of months. It's state of the art. If I had to send one of my own family members for treatment this is the place I'd choose."

I didn't have the energy to mentally process what she was suggesting. I just said, "Okay."

I was there for a week. Dr. Black was right, it was in fact a very nice facility. With a little effort it was relatively easy to forget I was in a locked ward. The food was good, the staff was kind, and the place was clean. Although none of it could offset the stigma I felt when it was all over. Sure, I'd been having some disturbing thoughts for a long time, been on countless psychiatric meds, and was in weekly therapy. Completing an inpatient stay felt like I'd been officially stamped CRAZY. I then feared that any bad day or bad mood would be a red flag to Lou or my family. I was damaged goods.

When I got home, I was relieved to be with my kids again. That was by far the most difficult part of being away, everything else was more or less unchanged. The same routines and problems were there waiting for me. I was still the same person, just well rested.

Over the span of two years there were two more psychiatric hospital stays for feeling hopelessly suicidal and detached from reality. Lou and I were fighting all the time. At least twice a week the fights were intense, not just petty arguments. Sometimes I lost complete control and went into a rage, something that had never happened before. It was completely out of character as I'd always been a classic people-pleaser who avoided conflict. We were arguing back and forth when I snapped without warning and began repeatedly punching a hole into the wall until he tackled me to the ground. My hand was fractured. Another time I was standing at my computer desk during an argument and in a flash, I beat the keyboard to pieces with my fist.

I wanted out. I didn't give a shit about God or vows. This was not sustainable. More than four years had passed since the TV show and during that span of time, my life had become a mental health nightmare. I was clinging to my kids, trying to give them meaningful interactions, determined to stay alive for them no matter how hopeless things were.

Despite our constant clashing I felt that Lou deserved to be happy, too, but I didn't know how I'd ever get him to see that it wasn't going to be with me. I didn't hate him. He had always been and still was, a good dad. He worked hard and took pride in making our house as nice as possible. Surely some part of him recognized that we had never been a good match. I sat in Carol's office and cried for all five of us, knowing a divorce was inevitable and going to be hell for everyone involved.

There were no easy answers. I didn't know how to leave or how to even start the process. It was overwhelming to consider so I shut it off and turned to my art supplies for relief. In the privacy of a sketchbook, I could work out some of the darker thoughts in my mind. On canvas paper I worked in acrylics, creating non-descript figures and abstractions.

I often wondered, *Who am I? Is my personality forever scrambled like my brain chemistry?* Those questions were the inspiration for a non-figurative self-portrait. I'd learned the concept in my undergrad studies, and that a self-portrait doesn't have to be literal. It can be anything that is representative of you or some part or quality of you. The finished piece was a painting of one of my prescription bottles wearing my ball cap. (A ponytail and ball cap had become part of my everyday attire.) It came across as somewhat dark to other people, but I liked it. It was exactly as I'd imagined it and accurately portrayed the questions that plagued me. *What or who is the real me beneath all the psych meds? Am I lost forever?*

Art seemed to quiet the noise in my head, particularly if the kids took part. They loved to paint. It gave us a chance to be together and do something fun. I felt fully present in those moments in spite of a baseline of despair that had become my new normal. Sometimes I took them to the Cincinnati Art Museum or the Contemporary Art Museum. I missed the carefree days of art school that seemed like a lifetime ago.

I needed something to work toward, some way of feeling in control and *normal.* I needed to prove to myself (and everyone, for that matter) that I wasn't a lost cause. After researching my options, I decided to apply to grad school and get a master's in teaching. Combined with my Bachelor of Fine Arts, I could get a teaching license and become a high school art teacher, something I'd been interested in for a long time.

The exam I'd have to pass for admission into the program was tough. It covered every type of art (even furniture and architecture) from all over the world, from as far back as the Paleolithic cave paintings in Lascaux, France. I went to the library and borrowed the biggest, most comprehensive art history book in the collection. It was an oversized, hardbound book, three inches thick with full color illustrations. It covered art and artists from the beginning of time. It detailed every medium and material as well as the terminology used to critique various styles and processes. It was exactly what I needed to know for the graduate exam.

I spent hours and hours studying the art book. Starting from page one, I read every word and took notes in a spiral-bound notebook. I carefully examined the accompanying illustrations, making notes on those as well, sometimes sketching the images next to my notes. It took several weeks to get through the 900-page book. It took several more weeks to study my notes and commit it all to memory in preparation for the exam. I needed to score at least 158 out of 200 to pass and was ecstatic to learn I scored 174. After completing the other application requirements and going through an interview process, it was official: I was accepted into the program and would start fall of 2011, less than six months away. It gave me hope. *I might be bat-shit crazy, but my brain isn't totally useless.*

CHAPTER THIRTY-FOUR

Maybe it was the momentum created by my focus on grad school or maybe we'd finally reached a tipping point but things with Lou were deteriorating at lightning speed. I supposed it was a little of both. In an all-too-familiar scenario I put the kids to bed while he waited in our bedroom, the obligation for sex looming like a neon sign.

Several weeks prior he pushed for sex, and I gave in, knowing it was a faster option than having an argument at 10 p.m. But the act was cut short when I started having a panic attack. I felt as if he were crushing me, and I couldn't breathe. My entire body began shivering uncontrollably even though he hadn't done anything out of the ordinary. Nothing like this had ever happened before. Fortunately, Lou stopped and didn't try to continue which was perfectly fine with me although he seemed somewhat annoyed.

Since then, he'd backed off a bit while I became more assertive in telling him I wasn't in the mood. But as days turned into weeks, I knew the reprieve couldn't last forever. The kids were tucked in, and I started my nightly routine of removing my contacts, brushing my teeth. A weight settled on my chest. Instinctively I braced for a confrontation. Our fights were so frequent and so unresolved that they rolled hopelessly one into the next.

"Let me guess: You're not in the mood." Lou grumbled as I entered the bedroom.

My anxiety flipped to anger like a light switch. "No. And it's a good thing I'm not because you just killed it with that shitty pickup line."

Ding ding! We were off and fighting. It was the same old shit. The same accusations, the same shitty responses volleyed back and forth. I stopped participating and sat on the floor. Lou paused mid-sentence just long enough for me to interject, "I can't fucking do this anymore. I can't. This is like the *Groundhog Day* movie; every fight is the same thing. How do you not see it? It's a fucking script for Christ's sakes! I'm exhausted, I can't do it. I can't. I won't."

As if I hadn't said anything at all, Lou continued ranting. I sat with my head in my hands unable to listen. My thoughts were getting louder and played on a loop in my mind: *I can't do this anymore. I can't do this anymore.*

Lou's tirade turned to background noise. I felt eerily calm. I got up off the floor and went to my dresser drawer for a fresh pair of socks. By the time I was dressed Lou was demanding to know what the hell I was doing.

"I'm leaving. I'll be back in the morning, early, before the kids wake up."

"Are you out of your fucking mind? Where do you think you're going?" His eyes were filled with rage, something that normally caused me to shut down immediately. But in that moment, I looked at him and felt a wave of empathy and sadness not just for him but for both of us.

"I'm going to Rachel's or Jayne's, depending on which of them answers my text first. I'm going to sleep on their couch, and I'll be back at 6:30 a.m. The kids won't even know I left."

He stared in disbelief. My words came with ease and clarity. There was no anger, no sarcasm, no desperation. "I can't fight with you; I don't have it in me. Please. I promise I'll be back at 6:30. You have my word. We'll talk tomorrow."

"Unbelievable! Fucking unbelievable! You're just going to walk out of here and leave."

I calmly repeated my plan, picked up my keys, and walked out of the house.

When I returned the next morning, Lou and the kids were still sleeping. I grabbed a pillow and stretched out on the couch knowing my mind was too awake to fall asleep. Thoughts flowed slow and steady like a news ticker: *It's Sunday May 22, 2011. Rylie died exactly nine years ago today. The kids will be up soon. We'll have yogurt and fruit for breakfast then get ready for mass.*

Mass. I'd begun attending regularly again for the sole purpose of getting Violet and Max a deeply discounted Montessori education in the parish's private school. I didn't feel guilty about it. Parents do what they need to do.

Later that afternoon I put on a video for the kids so Lou and I could talk privately in the next room. He was quiet and serious but didn't appear angry, which was somewhat surprising.

"This isn't working anymore," I said carefully.

"So, this is it?" he asked with a bit of an edge in his tone.

I had to find a way to get through this conversation without it blowing up into a fight. I wasn't even angry; I felt sad. "I don't see a way around it aside from some miraculous intercession from above."

He shook his head. "I can't believe you're just giving up."

"We each deserve to be happy and right now, we're not. Can you honestly say you're happy in this relationship?"

He was quiet for a moment. "No. But I'm not going to just throw it all away!"

"I love you, and I know you love me. That's not a question. But when you love someone, you want them to be happy. I can't be the person you need; I have to admit that. You deserve someone you can be happy with and so do I for that matter. Fighting every day about the same issues, over and over and over is not happiness. It's affecting the kids now; you heard Violet the other day when she came to our room. She asked us to please not fight..."

Revisiting that memory hit me like a truck. I started to cry.

"Do you know what this is going to do to them?" he fired back.

"What's it doing to them right now? They shouldn't have to hear us fighting. Even when they don't hear it, they can sense the tension between us. You see it as well as I do—they looked nervous and scared." He shook his head and looked away, but I continued. "This is a no-win situation and we're all in it, we're all suffering either way."

"You're not suffering, you're ready to run off and eat pussy!" His accusation was hissed through clenched teeth.

I took a deep breath, desperate to keep the conversation civil. "Please stop; can we please have a normal conversation for once? Like adults? I'm begging you. The kids are down the hall, and they don't need to hear another argument."

He didn't respond. We sat in silence for several minutes before he said something I totally hadn't expected.

"If we split up, your family is going to turn on me. They're going to hate me, and you all are going to talk shit about me constantly."

"What?"

"You know it's true. Just like when your uncle got divorced, everyone talks shit about his ex and makes fun of her. You'll hate me and they will too."

"Lou, I don't want to hate you! I don't even want to fight with you anymore which is why I'm sitting here trying to have an honest and open conversation. What happens between us is no one's business but ours. My family likes you and I'm glad. The only way they would turn on you is if you did something really awful to me or the kids."

His face changed slightly as if he were considering the truth in my words. I let it sit and attempted to steer the discussion back to center.

"Please be completely honest... are you really happy in this marriage? Do you really think it's working?"

He paused for a moment. "No."

With that single admission, the conversation began to flow. We agreed not to tell the kids until I found an apartment and secured a move-in date. After that we'd share custody fifty-fifty.

"What about the holidays?" he asked.

"We can share them, like alternate each year or something," I suggested.

"I guess I won't be at your mom's for Christmas Eve."

It seemed the idea of breaking up with my family was as difficult for Lou as ending the marriage. Maybe more difficult. I offered an olive branch. "Hey, maybe we can just be friends like Megan's parents, and you could still come to Christmas Eve. Who knows?" Megan was Randy's girlfriend.

We'd always marveled at the ease with which Megan's divorced parents interacted at family events. They'd each show up with their new spouses in tow and it was as normal as could be. This got his attention. "You'd actually be okay with that?" he asked.

"Well yeah as long as you weren't being a dick." I laughed. When he cracked a smile, I felt safe enough to continue, "Anything's possible, right? Maybe someday we'll both show up with our new wives or girlfriends and it will be no big deal."

He snorted in amusement. "Yeah, you'll end up with someone gorgeous and a little younger and I'll have some ugly old bag."

We both laughed at his joke although he seemed to be only halfway kidding when he added, "I'm serious. You wait and see; I guarantee your wife will be way better looking than whoever I get."

This was typical Lou. Everything was a competition in his eyes. "Oh stop, that's way down the road." We sat in silence. Maybe this wouldn't be as bad as I feared.

But that's not the way divorce works. The next few weeks were polarizing. Things looked hopeful one minute and dire the next. Lou and I had many calm conversations where we seemed to be on the same page about the split but then there were arguments, anger, and hurt.

I found a tiny apartment nearby and secured a move-in date. It was time to break the news to the kids. I told Randy first. He was twenty-two and engaged to his girlfriend of six years, Megan. Somehow, I thought the news of the split wouldn't come as a surprise to him since he had witnessed firsthand how rocky the relationship had always been. I was surprised when he started to cry. "You've seen us fight and have issues your whole life; I guess I thought you wouldn't be surprised," I said gently as I hugged him. He said yes, he knew there were always fights but we had always stayed together so he believed that's just how it would always be. His response made much more sense than my stupid assumption. I felt awful.

The entire situation was complicated by the fact that this was not only a divorce, it was my second *coming out*, and a very public one at that. Being married to Lou was the only thing keeping me locked into the category of bisexual. But the marriage was over, and the future was strictly women for me. By definition, that made me a lesbian, a label I was finally ready to embrace.

I told only the closest people. I figured everyone else could find out later on, organically, as I started to date and as word spread. One of the coming-out conversations I was most fearful of having was with my eighty-four-year-old grandma, my dad's mom. She had recently moved from West Virginia to Kentucky to live with my parents. We were very close and always had been, but I was scared to tell her I was gay. When I finally went to see her, she was outside on the patio alone. I sat down across from her and started to talk but was too nervous to use the word *gay* or *lesbian* and instead phrased it as "I'm not going to date men. I'm only interested in women."

She didn't flinch. "Women. Okay."

I wasn't sure what to make of that, so I took a more direct approach. "Are you going to disown me?" That's when I got a big reaction.

"Disown you? I can't believe you asked that! I'm your grandma. I love you and I'm *for* you." I gave her a hug and thanked her. No further discussion was necessary.

Divorce is a special kind of hell when kids are involved. Breaking the news to Violet and Max was a painful experience that will remain forever burned into my memory. Lou and I had agreed we would tell them together but when I called the kids into the room, he angrily looked at me and said, "You wanted this; you can tell them." He then flopped onto the bed and glared at the ceiling, refusing to take part.

I barely had the words out of my mouth when eight-year-old Violet began to wail and cry. "You said you weren't getting divorced!" she repeated over and over. I picked her up and hugged her against my body; she was sobbing uncontrollably. Suddenly I realized what she was referring to and felt like the worst parent of all time. A couple of months earlier she had come to the doorway of our bedroom when Lou and I were arguing and asked if we were going to get divorced. We hadn't noticed her standing there and quickly said no without a pause, more concerned that she had heard us fighting again.

As Violet's entire world crumbled, she shook and could only repeat the same thing over and over: "You said you weren't getting divorced!" Lou stayed silent, didn't move from his position three feet away glaring up at the ceiling. I caught his eye once and motioned him to comfort his daughter, *just hug her for Christ's sake*. He refused. "That's all you," he said dismissively. Six-year-old Max started to cry too.

At that moment I hated Lou more than I'd ever thought possible to hate another person. He'd always been a good dad, something I never doubted, but watching his kids cry and refusing to comfort them was some sick, narcissistic attempt to hurt me. Sure, he had every right to hate me and not want to be friends, I'd give him that; it was a fucking divorce not a vacation. Yet he had no right to withhold his love from the kids when they were experiencing the most traumatic news of their young lives.

I held them both on my lap, telling them I loved them and that it was going to be okay when nothing at all was okay.

CHAPTER THIRTY-FIVE

I may have hated Lou, but I also hated myself as I watched all three of my children experience the pain of our separation. Every day my mind was stuck in a loop of self-blame:

You are the cause of their pain. You started the divorce. It's your fault.

But it was also painful for them to have two parents who didn't get along and fought all the time... two happy homes have to be better than one miserable one, right?

No, kids only want their parents together in the same house no matter what. You put this in motion, you are causing their pain. You moved out.

But we are splitting their time equally between both homes!

Yes, but in their minds the house is their home; their memories will always be that you moved out.

Maybe it would've been easier to manage those thoughts had they not been true (intentions aside). It never stopped. I cried, I drank, I talked about it in therapy. I'd spent years imagining a new life, but nothing could have prepared me for the pain that came with it.

I thought about the phrase, being in the *middle* of a divorce. There was no *middle* for me or Lou, the marriage was over. The kids were the ones experiencing the *middle* as they shuffled back and forth between us. Nothing was *equal* for any of us in the fifty-

fifty shared parenting arrangement. How could Violet and Max be happy with one parent while simultaneously feeling the absence of the other parent? How do any of us create happiness in half of our waking moments while experiencing grief in the other half?

One particularly rough evening when the kids were with Lou, I thought I might go crazy being away from them. *How do people do this? How will this ever feel normal?* I wondered. The friends I now socialized and worked with were all younger and didn't have kids. But then I thought of Samantha.

It had been nine years since I last had seen her: the visit she made when Rylie died. She went through a divorce later that same year setting off a series of moves and career changes. I had Violet, then Max. Somehow in the midst of our lives undergoing drastic changes we lost touch. But several months before I split from Lou, Samantha found me on Facebook and posted a comment under a photo of me and the kids: *Your kids are adorable! You look great. Are you aging backwards like Benjamin Button or what?*

More recently I opened the app and sent her a private message: *Well, I finally did it. I'm moving out, getting divorced.* She replied back with some encouraging words and her phone number and said to text or call if I ever needed anything.

Now alone in my little empty apartment I picked up the phone and sent her a text:

How did you survive shared custody and being away from your kid? It's fucking AWFUL.

I put the phone down figuring it might be hours or maybe even a day before I'd hear back from her. But within minutes my phone rang. Not a text, she was calling.

"I wish I could give you some sort of shortcut or wisdom to make it less painful..." she said, "but it's so hard. It *will* get easier though, somehow. I swear. It just takes time unfortunately."

Her son, then fifteen, was only six during their split. She shared some of the heartache of that experience and how difficult it was in spite of the fact that she and her ex were amicable. "We worked so hard to keep things friendly between us, thinking that would make it easier but it's never easy for the kid. I don't think that really sunk in for me until he started referring to his overnight bag as *the divorce bag*..." She chuckled. "We can kind of laugh about it now because it's been so long but back then it really tore me up. It still breaks my heart a little when I think about it."

It felt good to talk to someone who had been down this road, and it felt even better that it was Samantha on the other end of the line. We talked for several hours that night as if the nine-year hiatus had only been nine minutes. I brought her up to speed on the events leading up to my exit, including the spiritual crisis and mental instability. She updated me on her life: the restaurant she bought, ran, and eventually sold after inheriting the family farm; her son's artistic and musical talents; and an asshole ex-boyfriend she recently dumped.

In a time when everything felt new and uncertain, reconnecting with my lifelong best friend brought a sense of comfort and familiarity. It was in the sound of her voice, the cadence of our conversations, and the safety of a shared sense of humor. "Thank you for picking up the phone and calling tonight," I said as we prepared to hang up. "I'd probably still be sitting here in the dark, crying. Talking really helped."

"Oh, trust me I get it, this stuff sucks! Try not to get bogged down in guilt, though; that only adds to an already difficult situation. Text me, let me know how things are going. I'm here if you need anything."

The call ended, marking a new chapter in our decades-long friendship. Feeling a little lighter, I replayed our conversation in my mind while locking up and getting ready to shower before bed. It was late July and the humidity was stifling. I stood under the cool water and made a mental plan for the next day: wake up early, get the remainder of the boxes unpacked, and make the apartment as welcoming as possible before the kids return in the afternoon.

A panicked thought interrupted, *Oh no, I've been in here too long!* Then I remembered there was no one to complain about it. No one was waiting to grumpily ask what took me so long. In fact, the water bill was included in the rent—I could shower until the water ran completely out if I wanted to! My shoulders relaxed immediately, and I laughed, amused by my unnecessary panic and feeling the first of many moments of *freedom.*

The next morning, I was up and energized, determined to get through all of the boxes. The space was small, but I moved things around until it flowed. I opened two boxes containing art supplies and art books. The books stacked neatly in a tall free-standing bookcase but where would I keep my art materials? Just like the shower the night before, I felt a jolt of panic followed by a reality check: *I can put this stuff wherever the hell I feel like. No one is going to argue or tell me it doesn't belong there or that it needs to be stored away.*

There were many more eye-opening moments like that in those first few weeks. Some nights after work my coworkers would invite me to get a beer or some hashbrowns at Waffle House. I no longer had to make up an excuse and say no. And when I said yes, I didn't have to keep a constant eye on the time. I no longer had a curfew. There were no accusations, inquisitions, or passive aggressive comments. *So, this is how normal people live and interact in the world... wow!*

It was becoming clear to me for the first time just how compromised my life had been. One afternoon I emptied a pile of my clean laundry on the bed and started folding it and putting it away. As I folded several pairs of underwear I thought, *God I hate these.* I hated the color and the style. I liked boxer briefs and owned a couple pairs, but all of the other underwear were purchased because they were what someone else wanted me to wear. They were items deemed "sexy" by the person who didn't have to wear them. Except they felt anything but sexy; they felt awkward, embarrassing, and uncomfortable. I immediately dropped what I was folding, grabbed a large black garbage bag from the hall closet, and pulled out the entire top drawer of my dresser. I threw away all of the underwear and bras except for three boxer briefs and two sports bras. I didn't care; I'd go to Target and buy what I liked. Maybe I'd even get boxers from the men's department. Who was going to complain or judge me?

I grabbed a second garbage bag and removed the remaining drawers from the dresser. I began to toss out shirts, shorts, pants, sleepwear, tank tops, anything that was purchased because Lou liked it or because Lou said I should wear it. He always complained that I chose dark colors like black, gray, or navy blue. He told me I needed to wear pink and pastels—colors I hated. He often nagged me to "do something" with myself, meaning wear makeup, style my hair, paint my nails. *Not anymore!* I thought. *I can wear what I like now.*

But... what did I like? I was stumped. I called to mind all of the basic categories of favorite things: cars, music, movies, books, clothing, shoes. Most of my favorites were things a friend or family member liked. *Holy shit, I don't even know who I am. This is bizarre.* I tied the garbage bags closed and made my way to the dumpster. *Well, looks like I better figure out clothing first.*

For the four years before then, clothes shopping had been getting easier in some respects and more miserable in others. My weight had been dropping steadily and then took another significant drop with the stress of the divorce. I was at 137 pounds, a number I hadn't seen since my junior year of high school. Being a smaller size meant there were more choices available, and things were physically easier to wear.

The bigger problem with buying clothes was that it was getting more and more difficult to shop in the ladies' department. It had always been a dreaded experience from as early as I can remember. Just walking through the aisles made me anxious and irritable. I didn't want any of it. I felt ridiculous. In the past when Lou shopped for clothes, I felt a weird sense of jealousy. I'd think, *I wish I could wear these clothes... it would be easy to choose things from this side of the store.*

I chucked the garbage bags into the parking lot dumpster and checked my watch. Maybe I'd make a trip to Old Navy. It was an easy place to shop, and I had the freedom to venture into the men's side of the store. I thought about the large selection of T-shirts and jeans. *There's one thing I know about myself that's been the same forever: I love T-shirts, jeans, and sneakers.*

CHAPTER THIRTY-SIX

When I didn't have the kids at my place, I relied on a few close friends for company and support. Dating was completely new, and I had zero experience. At least it was easy to talk to women; I had no issues in that area. Terry, my freshman year boyfriend from high school, found me on Facebook a few years before I left Lou. He was "out" and gay now, living with a man he'd been dating for three years. We reconnected our friendship despite Lou's protests (which had no basis for jealousy considering Terry identified as gay, not bi). Being single meant I was free to hang out with Terry more often. We still enjoyed the same movies and books and still made each other laugh nonstop. He loved to cook, and I dropped by regularly to hang out in his kitchen and share a delicious meal. Sometimes we walked from his house to the gay bars nearby. If I had too much to drink it was easy to sleep on his couch until the next morning.

For my first Halloween as a single person, Terry and I decided to dress up and go to a Halloween-themed drag show. He made himself an excellent costume and went as Tim Curry's character Frank-N-Furter from *The Rocky Horror Picture Show*. I decided to take a more generic approach and go "in drag" meaning dressed as a different gender.

It was incredibly exciting to give myself a sound reason to purchase men's clothing. Ever since I was a little kid, I had wanted to wear a necktie. Finally, here I was at age forty getting my chance. I spent an entire day browsing the men's department of several stores and settled on a black and gray necktie, black suspenders, and a fedora. I bought a man's undershirt tank top and a white, pinstriped, button-down shirt. I was too short to buy a pair of men's slacks off the rack and there was no time or money to get something altered. I settled for a pair of flat front black slacks I already owned. Putting on the full outfit felt as comfortable as a pair of favorite well-worn sneakers. I slicked my wet hair back into a very tight ponytail and stuck it under the hat.

We made it to the show and watched performances by several drag queens—those who dress as a female and perform a lip sync on stage while dancing and interacting with the audience. I was surprised to see a drag *king*: a person (in this particular case, a lesbian) dressed as a male and performing on stage. I'd only ever known of drag queens but was completely enthralled by the king. I watched him interact and flirt with women in the audience as they yelled and clapped and waved dollar bills at him. I thought to myself, *I'm going to do that one day*. There was no question, I knew it like I knew the sky was blue. At the same time, some other part of me was fully aware that performing *anything* publicly on stage was completely out of character for me. For my entire life I was a person who wanted to go unnoticed; I have always been quiet, shy, and avoided embarrassment at all costs. Yet I was totally at peace with the revelation and knew it was in the future, so there was no need to fret about the details.

Terry helped me settle into my newfound social life and introduced me to many people. He became a protective big gay brother in some ways and never hesitated to voice his opinion on the women I dated.

My first relationship was a whirlwind and burnt itself out very quickly. I fell hard but always knew (though often refused to believe) it couldn't go anywhere long term. At least it was good to get the first heartbreak out of the way though. I was right back out in circulation.

I created a profile on a couple of dating apps. That produced a few opportunities but those were never well-matched. It was easy to know in the first few messages if it was not a dating connection but instead had potential for friendship. At least one good friendship came about that way.

There were two unbreakable rules I created for myself: One, I won't introduce anyone to the kids as my girlfriend, and two, there will be no adult sleepovers when the kids are at the apartment.

Violet asked me early on if they would have a stepdad one day. I remember laughing internally and thinking, *hell fucking no, halleluiah!* Without making it a big deal I said, "No, I like girls. So someday I'll have a girlfriend." She made an unpleasant face. "Eww, a girlfriend? That's gross."

I played it cool, deciding the more I normalized it, the easier it might be. "Why is that gross?" I asked very matter of fact. She thought for a moment before answering.

"I don't know, two girls kissing is gross." Considering she had just turned eight, I kind of hoped she thought kissing in general was gross. But I didn't go there.

"Well, the good news is that *you* never have to kiss a girl if you don't want to. Or a boy for that matter. Some people grow up and like boys, some people grow up and like girls. And some people grow up and like both. Everyone is free to like who they like. No one else gets to decide that for you."

Hearing my own words felt empowering. I may have turned their world upside down with the divorce, but I was determined to give them the freedom to be themselves.

Violet looked at me for a few seconds and processed this new piece of information. "Okay!" She smiled and went right back to playing.

Days later we revisited the conversation when both kids asked if I would marry a girl someday. I told them yes, that was my hope. I explained how I'd have to find the right one.

"Will she be funny?" they asked.

"Oh yes, she has to be funny," I said.

"Will she like us?"

I felt a protective urge, a parental reflex, to yank them out from under the weight of that question before they were crushed.

"She can't just *like* you guys. She has to *love* you just as much as I do."

Their eyes widened. "Really?"

"Oh yes. I have to search very carefully to find just the right person and if she doesn't love you like I love you, then she is definitely *not* the right one."

Smiles of relief spread across the two little faces as their bodies visibly relaxed. My eyes watered with emotion. How scary and uncertain it must feel to wonder what kind of stepparent you might have one day.

CHAPTER THIRTY-SEVEN

By January the kids and I were starting to find a rhythm in the continual shuffling back and forth. It didn't ease the heartache of separation though. We were still navigating rough waters with no end in sight. When they were with me, I made every effort to be present, to take them to the park or the mall, to play a game or watch a movie together on the couch. I set up a permanent Play Doh station, an old coffee table someone gave me, with a bucket of Play Doh tools and accessories. I showed them how to use my camcorder and let them make up little TV shows. After a trip to the grocery store one day, I taught them how to cut up fresh fruit (without chopping off their fingers) and we played Iron Chef (fruit salad edition).

Somehow I understood that even though this period of our lives was pure hell, I had the rare opportunity to give them my full attention and interaction. I was no longer on Lou's schedule and subject to his demands. We could do what we wanted when we wanted, with no one else to interfere. It certainly didn't cure the pain of a broken home, but it was our only hope for little moments of reprieve.

I had to find a different way to create quality time with Randy. We texted and talked regularly and started meeting for lunch every week. When our work schedules aligned, I'd join him and Megan for a movie or concert. He'd moved out of Lou's house in the fall after deciding it was too depressing to be there—a constant visual reminder of what used to be his happy two-parent home.

I felt awful not having a bigger apartment with an extra room to offer him. (The only bedroom was stuffed with a double bed for me and bunk beds for Violet and Max.) But I gave him the spare key as if it were his home too. "You can come and go whenever you want, hang out, eat, crash on the couch, I said. He never took me up on the offer and I can't say that I blame him.

****

My non-parenting hours were jam-packed with school and work. Some days were worse than others and this was one of them. The alarm went off at 8 a.m.—which is not early to most people, but I'd just got home from work at 11:30 the night before. It was a part-time job I'd had for a while but a very physical one, making it impossible to shower, decompress, and fall asleep before 2 or 3 a.m.

My eyes struggled to focus, still heavy with sleep. *Thank God I didn't go out last night,* I thought as I made my way to the bathroom. I'd been staying in more often because it was too expensive to buy drinks at the bar. It was cheaper to keep a bottle on hand at home even though I technically couldn't afford that either. *I have to,* I reasoned, *I need it to shut off my brain, the sadness gets too big if I don't.*

I dug through piles of laundry in search of something clean and suitable to wear to my other part-time job: a work study on campus. It was very low pay and only a few hours two days a week, but it was easy, mostly data entry. I picked up a dark blue polo shirt and pressed it to my nose. *Finally, something clean.* My shift was only four hours long and I made a mental note to take the shirt off and hang it up as soon as I got home. Payday was still several days away, and I was out of laundry detergent and quarters. My mom didn't mind letting me wash clothes at her house but that might run my gas tank down. It seemed like the gauge never made it above a quarter tank. There was just too much driving: two jobs, classes two nights a week, getting the kids back and forth from school or Lou's. It never ended.

There would be extra driving today too. I'd arranged to leave my campus job earlier than usual because of a doctor's appointment. When that was over, I'd pick up the kids from school, stop at the apartment for a quick snack, and then head right back out the door to their 4 p.m. therapy appointment. It would last until 5 with each kid getting thirty minutes with Patti, their therapist, and then back in the car for rush-hour traffic. If we were lucky, we'd make it home before Lou arrived to pick them up at 6. We'd exchange kisses and hugs, and I'd dig something out of the fridge to eat and change clothes and head out to my regular part-time job by 7 p.m.

Previewing the entire day in my head was overwhelming. I wanted to crawl back in bed and stay under the covers indefinitely. But there wasn't time for that, so I made my way to the kitchen in search of something breakfast-like that I could eat on my way to work. Dirty dishes filled the sink and were threatening to take over the small counter. I missed having a dishwasher.

The text alert on my phone sounded. I grabbed a banana and read the message on my way out the door. It was from Lou: *Max doesn't want to do therapy anymore and I told him that's fine. Violet can go for the full hour.*

My fingers angrily tapped out a response: *WTF? You just made that decision without talking to me? Max is six and stuck in the middle of a divorce. He may not want to go to therapy, but he NEEDS to. He needs to go, and you had no right to tell him he didn't have to without talking to me.*

I slammed the car into gear and tossed my phone on the passenger seat. If any of the kids needed therapy right now it was Max. I could tell he felt some resentment toward me for blowing up our family, which made perfect sense, given the circumstances. But he wouldn't talk to me about it, he just seemed irritated with me a lot of times and critical of the apartment and its glaring lack of amenities. His feelings were absolutely valid, and I understood why he didn't want to talk about it with me, which was exactly why talking with the therapist was so important.

My phone continued to sound alerts for texts, one after the other. I knew it was Lou. In these situations, he had a habit of firing off a series of shitty texts and if I didn't respond he sent them faster with increasingly nasty messages.

By the time I reached the campus parking lot I had seven unread texts from him. I felt nauseous and hadn't even looked at them yet. *I can't fucking do this. Why does he have to be such a controlling bastard?*

I got to my desk and called Patti to ask for help. "I'm so sorry, I can't force him to let Max see me. But I agree with you wholeheartedly. Max is holding on to a lot of emotion, he needs to be here regularly. These things take time and patience, sometimes months of sessions before a kid like Max will open up and start to process what he's feeling," she said.

"Can you talk to Lou? I know you can't force him, but can you try to convince him, get him to understand this is for Max's benefit not mine? He's only doing this to provoke me. He'd love it if Max hated me."

Patti agreed to make the phone call but having talked to Lou before, she was very realistic in her expectations. "I'll do what I can, but my hands are tied" she said before we hung up. We both knew it was pointless.

I looked at the stack of papers on my desk and willed myself not to cry. It was impossible to focus. I was miserable and my brain felt like an overloaded computer buffering indefinitely. In fact, that was the reason I was leaving early to see my doctor. My grades were all A's in the fall, I did great. But now, only a few weeks into spring semester, I was struggling with the assigned readings. I'd read a paragraph or a page, but nothing registered in my brain. I'd read it again, nothing. A third, fourth, and fifth time, and I still couldn't process the meaning of words on the page.

When my appointment time came, I described it to the doctor. "It's like the words are not going into my brain or something."

He took a quick glance through my chart. "You're overmedicated. You're on four different meds and one of them, Topamax, is a very high dose. At this level it's common to see cognitive dysfunction as a side effect."

He decreased the dosage and said it would take a few weeks to notice a difference. Until then I'd have to claw my way through my studies somehow.

I asked about another problem: My hair was falling out in huge clumps. He assured me it was due to stress. "It will grow back when your stress level decreases," he said. That was laughable. I'd be bald by the time that ever happened. His last piece of advice before our consultation ended was, "Consider a shorter cut. Your hair won't be as heavy if it's short. It may not fall out as easily."

I nodded an acknowledgement and left. Walking to my car his words echoed in my head—a shorter cut. I wasn't ready to consider that at all. It immediately brought to mind something Lou said to me months earlier, spoken with ease and normalcy, sincerity even:

"Just do me one favor. Please. If you do nothing else, please don't turn into one of those big bull dyke bitches and cut your hair off and start carrying a wallet on a chain. Promise me you won't do that to yourself."

I couldn't help but shake my head at the memory. It wasn't disbelief, that was a typical Lou comment. What was it about that word, *dyke*, that gave me such a visceral reaction? I pulled out of the parking lot, lost in thought.

Growing up I regularly heard the word *dyke* used as a slur toward any woman whose appearance (haircut, clothing, mannerisms) was more stereotypically male than female. The word was laced with a very pointed cruelty, sometimes in a serious, hateful context while other times in an equally hateful attempt at humor: big dyke... bull dyke... klondyke... ugly dyke... walks like a dyke... dyke bitch... acts like a dyke.

I understood the context at a young age. It was mostly an adult word but not on par with curse words. It's entirely plausible that I wouldn't have been punished had I used it in context and not directly to a person's face. After all, I was raised to be kind to others, to never be the instigator, never make the first strike, only resort to physical violence in self-defense. The word *dyke* was simply a descriptor. Since it also meant the woman was gay the word was a bit taboo. I was taught that gay people were going to hell.

Into my teens and twenties, it was a word that struck an all too familiar nerve in my psyche, instilling a hate-filled fear. It would exit my mouth with a quiet undercurrent of panic, a rush to establish the dividing lines between *us* and *them*: rule followers and rule breakers; Christians and sinners. There had to be just the right amount of malice to make a clear distinction but enough humor to make the hate palatable, enjoyable even. The funnier the better. The easiest way to distract yourself from a fear of something is to make a joke about it.

Laughter is a mask (and I grew up wearing several) but cruel laughter never erased what I secretly had in common with dykes. I hated that part of me because I couldn't erase it, and I didn't choose it. It had been there as long as the cloud shaped birthmark on my stomach.

And there I was, a self-proclaimed lesbian who hated women's clothing and all things that fall under the category of *feminine*. And somehow, I was still terrified of being called the D word. It made zero sense.

Coming to terms with understanding who I was as an individual was turning out to be no small task. The more I looked at my past, the more clearly I saw the dysfunction. One of my friends encouraged me to focus on the future, saying the past is gone and can't be changed anyway. This was true but thinking about the future felt uncertain and scary. Another friend's advice was to only worry about today, but I found no relief in that either.

What happened? I wondered. My dating experiences confirmed that I was definitely attracted to women, so I got the lesbian part right... *right?* Something was still misaligned though. It was almost like putting on a shoe that was technically the right size but still didn't feel like it fit properly. That thought was alarming and led me right back to the question of, *Who the hell am I and what the fuck is wrong with me?*

By the end of February, I was mentally wrecked. When I didn't show up for work one night, a friend and coworker found me drunk in bed, talking about wanting to be dead because it was the only solution. She drove me twenty miles up the highway to the same mental health facility for what would be my fourth inpatient stay.

A doctor there agreed with the notes in my medical record that said I was overmedicated on the drug Topamax. But he went one step further: He ordered the medication stopped immediately, all at once. He also ordered an immediate stop to Wellbutrin, an antidepressant I'd taken for several years with no issues. I was still taking lithium (a mood stabilizer) which he left unchanged, but he also added an antipsychotic drug called Risperdal. I'd been on psych meds for a number of years and knew that stopping anything cold turkey was not recommended. But I didn't question it, trusting that the doctor knew far more than I did.

On my second or third day there, the same doctor recommended ECT: electroconvulsive therapy or as it's commonly known "electroshock treatments." I didn't even realize it was still being done. I'd always assumed it was a painful and barbaric treatment from the past. The doctor explained that it was not painful, and that it was done with general anesthesia. A series of treatments can help medication-resistant depression, he claimed, its effect similar to hitting a reset button in your brain, like rebooting a computer.

In hindsight it seems a bit unethical to recommend a treatment like this to a person who is already in a mentally compromised state. Maybe that's why it sounded like as good an idea as any and I agreed. I received my first treatment the next day and was scheduled to get five more.

He was right, it was not painful. I was taken to a room and strapped securely to a table; electrodes were placed on my head in very specific spots. I was given anesthesia through an IV and went unconscious before they administered the shock. I woke up in another room sitting upright in a regular chair with no memory of how I got there. The nurse said this was just some short-term memory loss and was a common side effect.

My inpatient stay was one-week long and I received a second ECT treatment before being discharged. The following week I returned for two more treatments as out-patient sessions although I don't recall much else. It's hard to say whether it was the ECT or the sudden med changes or the combination, but things went from bad to worse almost instantly.

CHAPTER THIRTY-EIGHT

My memories of March 25, 2012, are spotty at best. Some of the pieces are focused snapshots, others are blurred, the rest are nonexistent, or I'm unable to retrieve them.

It was a late Sunday afternoon when Lou picked up the kids. I watched from the window as they walked out of the apartment building and climbed into his truck. I let go of a wave of tears I'd been holding back while they were with me. Sometimes my love for them overwhelmed me and made me cry. Have you ever loved someone so much that you can't bear to cause them pain or see them suffer? Maybe it's simply the depth of a mother's love, the physiological, spiritual, and emotional connection that happens when you cocreate another human being from within your own body. Maybe it was months of witnessing the ongoing pain they suffered as a result of my leaving the marriage and flipping their lives upside down.

Whatever it was, it successfully managed to override my logical thinking processes. Something inside was telling me that the pain had to stop—their pain, my pain, all of the pain—and I had the ability to turn it all off like a light switch.

I don't know how much time passed. I sat down on my couch with the two empty pill bottles, the lithium and the Risperdal, and wondered how long it would be before I fell over. I looked at my cell phone and thought about texts that would come in and the sounds of the alerts going off next to my lifeless body. It felt surreal. I wondered how long it would be until someone found me.

The next thought crashed through the calm like shattering glass: Randy is the only person who has a key to my apartment. Randy is going to be the one who comes in here and finds me. *No, no, no, no, no… this is not the plan! This is not how it's supposed to go.*

The pavement outside was cold on my bare feet. I drove to my parents' house. The concrete steps were cold too. I opened the door, and I don't remember words, just my dad standing in front of me. I put the two empty pill bottles into his big familiar hand. He's always calm in emergencies. There was an ambulance ride, then the emergency room, then chaos. It was hard to keep my eyes open, it was hard to speak. I was being told to drink something that tasted awful, like liquid plastic. Someone was yelling at me, "You have to drink all of this, or we have to pour it down you through a tube and that won't be fun." It wasn't fun. I was vomiting with a tube down my nose or my throat. I was choking. Someone said charcoal. There was a bedside toilet and people moving my body.

I woke up in the ICU. A nurse told me not to move under any circumstances because of a kidney dialysis line in my femoral vein or artery. It had been stitched to my leg to keep it securely in place. "If that comes loose, you'll bleed out faster than you can hit the call button," she said. Minutes later one of the hospital's staff psychiatrists was standing over me. He skipped all of the usual formalities and cut straight to the point.

"Well, you're alive. We dialyzed your kidneys three times. Do you know how many people are on transplant lists waiting for a healthy kidney?" He didn't actually pause for an answer but kept going: "You almost lost yours. Intentionally."

He paused and stared at me. I nodded an acknowledgment, unsure how to respond and still a bit groggy.

"You'll be here in the ICU another day or two and then I'm transferring you to the behavioral health unit. The nurse will be back to draw your blood shortly."

And that was it. He turned and left the room. The interaction felt more like a traffic stop than a doctor's visit.

By the time I was transferred to the locked ward of behavioral health, I felt as if I'd awakened from a bad dream or a trance. I couldn't believe what I'd done and couldn't for the life of me understand why. For the past several years I had lived with the feeling that the only way to "fix" myself was to be dead but also believed it wasn't an option. I knew, or at least thought I knew, that I could never do that to my three kids. I'd long ago accepted feeling trapped in this lifetime, unable to do anything about it. I racked my brain, desperate to remember anything that would explain my actions in that one moment.

For now I was grateful to be alive and felt clearer and more determined in my thinking than I had in a very long time. I wanted to be okay; I wanted to be with my kids, to finish grad school, and to find some semblance of normalcy.

The first few days were rough; this was *not* the state-of-the-art facility I'd been admitted to for previous inpatient stays. It was simply one floor of your typical city hospital. From the patient phone in the hallway, I was allowed to make phone calls at certain times of the day. I called Carol. She came to the hospital and was allowed to have a therapy session right there in my room on the ward. I scheduled two follow-up appointments with her in anticipation of my release, although that date was still unknown. I made calls to my employer as well as my department chair at the college to request a medical leave of absence.

I asked anyone who came into my room about getting transferred to the Cincinnati facility I'd been in before, but no one could offer anything definitive or helpful. That information definitely wasn't coming from Dr. A, the irritable ICU psychiatrist who, after I woke up, had chastised me for overdosing. He'd visited again after I was moved to the locked ward, making a point to remind me how foolish I was to overdose and nearly lose a kidney, something so many others were desperately waiting to receive.

I still couldn't make sense of what malfunctioned in my mind that night, but I was absolutely certain I didn't just randomly decide, *You know what? Fuck my kidneys and fuck those people waiting for transplants... I'll show them!* And then swallow two bottles of pills. I didn't feel safe under Dr. A's care and needed to get out of there and find some real help. Unfortunately, he was one step ahead of me.

The evening shift nurse, Sandy, came to my room. I liked her from the first time we met after I was transferred from the ICU. She had a quirky sense of humor and was the kind of person who didn't conform to the status quo. In other words, Sandy was unapologetically authentic and didn't give a shit. She also gave off a strong gay vibe. My hunches about these things were typically pretty accurate, but the only reason it mattered was that it made me feel safe and not judged for who I was and how I got there.

That particular evening, she took a seat in the chair at the foot of my bed, making herself comfortable. She propped one foot on her opposite knee the way my dad always did and listened intently as I told her of the phone calls I made, my determination to get out of there and get better, and my request to be transferred to the other facility.

"Well that all sounds great to me," she said, "but Dr. A has a different plan for you unfortunately. And he's an asshole."

"He won't transfer me?" I asked, confused.

"No. The other facility wouldn't take you anyway. You're a liability now. You were under their treatment and then you took an overdose. Psych docs won't touch you after that; they don't want the potential for lawsuits."

My chest tightened and I could feel my heart rate pick up. This was not what I wanted to hear but I was grateful for her no-bullshit approach. I thought that was all of the bad news, but she continued.

"You're going to be here for a couple more days and then Dr. A is sending you to Eastern State. He's a prick and he's trying to make an example out of you, trying to punish you for o.d.'ing."

"What? What's Eastern State? What do you mean?"

I sat speechless as she explained how the doctor started the legal process to have me committed to the state mental hospital eighty miles south. There would be a legal hearing in front of a judge, and I'd get a chance to plead my case but typically the psych doctors get what they ask for.

"But I don't want to die. I'm not suicidal! I got help, which is the whole reason I'm even here right now." I looked around the room for the garbage can, fearful I'd throw up.

"Listen, if I could help you I would. You don't need to be at the state hospital. That doctor is a bastard, and this is what he does. You're not the first one and unfortunately you won't be the last. He has some kind of God complex or something; it's fucked up."

I asked if she could make a statement or go to the court hearing on my behalf, but she couldn't do so without losing her job. Before heading down the hall to check on other patients she offered a last bit of reassurance: "You're gonna be okay. Keep it together, just get through it. You'll be okay."

Two days later just as my nurse friend had warned me, there was a court hearing scheduled. The hospital staff prepared my discharge paperwork. Two police officers put me in handcuffs and drove me to the courthouse. I was there almost two hours early for the purpose of meeting with the public defender who was supposed to speak on my behalf. But he showed up late and talked with me for about ten minutes. I sat helpless in the courtroom as he gave a robotic, meaningless motion for dismissal. Dr. A's petition was approved. I was escorted out of the courtroom by police officers and allowed to give my parents and Randy a quick hug before I was cuffed again and put in the back of the police car for the ninety-minute ride to Eastern State Hospital.

CHAPTER THIRTY-NINE

After arriving at Eastern State, I was taken to a large office for an intake evaluation. The admitting doctor was a tall, brown-skinned man with a few hints of gray in his dark hair. His demeanor was warm, calming almost. I sat quietly for several minutes as he read through court documents. He then turned his attention to me and asked a few questions, taking notes as I recounted the events of the past week and the weeks leading up to it. I waited nervously through more silence and watched as he flipped through what looked to be faxed medical records.

He put down his pen and turned his chair to face me directly before he spoke. "Well…" he started with a deep breath, "you do *not* need to be here." His voice was kind, almost apologetic. "You do not meet any of the criteria for the type of care we give here. If it were up to me, I'd send you right back out the door. But…" He picked up the court documents on his desk, waved them at me, and said, "I have a court order that says I have to keep you. Your doctor is recommending twenty-one days; I'm not doing that."

I struggled to keep my composure. He leaned slightly forward in his chair, locking his eyes with mine. His voice was even softer when he continued, "Keep your head down, follow the rules, and I can get you out of here in a week. Maybe five days." I nodded in agreement, fearful any attempt to speak would trigger uncontrollable sobs.

Less than an hour later I sat in a large dayroom and took stock of my surroundings. The building was very old and outdated; I'd later learn it was built in the 1800s. It looked like a Hollywood depiction of an asylum, like something straight out of *One Flew Over the Cuckoo's Nest* or *Girl, Interrupted*. It had high ceilings, stark white tile, and concrete block walls. The Cincinnati facility where I spent my previous hospitalizations was a luxury resort by comparison.

I understood quickly what the intake doctor meant when he said I didn't need the type of care they offered. Another patient, a tall woman with short, blonde hair and large glasses walked in circles around the room, her hands clasped behind her back. She stopped in front of me and smiled, then spoke a jumble of words I didn't understand. I offered a nervous smile and a hello.

Another patient, probably in her sixties, sat strapped in a large vinyl cushioned chair and smelled of urine. I remembered similar chairs from years earlier at the nursing home and the typewritten policies and procedures on how to use the restraints in a way that didn't harm the patient, documents I retyped anytime the director of nursing updated the language or the specifics. The condition of the woman's hands and the amount of waterproof pee pads underneath her made me question whether there was any such humane policy or procedure in this place.

"What's your name honey?" Another patient sat down in a chair diagonal from mine. She too was probably in her fifties or sixties. I answered her question and smiled politely. She told me her name and asked if I knew her son. She said he was coming to pick her up. A minute later, she asked me again. I gave the same answer as before, delivered with the same smile.

I got up and walked to a large, covered patio that was enclosed and secured but offered a bit of fresh air. I took a seat and thought I was alone until a young woman in her twenties appeared from further down the patio, walking in my direction. She had very short choppy hair that reminded me of a 1920's style from old black-and-white movies. As she got closer, I realized she was completely nude.

When she caught sight of me, she approached with a wide, genuine smile and sat down in a big empty chair across from me. I smiled back and she started a friendly conversation. Her name was Lily. She asked if I was new, where I was from, then offered her own stats: She had only been there a couple of days and had cut her own hair before she arrived. "I hate wearing clothes," she smiled and rolled her eyes. "I just want to be free... it doesn't bother you, right?" I smiled back and shook my head *no*. The word *free* made me recall the doctor's instruction to keep my head down. Just then Lily stood up, raised her arms, and turned in circles. "I love to dance!" she sang out to me, still smiling. I wondered what it must feel like to be that comfortable in your body, that brave. And I wondered what happened in Lily's life that landed her here two days earlier.

Our peaceful exchange was interrupted by voices from the doorway. Two employees appeared and asked Lily where her clothes were. She ignored them, still swaying and humming a tune. As they stepped closer one of the workers looked at me, "She keeps taking her clothes off; have you seen them?" I shook my head. Within minutes all hell broke loose. They began to struggle with Lily, attempting to physically move her inside. They told her she was going to the quiet room, which only made her scream hysterically and fight harder. I looked away, unable to watch them wrangle her like a wild animal. Why did they approach so aggressively? She wasn't rioting; she was nude. In an all-female locked ward. They moved in a ball of chaos, the three of them, through the doorway and down the hall. I heard the voices of more workers getting involved while Lily continued to cry out and resist. The volume faded as they moved farther away, farther down the hall, and then silence.

I waited a while before venturing back inside. My heart was racing, and I felt nauseous. I went to the nurses' station and asked if I could go to my room. The answer was no and that it would be unlocked in the evening after dinner. I circled the dayroom and the porch, sitting down for a few minutes after every three or four laps.

On one of my breaks the patient who said she was waiting on her son took a seat fifteen feet away. I picked at my cuticles, fearful she would question me again, but she didn't seem to notice me. She was staring straight ahead with her arms folded and her brow furrowed. Several minutes later I heard mumbling and saw that she was talking to herself and seemed very agitated. Her voice got louder, and I realized she was arguing with someone who wasn't there, as if the person were standing in front of her. Her words got louder and louder, the imaginary argument escalating until she sprung up out of her seat and began punching the air. She was yelling profanities, lunging forward, her arms windmilling towards the invisible enemy, fists clenched. I stayed perfectly still hoping to blend into the surroundings like a piece of furniture. I braced for a staff member to intervene, but no one paid attention. The people at the nurses' station barely looked up and went right back to what they were doing. As quickly as it started, the imaginary fistfight was over. The woman spat out a couple final profanities then sat back down in her chair, exhausted.

What IS this place? I wondered. *Did I arrive here by time machine?* It was becoming increasingly difficult to believe it was 2012 within these walls.

But it wasn't as simple as outdated decor. It was the atmosphere, the *feel* of the dynamic between us and them: the inmates and the staff. We weren't here by choice. Hell, I felt certain that none of us were "crazy" by choice.

Hours later the rooms were unlocked and a staff member escorted me to mine. Like the rest of the hospital, the room was large with concrete block walls and high ceilings. She pointed me to my bed, a simple cot with one thin blanket in the corner farthest from the door. I had three roommates, one cot in each of the other corners. One of the cots belonged to the woman who believed her son was coming, the same woman who had the fistfight with the invisible person. On my third night in the room, I jolted awake to the sound of her fighting again. In silhouette she shouted profanities and swung her fists through the air, moving to the center of the room. And like last time, I froze in place, terrified she would mistake me or one of the others for her invisible target.

****

On day seven at Eastern State, I was released. The intake doctor was true to his word; I kept my head down and he got me out as quickly as he could legally do so. I walked out of the building and didn't look back. My parents waited for me in the parking lot with Violet and Max in the back seat. When I climbed in between them we latched onto one another and rode like that all the way back home, ninety minutes north. We had been separated for nineteen days, the longest I'd ever been away from them.

During that time, they were never told about the overdose, only that I was sick and in the hospital. We had communicated through a spiral notebook my parents carried back and forth when they had visited during inpatient stays. The kids would draw pictures and write messages anytime they wanted. During the visits I'd read their entries and write back so my parents could show them the next day.

In what would be the luckiest timing of anything in my life, Lou missed this window of opportunity to pursue full custody. He was preoccupied with the woman he was dating and agreed to let me have the kids for the first five days I was back. We then went right back into the fifty-fifty arrangement we'd been following.

I stayed with my parents for the first week after my return but by the second night I felt emotionally unstable. There was a lot to process, and a lot of damage done as a result of my actions, regardless of the fact that I'd been mentally compromised. I still didn't understand what had happened internally, mentally, that prompted me to overdose.

I held myself together until after the kids were in bed. I could barely breathe under the crushing weight of guilt and started to feel the first hints of panic. Afraid of alarming my parents with a burst of tears and emotion, I took a walk through the neighborhood. Walking in the dark with my head down, I could cry without drawing the attention of passing cars.

What do you do when your life is so wrecked that it's unrecognizable? Who do you reach out to when everyone you love and trust has suffered—has been traumatized—as a result of your actions?

I kept walking, head down, my vision blurred by tears. My mind churned in search of the tiniest sliver of logic. Eleven months ago, I set out to create a new life. Where was it? Did I fuck it all up before it had a real chance? What had I done to Randy, Violet, Max, and my parents?

For years I'd been on countless meds, had inpatient treatment, outpatient treatment, talk therapy, art therapy, electroconvulsive therapy. For what? For *this*?

I don't know where the next thought came from, but it entered my awareness as if spoken by someone else. It came in through the noise of my distress with a calm firmness, like tough love:

You've exhausted all of those options. No more hospitalizations or you're going to lose custody of the kids. YOU have to do the work.

Another wave of panic swept through me as I realized this hard truth. *What's the work? What do I do?* I wondered. I paused, waiting for more information, but there was nothing. That was it.

The panic eased and my logical left brain kicked into problem-solving mode. *Okay, if inpatient is no longer an option, what do I do if things get really bad again?* The clog in my brain started to dissolve and clear thoughts began to flow, slowly at first and then a steady stream. There were things I could do (the work) on the front end, like preventive maintenance, instead of trying to fix things post-crash: stop drinking, cut off toxic friendships and relationships, no more looking backward, focus on what's in front of me right now.

After leaving the ICU I was put on a standard dosage of a single medication, an antidepressant I'd taken before that had had good results. That was it, just one medication. Part of my *work* was to make sure I took the pill every day at the same time, no careless missed doses or late refills.

The crying had stopped. I felt clear, still a little nervous but clear. I took stock of my whereabouts and looked at my watch. I'd been walking for nearly two hours. I crossed the street and started in the direction of my parents' house hoping they were in bed by now and not worried. Things were still incredibly messy, but it felt like I had a solid starting point or at least some type of direction. *I'm still a good mom,* I thought. I blocked out a contradictory thought that came next and repeated the only truth I possessed: *I am still a good mom; I can do this.*

CHAPTER FORTY

In July of 2012, a year after Lou's concerned plea, I finally took the leap to short hair. I suppose it was two leaps, technically. I first went to my longtime stylist and asked to go pretty short. She went very conservative but not as short as I'd hoped. After a couple of days, I couldn't shake the feeling of looking like a soccer mom and that was *not* the look I wanted. I went to a second stylist, the mom of a close friend, and she cut it as short as I'd requested. It's still hard to fathom how I got the nerve to actually do it. Maybe I felt empowered by old Joan Jett concerts I'd been watching on YouTube. The clips were from the early 2000s when she adopted a crew cut and later a shaved head.

As a kid I had been obsessed with Joan Jett from the time "I Love Rock 'n Roll" came out in 1981. I thought she was beautiful, and I loved her entire look: black leather, chains, spiked wristbands, high-top sneakers, electric guitar. She was the epitome of a badass and I was never more content than sitting in my bedroom staring at her album covers, listening on repeat.

Somehow, I drifted away from Joan and her music by the time I was in high school. But there I was in 2012 getting caught up, thanks to the internet. The new androgynous Joan threw my ignorant little mind into a tailspin. I found her more attractive than ever. Her big brown eyes were so much more prevalent without the old shaggy hairstyle covering them. She was a mix of qualities that was totally foreign to me. Her heavy black eyeliner and blue eyeshadow was feminine while her energy and buzz cut were very masculine; it was attractive, sexy, and strong. I was mesmerized.

It was the first major crack in what I had been conditioned to associate with masculine women or masculine lesbians. Maybe it was the new freedom I enjoyed as a single person that allowed me to watch her without shame or secrecy or homophobia. After all, I had labeled myself a lesbian and was doing my best to find my place in the LGBT world. I had managed to let go of some of my homophobia but had internalized the rest.

The "rest" made itself known the minute my long hair became short. I didn't see Joan Jett in the mirror even if I wore eyeliner. I didn't see strength, beauty, or power. The words "fat dyke bitch" rang in my ears every time I looked in the mirror, every time I caught my reflection in a window or the rearview mirror. "Fat, ugly, bull dyke."

My mask of femininity was gone and with it went any ability I had to influence how people perceived me. I was sure that no other human could ever look at me without assuming I was gay. So why was that a problem? I sure as hell didn't want to date men.

It was harder than ever to leave the house. I hated what others saw when they looked at me: a masculine woman. I didn't want the stares and assumptions, not for me or my kids. Picking them up from school and going to their school events was painful. I felt embarrassed by my appearance and the fact that all of the other parents and kids witnessed the drastic change that had taken place over two years. It was glaringly obvious to my own kids, particularly eight-year-old Max, the youngest.

"The jacket is a bit much" he commented one afternoon as we left a school function. He was referring to the well-worn brown leather bomber jacket I was wearing. I'd picked it up in the men's section of Goodwill days before. "What's wrong with it?" I asked, not wanting to assume the obvious. "It's just... too much" he said and turned to stare out the car window.

The last thing I wanted to be was an embarrassment to my kids. I wondered if other kids made comments to him or asked why his mom dressed like a man. I imagined he heard commentary from his dad as well.

But where is the line? I wondered. No one, adult or child, should conform to another person's taste in clothing or style. I believed this strongly despite my own compromises over the years, caving to what Lou wanted. But I fought hard when it came to the kids. I remembered a time in my early days of parenthood when Randy, the oldest, was three or four. We were shopping for new clothes to replace items he'd outgrown. He grabbed a red and black striped shirt from a rack and said, "This one!" It didn't have cartoon characters or illustrations on it, so I assumed he was just being playful. I smiled and turned my attention back to the racks. He repeated his words with obvious frustration.

"You want to wear that?" I asked. His little face lit up. "Yes!" He hugged it to his chest.

Until that point, I assumed preschoolers only liked clothes with recognizable objects or characters. I handed him the shirt and figured if he knows what he likes then why not let him decide. We took it home and it was his favorite shirt until he outgrew it.

When I did assert a little parental control over his wardrobe, I realized the impact. On Randy's first day of kindergarten, I dressed him in a short-sleeved polo shirt and jeans. He came home that day insisting that I never make him "wear any more of those shirts with the stupid little collars." No one had made fun of him. It just wasn't what he liked, and it affected his comfort level on a day when he had to navigate a brand-new environment. It was a valuable lesson for me and one that I could personally relate to even back then.

Later, when Randy started middle school, clothing became a constant battle between him and his dad. Randy wanted to shop at

Hot Topic. Lou wanted him to shop at Abercrombie or American Eagle. I fully supported Randy and admired his individuality. "Be yourself, don't try to be what someone else wants you to be," I'd tell him, determined to give him the confidence I lacked. To his credit, he listened. He was the only boy on the school football and basketball teams who wore goth and emo styles.

But that was Randy. I returned my thoughts to the present, to my Max, sixteen years younger than his big brother and still staring out the passenger window, his face turned away from me. I could hardly blame him. My boys' childhoods couldn't be more different. Max was a serious kid, a bit of a black-and-white thinker with newly divorced parents and a mom who dated women and dressed like a man. My heart hurt for him. I wasn't sure how to be sensitive to his needs *and* maintain my sanity.

"It's okay if you don't like the way I dress," I said gently. "People should wear what feels most comfortable for *them*. Being yourself is the most important thing you can be."

I knew my well-intended words didn't change the obvious. His life would be much easier if his mom looked like the other moms. But that was something I couldn't change without risking my ability to *be* his mom.

I made a mental note, a silent promise, to try to remember to leave my jacket in the car whenever I picked the kids up from school. I don't think I looked any less masculine without it but if it lifted a little of the burden from Max's shoulders then it was worth the effort.

I had cut my hair and changed my wardrobe, but the more I searched for a clearer understanding of who I was, the more confusing it became. No one had any answers and sometimes even my friends, the gay ones, couldn't figure me out.

On one occasion I was having a conversation with a woman I was dating and something I said—whether the phrasing or the meaning it conveyed—invoked a strong response from her that I'll never forget. She said, "You sound like a guy, stop being that way. I'm with you because I like women, not men." I was so caught off guard by this comment that I didn't even ask for clarification. She laughed in an effort to take some of the sting out of her remark, so I laughed too, and we moved on, or at least I pretended to move on. I replayed her words in my head for weeks trying to understand. It felt like the explanation was right in front of me, but I couldn't see it.

One of my closest friends, Jayne, was also my coworker. She was questioning her sexual orientation after several years of dating men. We frequented the local lesbian bar after work on Wednesday nights to watch the weekly drag show, both of us enamored by the beauty and larger than life personalities of the women on stage. One of the queens had taken a young drag king under her wing and gave him one or two numbers in the show. Jayne and I both enjoyed his performances and the girls in the audience went crazy for him. This particular king was played by a lesbian. It proved to be a real mind fuck for me when I noticed myself noticing him.

"I think I have a crush on him, which is really... bizarre," I confessed to Jayne as we watched the show from the back of the bar.

She smiled and raised her eyebrows, clearly amused by this piece of info. "Oh yeah, you typically go for the girly girls, but he is super cute though."

"I know. It's weird." I was still puzzling it out in my head.

Jayne sensed it was more than an off-the-cuff comment and, keeping it light, offered some reassurance: "You're just branching out, it's all good. Variety, right?"

I struggled to find the words to explain. "No... you see, it's like I look at him and my brain says *oh he's attractive*, but if I think beyond that... like try to think about him sexually it feels... gay."

Jayne's eyes widened and she choked mid sip of her drink. "What? Newsflash, you ARE gay. You're a lesbian!" She howled with laughter.

I laughed not only at her response but at the oddity of my own words. I was still mystified. We made our way to the bar for refills and moved on to the next topic of conversation. The puzzle remained in my head. *Maybe I don't* like *him, maybe I just want to be* him. Something clicked into place.

CHAPTER FORTY-ONE

For most people, the experience of looking into a mirror typically goes like this:

The person has a general sense of their appearance as they approach the glass, they look at their reflection and in a fraction of a second their eye sends the image to their brain which immediately signals the recognition, "That's me." Then the person brushes their hair or washes their hands, completely oblivious to that little exchange between eye and brain.

For the first forty-one years of my life, my experience was quite different. It went like this:

I'd have a general sense of my appearance as I approached the glass, I'd look at my reflection and in a fraction of a second my eyes would send the image to my brain, which signaled a complex and overwhelming mixture of shock, disappointment, disgust, and the word *ugly*. This discord between my eyes and brain blared like a car alarm at 3 a.m.

But one afternoon alone in my apartment I experienced something in front of my bathroom mirror that would change my life permanently.

I watched many professional drag performers on YouTube. Aside from their actual stage performances many of them showed how they applied their makeup to achieve a stereotypical feminine or masculine look. From an artistic standpoint, it was impressive and very creative in the ways in which some individuals improvised tools and techniques. I watched self-professed lesbians demonstrate how to use products like eyeshadow and contouring makeup to create the appearance of male facial hair and chiseled facial features. Some of them shared techniques for creating the appearance of a masculine chest using things like elastic medical bandages, duct tape, or extremely tight-fitting garments called binders.

I was beginning to think seriously about becoming a drag performer, a drag king. There was a local drag troupe holding auditions the following month, so I decided to give it a try. I had no idea what I was doing and zero background or experience in stage performance. I rarely danced in clubs with friends so dancing on stage was going to be quite a stretch.

With no particular prompting, curiosity got the best of me, and I decided to test what I'd learned in the videos. What would I look like as a drag king? In other words, what would I look like as a man?

With scissors, duct tape, and lots of patience I flattened my breasts and put on a men's basic white tank top. Digging through an old bag of makeup I found an eyeshadow palette with various shades of brown and tan and a small palette of black. Then I spun my ball cap backwards on my head and went to work. With a large blush brush, I used tan shades to contour along my jawline, up into the cheek area, at the temples, and along the brow. Using a stippling technique with browns and black I created the appearance of a five o'clock shadow. Finally, the darkest browns and black were stippled over and over to build the illusion of a mustache and goatee. I took a step back from the glass to evaluate my work.

The instant I saw my reflection my brain shouted, "THAT'S me!" I was dumbfounded. I recognized the person staring back at me. *That is me. That's the face that matches who I am on the inside.*

It was the face of the person I always expect to see in the mirror but never do.

The recognition was so monumental I grabbed my phone and snapped some photos. I texted the photo to Samantha with the message "I'm trying some new makeup techniques, what do you think?" She responded instantly. "Omg you're hot!" I couldn't stop laughing. I texted it to another friend with the same message. She replied, "Who the hell is that?"

It was impossible to stop smiling. I stared into the mirror in disbelief, feeling as if I'd found someone who had been gone for decades. *Finally. There you are.*

Part Four

I Am Jay

CHAPTER FORTY-TWO

Everything was distinctly different after that. Although the recognition in the mirror was instantaneous, the implications were not. It was coming about much slower, like watching a Polaroid picture develop.

In the meantime, I had a very different event ahead of me and it was a big one: Randy's wedding. He and his fiancée, Megan, had been together for seven years and I'd long considered her one of the family. Everyone had been waiting for this big day and it was now just a few weeks away.

Just as it did with my own wedding two decades earlier, time was running out and I had six days to find something to wear. Terry had been bugging me for weeks, asking if I had an outfit yet. He insisted that the mother of the groom should be in a dress, not slacks. I didn't know how to explain myself but accepted his offer to come along and help me find something. As we pulled into the parking lot of the first department store my chest tightened and I started to have a panic attack. Once inside, it didn't get any easier. The usual discomfort I felt when walking into the women's section had compounded and was worse than anything I'd experienced before. The racks, displays, mannequins, and wall-sized photos loomed over me, closing in from every direction. I wanted to cry. *How the hell am I supposed to find something appropriate that doesn't make me want to crawl out of my skin?*

I quickly grabbed some black slacks, a couple of blazers and blouses, and headed for the dressing room. In complete defiance, Terry slung two dresses over the dressing room door. "Just try them on," he ordered. Nothing looked right. I even caved to the pressure and tried on one of the dresses, but it pushed me over the edge. I rushed out of the store and back into the car, chest heaving. Terry watched from the passenger seat as I worked to steady my breathing. "Are you okay?" he asked, even though the answer was obvious. I put the car in drive and made my way to the Applebee's restaurant at the opposite end of the shopping center.

"I need a drink."

As much as Terry and I butted heads over what I should wear, I wasn't angry at him. I couldn't be. I knew he didn't understand the issue I was having. Hell, I didn't fully understand the issue I was having. It was difficult to put into words.

We took a seat at the bar inside the restaurant. My post-hospitalization, no-alcohol rule lasted three weeks before I compromised to allow beer only, which lasted maybe two months. I ordered two shots of tequila. Terry's eyes widened, "It's 11 a.m. for Christ's sake!"

"Can you try to imagine for just one minute… what if you had to actually put on a dress and go to a very important formal occasion?" I desperately wanted him to understand that whatever this was, it was not simply me being a stubborn, selfish asshole who didn't give a shit about their son's wedding day. A stubborn, selfish asshole wouldn't be distraught, they would easily buy what they wanted and be done.

Terry was not having any part of this analogy. "Oh my God! I'm not the mother of the groom, you are! It's not the same!"

He had a point. It wasn't the right comparison. "Okay, well just forget the wedding for a second and hear me out. Have you ever been in a situation where you were forced to wear something that was completely and entirely uncomfortable for you? Something that didn't feel right on your body... something that logically should be totally fine and everyone around you says it's fine, says that you look fine, but *you* know that NOTHING about the outfit is fine..." He listened in silence and looked as if he were considering my words. I continued, "maybe the clothes even fit okay, but you look in the mirror and you're mortified; you can't get the clothes off your body fast enough. There are no words to explain it, you just *cannot* wear it."

His tone softened. "Well, we have to find you *something*."

We had a light lunch and headed back out on our search. Several stores and several hours later I had an acceptable outfit: black dress slacks, a black top with (fake) diamond and silver accents on the front and a black dressy jacket. It was a lot of black, but the bridesmaids were wearing black too. It was part of the overall black and red theme.

It's funny how formal occasions come with the obligation to wear a full face of makeup. I had to decide what that was going to look like for me now that I only used eyeliner if anything at all. There had to be some kind of middle ground. I made an appointment with a professional for the morning of the wedding day. When asked what I had in mind I answered, "I want to look like I'm not wearing makeup: no bright colors, no rosy cheeks, no unnatural lip color, no gloss, no iridescence, no sharpie marker eyebrows."

****

What a difference a day makes. Twenty-four hours after celebrating Randy and Megan's wedding, I was back in front of my bathroom mirror to recreate the familiar face I saw four weeks earlier. It was time for the drag troupe audition.

I wasn't nervous at all about walking out of my apartment in men's clothing and a full face of drag king makeup. It was the opposite; I couldn't wait to get outside. It felt comfortable and natural. The audition however was something to be nervous about.

The current members of the troupe and the other potential newcomers were all friendly and welcoming which made it much easier when I didn't make the cut. It was okay; I could see how good the others were, and I had zero experience. The lead member of the troupe encouraged me to keep working and go to some of the drag amateur nights in town. He said it was similar to an open mic night for musicians, except it was drag.

I left in a great mood. Each time I stopped at a traffic light I noticed my reflection in the rearview mirror: *my* reflection. It was more *me* than I'd ever been in my entire life. I took a couple more photos when I got home and texted them to Samantha. She was waiting to hear how the audition went. I was never more grateful to have reconnected with her after the nine-year gap. She listened and supported me.

Most importantly, Samantha never asked what it all meant or why it was so comfortable. She didn't psychoanalyze or voice any worries or concerns. I knew she saw the real me even before I put on the face. I thought back to a visit we had had a year earlier when I was just settling into the apartment. I took the kids on a weekend trip to West Virginia to visit my grandparents. The first evening we arrived in town we stopped at Samantha's house. She had only seen photos of the kids and hadn't yet met them in person. We hadn't seen each other since Rylie's death when she came to stay with me during those first difficult days.

The kids warmed up to her quickly and we all went out to dinner together. Later that evening I texted her a thank you for dinner and the visit. She replied in kind and added, "It was like hanging out with twelve-year-old you." Those words hit me in a way that I couldn't fully process. But I knew it was meant as a good thing, a compliment almost, and I liked it. It fit despite having turned forty just four days earlier.

I stood in front of the mirror again, relieved the audition was over. I reluctantly washed off the male face and went to bed thinking about the possibility of amateur drag nights, hoping it would happen soon. The next day I went to my therapy appointment with Carol and showed her the photos. It certainly gave us plenty to talk about, but she went easy, she didn't push. She seemed genuinely supportive and interested.

Things felt easy when I could process this mirror dichotomy through the lens of drag performance. But when I thought about it in the larger context it was like staring directly into the sun. Yet each time I faced a mirror and didn't see the hard chiseled lines and faux five o'clock shadow, it became more painful. I did not want to see myself in black dress slacks and an embellished top. I did not want to see a masculine woman. That's not who I was.

CHAPTER FORTY-THREE

I was very cold and lying on my side on a cement floor. Several feet in front of me were my shoes and they were soaking wet. I still hadn't registered where I was, but the regret and panic kicked in immediately. *Fuck, fuck, fuck* repeated in my brain. Within moments I realized I was completely naked and partially covered with a strange dark green blanket. I was on the floor of a tiny jail cell.

Using every ounce of strength I had I sat up and looked around for a clock. *Oh my God, what time is it? I have to get the kids.* The only items in the room were my wet shoes next to a stainless-steel toilet.

In a panic I tried to stand up. My head throbbed, my neck hurt, and my shoulder felt like it was nearly dislocated. I touched my forehead, and it felt bruised. My forearm felt bruised, my wrists were red and sore. *What the fuck happened? How did I get here? What did I do? The kids… oh my God.*

I managed to get upright, wrapping the green blanket around my body and made my way to the door of the cell. It was nothing like I'd seen in movies. The walls were concrete blocks, and the door was solid steel. The only bars in sight were ones that covered a small rectangular opening in the door. I stood on my tiptoes to peer out into the hallway. "Excuse me, Officer?" After several minutes a man in uniform returned demanding to know what my problem was. I politely asked him the time. It was 5 a.m. I asked if

I could please make my phone call. His response was, "Yeah when I feel like it."

I thought I might throw up. Until that moment I thought the state mental hospital was the absolute worst predicament of my life. Waking up in jail with no idea how I got there and only two hours left to get the kids was a million times worse. If Lou found out, especially after the fight we had had the previous day, he was absolutely going to win full custody. I'd be lucky to get supervised visitation.

Keep it together. Keep it together. Don't freak out.

Foxhole prayers. Those are the prayers soldiers say on the battlefield when they are begging God to save them from certain death. I was fully aware that my desperate pleas to a god I told to fuck off years earlier, were a variation of foxhole prayers: twisted, alcoholic, shameless *jail cell prayers.*

I made every bargain, every promise, and every apology to God. All the while some other part of my brain yelled at me like a drill sergeant: *Mean it, believe it, thank him now! You better have faith if you want help, you worthless piece of drunken shit! Thank him for getting you out of here and believe it, mean it!*

An hour later the cell door opened. I was allowed to make a phone call. A recording instructed me to speak my name and then it put me in a hold status while it connected the call. I heard my mom's sleepy voice say hello and then a recording asked if she wanted to accept a call from the county jail. She said yes and we were connected.

"What happened?" There was fear and exasperation in her voice. I held back tears.

"I don't know. I have no idea."

"Was it a DUI?"

"No, I didn't even have my car with me, I walked to the bar, but I don't remember what happened after I left. I need help, I'm supposed to get the kids from Lou at 7, before he goes to work. He cannot find out I'm in here or he's going to take them away from me. Please, can Dad go get them and just tell him I'm sick? Please?"

"Yes, yes he'll go get them."

I returned to my cell to find I'd been given a cellmate. She looked at me and laughed. "Yeah, I heard you come in last night. You fuckin' puked like the exorcist, man. Those cops were PISSED. They rolled a big fuckin' trash can down there and everything."

I still had no recollection of the arrest whatsoever. I'd gone to a lesbian bar and spent the evening on a barstool, drinking and talking to a blonde woman on the stool next to me. Around 11p.m. she asked if I wanted to go to another bar with her and her friends. She was going to call a taxi for all of us. The very last thing I remembered was saying yes, getting off the barstool, and following her out the door.

Surely there had to be more; it can't be possible to get arrested and throw up like that... to have my clothes taken and not remember even a few seconds of it? There was nothing. My mind was as blank as it was after an electroshock treatment. Hell, at least that was only a few minutes lost. This was six hours missing, just deleted, like words on a computer screen.

I told my cellmate that I didn't even know what I was arrested for. She assured me I'd find out soon; I'd see the clerk or someone who would inform me of the charges and either set bail or set a hearing.

My heart nearly stopped. "But it's Saturday. Will I have to wait until Monday?"

"Hmm, I don't know. Maybe. But usually there's someone here every day. Maybe you'll get lucky."

More panic. More foxhole prayers. I fought off nightmarish scenes of losing custody of the kids, of having one hour of supervised visitation a week, of Randy and Megan distancing themselves from me, of the kids growing up without me and hating me for being a piece of shit who ruined their childhood.

My cellmate continued talking. She said she got arrested more than three months ago and was still waiting for a hearing. Multiple times there was a date scheduled but her lawyer, the public defender, asked for a continuance each time. He didn't even bother to tell her. Each time she found out from one of the jailers on the day of, as she waited to be escorted to the hearing. She started to cry. "It's fucked up! I can't even get a fair hearing because of this sorry ass fucking public defender! I'm just rotting here, and he doesn't even give a shit. No one does."

She was absolutely right. I felt terrible for her and couldn't imagine being there for over three months. We sat together in silence. Somewhere outside our cell another inmate was calling for a guard. By the proximity and direction of her voice I guessed she was across from us but one or two doors down. She was repeatedly asking for a tampon. Then a male voice, a guard, shouted back, "Shut the fuck up, you'll get one when we feel like it!"

We looked at each other. "See what I mean?" she said. "This place is fucked. We're just garbage; no one cares."

Hours later our cell door opened, and a guard tossed a set of pink jail scrubs at me. I was escorted to a booking area where they took my mugshot. Apparently, I was too drunk to get it done when I came in. Afterward, I was called to a counter where a woman sat behind glass. She verified my name and Social Security number and asked if I understood the charges.

"Ma'am, I don't have any idea what I did. I don't even remember getting arrested, I woke up and was here."

The corners of her mouth curled in a half smile, and I wondered how many times she'd heard people give that explanation. But her demeanor was somewhat friendly, and I was grateful. She read the charges: "Well, let's see… looks like you sold some cigarettes to a minor… from a vending machine. And disorderly conduct. How do you want to plead?"

I was thoroughly confused. Cigarettes? I don't even smoke. I frequented that bar and knew it had a cigarette machine in the back room, but I never went in there that night. I never left the barstool in the front of the bar until going outside to wait for a taxi which was my last memory. *What minors?* I wondered. It's a twenty-one and up bar that checks IDs at the door. There couldn't have been any minors, and I know for a fact that I didn't purchase cigarettes. I didn't even have cash on me, just a credit card which was likely still with the bartender.

I explained a little bit of that to the woman behind the glass and asked if the charge was a mistake. All she said was, "So you want to plead not guilty?"

"I… I don't know, I don't understand why that's on there. It has to be a mistake."

She looked at me with a mix of pity and exasperation. "Soooo, you want to plead not guilty…" She said it like a statement this time. I suddenly understood she was trying to help me despite the fact that she was probably not supposed to help me, particularly not with advice on pleading guilty or not guilty.

"Yes ma'am, not guilty."

I signed the paperwork. She said she would communicate with the judge over the phone then call me back up to the window. I looked at a clock on the wall, it was 11:30 a.m. Twenty minutes passed before I heard her call my name. She pushed a paper through the opening beneath the glass. "This is your court date. Since you have a clean record, you can ask for diversion. If the judge agrees, you'll pay some fines, do community service, and the charges will be dropped. If you stay out of trouble for another six months, you can petition to have the record expunged. Sign here."

She offered one parting piece of advice. "Do *not* miss that court date. And stay out of trouble. The officer will take you back to your cell and you'll be free to leave this afternoon. You can have another phone call to arrange a ride."

Two hours later the cell door opened one last time; I was never more grateful. As I was escorted down the hall the officer explained that my vomit-covered clothes were sealed in a special kind of bag that dissolves into laundry detergent. "You just throw the whole thing into the washer," he said. With no clothes to wear home my only option was something from the storage room. When you're given jail scrubs your street clothes go to the jail's laundry facility but sometimes people are released or transferred before the clothes make it back. The officer asked my pant size and ten minutes later returned with my bagged dirty clothing, a T-shirt, and a ratty pair of men's jeans that were two sizes too big.

I signed for the return of my belongings: house keys, my wallet, and my phone. All of the items had been shrink-wrapped to a twelve-inch by twelve-inch square of corrugated cardboard.

I made my way out the door and into the bright afternoon sun. My dad was leaning against his car in the parking lot. I felt sorry for him standing there watching his firstborn walk out of the county jail: one hand securing the baggy blue jeans of an unknown inmate; the other hand carrying a specialized jailhouse laundry bag full of pukey clothes; the shrink-wrapped cardboard tucked under one arm. I was disappointed *for* him. Without saying a word, he squeezed my shoulder, and we got into the car.

I broke the silence. "What the fuck is wrong with me?"

He didn't lecture, criticize, or ask questions. He didn't glare at me or shake my head. He spoke with firm encouragement.

"I'm taking you to your apartment. You get a shower and clean up and then come back out to the house. The kids are waiting for you."

CHAPTER FORTY-FOUR

I turned on my cell phone and found multiple voicemails and texts from the girl who had been drinking with me. One of them read, "I'll go to court for you as a witness! There are two other girls who saw it too, we will all testify! Call me!"

She answered immediately. I told her I remembered her suggestion that we get a taxi to another bar before standing up and walking out the door. That's when the blackout began. She filled in the missing pieces: We were sitting on the sidewalk waiting for the taxi. A police car slowly drove by and the officer in the driver's seat stared at us for a few seconds then went on. He circled around again, slowed to a stop right in front of us, stared, and then went on. She said we were just sitting there, not saying anything at all. He came around a third time and did the same thing. As he started to pull away, I silently raised my middle finger.

There was a loud bang—the slamming of a car door—as the officer jumped out of the car. She said he made a beeline for me, grabbed my upper arm, yanked me up off the ground and slammed me into the side of the car. I asked her if I said anything or fought back. She said no, that was the fucked-up part. He shoved me around like a rag doll, knocking me face first into the lid of the trunk, cuffed me, and threw me into the back seat. He slammed the door, looked at her, and said, "And that's how we do it around here."

It was difficult for me to believe that I couldn't remember any of it, particularly since it was so physical. I hadn't told her about my bruises but everything she described matched my injuries. She was outraged by the fact that he could have just arrested me for flipping him off and been done. Instead, he made a show of roughing up an incredibly drunk female who could barely stand let alone resist.

I asked if I went back into the bar at any time and bought cigarettes. She said no. I asked her if I bought any when we were inside the bar and again, she said no, she never saw me with cigarettes. Like me, she wasn't a smoker. I asked the ages of her and her two friends, and they were all twenty-five.

I got off the phone. *How is that possible?* I wondered. It had to be true, I barely knew this girl so there was no motivation for her to make it up. Plus, I had the bruises to match. I'd heard stories about certain police officers and unfair treatment or harassment near the gay bars in that part of town. I was wearing men's clothing, sitting next to very feminine blonde women outside a well-known lesbian bar. Was that somehow emasculating to be flipped off by a drunk, masculine woman? There's no way to know.

Fighting the charge or the unfair treatment was a moot point. I couldn't take the risk. I needed to jump through all the necessary hoops to get it expunged or I'd never get a teaching license. I was in my second year of grad school with student loans for a career that might be over before it ever began. More importantly, I could not risk Lou finding out about the arrest.

For the rest of the day and well into the night my brain was in overdrive. One half analyzed every detail, the other half fired a mix of corresponding and conflicting emotions. There was immense shame in acknowledging my desperate prayers for help yet, simultaneously, an immense gratitude for having them answered. There was shame for calling my parents from jail but gratitude for their help. I was outraged by the actions of the arresting officer and horrified that I'd consumed enough alcohol to induce a six-hour blackout and flip a middle finger at a cop.

But everything pointed at only one source for blame and that was me. I couldn't shake the very real possibility of losing my kids; not just the two younger ones but Randy and Megan too. They were the only thing of value in my life. Nothing else mattered.

The next day I got online and looked up meeting times and locations for Alcoholics Anonymous. Two years prior I'd casually dropped into some meetings after one of my inpatient hospitalizations but was only there to "take a break" from drinking as I saw it. It was now painfully clear to me that I did not have the ability to take a break. Just like the overdose six months earlier, my life was hanging in the balance. Something had to give.

I found a meeting that started at midnight, seven nights a week. It fit perfectly with my work schedule, so I started attending every night. If I had the kids, we spent the night at my parents' house so that I could easily go to the meeting and back while they were asleep. I got a sponsor this time and started working the steps and reading the big blue AA book.

2012 had proven itself to be a year from hell, maybe the single worst year of my adult life. Thanks to AA at least it could end on a high note. I ushered in 2013 sober, in the audience at a drag bar, and it became the year I fulfilled my dream of taking the stage as a drag king.

****

During the first half of the year, I was part of a Ladies Night show in Cincinnati featuring mostly kings. At the same club on Sunday nights, I was part of the "B cast" (non-headliners) for some of the big-name performers in town. Those were without a doubt some of the most memorable months of my life. I danced and flirted with women for tips, hung out with drag queens, and was even invited to perform at bars in Detroit, Michigan, and Dayton, Ohio.

As I got to know the other performers, I learned that some of the queens were transgender women. They were individuals who were assigned male at birth but had transitioned to female at some point in their lives. Until then, I ignorantly assumed what most people outside of the community assume, that all drag queens are men dressed as women.

I was still a little confused. Why would a (trans)woman want to dress up and perform as a drag queen? One of the women helped me understand by explaining that a drag queen is a character, a persona she creates for the purpose of entertainment. She doesn't dress or wear her makeup that way in her day-to-day life. Like any other stage performer, they get into character and costume backstage and when the show is over, they change and go home.

It made sense. But I was struggling with how to apply that to my own drag experience. I couldn't figure out how to create a character. I was just *me* when I put on the face and binding. How do I not be *me*?

Unlike the rest of the performers, I always arrived at the club in full face and left that way when the show was over. It was so comfortable, so natural. Instead of going home, I'd go to an all-night diner for a soda and some hashbrowns. There were plenty of stares but for the first time I didn't care. I wanted people to see me. I was happy.

Maybe I was too happy or having too much fun. Whatever the reason, I got very careless with my sobriety. For months I was in the bar at least two nights a week, sometimes more. Yet I never considered drinking. On one occasion I even sold Jello shots to the Ladies Night crowd. Drinking didn't feel like a temptation, so I thought I was safe. "Safe" makes it easy to let your guard down which for me meant skipping some AA meetings.

I was too new to AA to understand that it's not the absence of alcohol that keeps you sober; it's doing the actions required of each step and showing up at meetings for accountability. Within a few short months I'd stopped doing both. The drinking started in May and ended six weeks later with a humbling phone call to my parents. I packed some clothes and retreated to their spare bedroom for a week or two to regroup.

Even as drag was a positive force, allowing me a small preview of how natural it felt to show up in the world as a man, I wasn't doing the work on myself that AA requires. I slacked off keeping my character in check, did some things I'm not proud of, and fell into alcohol as an escape. It was a hard lesson but an important one: For an alcoholic, drinking is rarely about the actual drink. I drank because I couldn't stand myself.

Instead of fixing my problems or changing the behaviors that created them, I jumped ship. I abandoned myself over and over, as if I looked in the mirror and said, *Hey, shithead, you suck... you did this thing or that thing... you fucked over this person or that person, and you can't fix it because you're a giant asshole. So you know what? I'm outta here, fuck it.* Then I'd drink myself far, far away.

I have to admit, the first few minutes of relief was always great. It felt like shrugging off a heavy coat, the weight clearing my shoulders gliding down my arms and onto the floor.

Of course my mess was always there the next morning, right where I left it. And the cycle would begin again.

After the relapse I had no choice but to keep myself out of the bar scene. I'd miss the friends I made, the makeup and costumes, and the fun interactions with all those ladies in the audience but for now I couldn't trust myself around alcohol. I narrowed my focus to three things: the kids, AA, and grad school. The only thing standing between me and graduation were two summer classes and student teaching in the fall.

CHAPTER FORTY-FIVE

The final semester of grad school was an intense grind of full-time student teaching, thesis work, parenting, and scraping by on literal pennies some days (pretty sure the sight of coin wrappers still triggers a flash of panic). But in December of 2013, I graduated with a 3.9 GPA. I passed the licensing exam and was officially a certified art teacher.

While I'd always planned to walk in the graduation ceremony in front of my kids and parents, I scrapped the idea weeks earlier when it was time to order a cap and gown. The thought of all those eyes on me as I crossed the stage was too much. I couldn't do it. My weight had been steadily increasing for over a year. My short hair was still an issue. I felt fat and ugly and didn't want to be seen by anyone.

In fact, I rarely left the house unless I absolutely had to: school, kids, groceries, AA meetings. That was it. But now school was finished and there was much more time to fill. And much more time to *feel*.

I ventured out to the grocery one Saturday morning, alone, since it was Lou's weekend to have the kids. I made my way over to a Starbucks counter with a gift card I'd received as a graduation gift. After placing my order, the barista grabbed an empty cup and a marker. "What's your name?" she asked. "Jay," I said, after a split-second pause. She wrote neatly on the cup and added a little smiley face after the y. I'd been testing out this new name for a few months and it felt good. Phonetically it was the first initial of my birth name, so it wasn't entirely different and didn't require much explanation when I used it around the kids.

"Caramel Frappuccino for Jay!" another barista yelled. I picked up the frozen drink and walked away. Yep, the name felt very right.

"Ma'am, ma'am! You left your keys!" the cashier waved wildly at me. I cringed. *Ma'am* did not feel right. Neither did *Miss, Ms., she,* or *her.* Those words had been increasingly difficult to hear, and I was mystified. They were jarring, strange even. I couldn't make sense of it.

I rushed through the aisles grabbing what I needed and made my way to the checkout lanes. It was a typical crowded Saturday with every lane full of people. I took my place in line behind a mom and her preschooler. The mom was emptying her cart onto the belt while the little boy looked at me. I smiled. He responded with a half-smile but didn't look fearful. I turned my attention to the rack of tabloid papers and magazines and then back to his mother's cart which was now empty. She was opening her wallet and preparing to pay. The little boy was still staring at me inquisitively. I smiled at him again and watched his little hand begin to tug on his mom's shirt. She was preoccupied with counting out correct change and tried to shrug him off. He spoke anyway, his eyes never leaving mine. "Momma, is that a boy or a girl?"

The woman quickly turned to him and followed his gaze directly to me. Her embarrassment was instantaneous. She looked away, pulled his hand from the hem of her shirt and pretended not to hear his question. "Come on, help me push this cart, let's go," she said.

"But is that…" The poor kid just wanted an answer to a valid question. She pulled him along, talking over him about something totally unrelated. As a mom, I couldn't help but feel embarrassed for her. I'd experienced a similar situation years earlier with one of my own kids, then three or four, loudly asking an innocent question about a stranger's leg deformity. I'm pretty sure it's a scenario every parent encounters at least once.

I stepped up to the register and locked eyes with the young cashier. She seemed to be nervously waiting for my reaction, so I smiled, forced a laugh, and said, "Gotta love kids, right?" She nodded and visibly relaxed. I glanced behind me and wondered how many people just witnessed this embarrassing situation.

The cashier was new and didn't know how to take off the two coupons I handed her. She flipped on the help light and apologized. Wanting desperately to be done, I was about to tell her to forget the coupons when the manager appeared. "This lady has two coupons, and they won't work but she bought the right items…" There it was again: an internal cringe at the sound of *lady* and *she*. Then the manager spoke, "I'm sorry for your wait, *ma'am*. I'll take these off manually and we'll get you on your way."

The next person in line sighed and glared at me. I wondered again if they had heard the little boy's question. Maybe they were only judging me for the malfunctioning coupons. I grabbed my bags and hurried toward the exit.

On the drive home I tried (for the umpteenth time) to make sense of those little gendered words and pronouns. *Why did they bother me so much?* It hadn't happened overnight either. The discomfort had been increasing over time. *When did this start and why?*

I put my groceries away and flopped on the couch. Words, language, emotions, memories, all swirled in my mind. Usually these conundrums were about labeling my sexual orientation. Surprisingly my attraction to women was the only constant throughout my entire life. It had never changed.

"Are you a lesbian or a boy?" The question popped into my head. A drag queen had asked me that backstage one night while we waited our turn in the lineup. It seemed like an odd question at the time. My answer was tentative and unsure: *"Umm, a lesbian?"*

I thought she must be referring to my masculine appearance, but I was too embarrassed to ask for an explanation.

I silently counted how many months had passed since my last performance. Almost nine. To my surprise I didn't miss the bar or the stage; I missed the familiar male face in the mirror. I felt so at ease and confident with the faux-chiseled features and five o'clock shadow created by makeup powder and a few brushes. I opened my phone and scrolled the camera roll until I found the selfies I'd taken. *That's the face that matches who I am on the inside.*

I tossed my phone on the table, suddenly aware that without drag there was no socially acceptable reason to get made up like that again. This was all too much to think about. I got up and started cleaning in an effort to put my mind somewhere not so depressing.

It worked for a while. I put on some music and washed dishes, picked up the kids' room as well as my own, and did a couple loads of laundry. I'd all but forgotten about pronouns and drag until I started to clean the bathroom. As I scrubbed the sink, I caught sight of my reflection in the mirror and felt the familiar jolt of surprise and disappointment. The feeling was always the same: like being around a bunch of people, interacting and feeling totally fine until you leave and realize you've had a giant piece of toilet paper hanging from the back of your pants. Or a big chunk of broccoli stuck in your teeth, or food in your hair. Whatever the case, it's an embarrassment that causes you to think, *Oh my God I've been walking around looking like THIS??*

I was back at square one. *What the fuck? What is wrong with me?* The never-ending feeling of shock at my reflection had been happening for my entire life. *Why then does it continue to be shocking? And why is the same thing happening when someone refers to me with feminine words like she and ma'am?*

There was an explanation, I was sure of it. My best Virgo quality has always been my ability to analyze the hell out of anything. Combined with what I'd learned in AA—methodical self-inventory—the answer was within reach.

I started with my appearance. *What's the problem? Do I want to grow my hair out and go back to wearing women's clothes? Hell no. Never.*

Okay then I'm a masculine lesbian. No! That's not right either.

Well, if I'm not a lesbian then does that mean I like men somehow? NO! Hell no. No.

Then what the fuck am I? I like women, I'm not a lesbian. When I'm made up like a drag king that's what matches who I am inside.

And then the answer fell right into my lap like a pair of glasses that had been pushed up on top of my head the entire time I'd been frantically searching: *I'm a straight man. Not a gay woman.*

The realization clicked into place, like carefully tapping the first domino in a forty-two-year-long line of standing dominoes: the recognition of my internal *self* when in drag; the confidence, ease, and comfort in that persona; the discomfort of being named after my grandma; the awkwardness, embarrassment and disconnect with women's clothing, makeup, hair, and accessories; feeling like a guy in my friendships with women; the toys, interests, and Halloween costumes of my childhood; the occasional feelings of jealousy of my brother as my dad's only son. The list rolled on and on.

My life *finally* made sense.

CHAPTER FORTY-SIX

I t's too much, it's too big." I said to my therapist between sobs. "I just spent years upending my life to go start a new one as a lesbian, and now I'm back at square one."

Falling dominoes are cool, but it's a big fucking mess to clean up.

Carol was kind and empathetic. She admitted having no previous experience in this area and gently suggested I consider seeing someone who specializes in gender identity. I thanked her and explained the last thing I wanted to do was start over with a new therapist. She agreed to keep seeing me and offered to educate herself on the subject as best she could.

I was doing the same. Reading and researching online was a good starting point but eventually it became redundant. I needed firsthand information. On YouTube I found trans men with video channels dedicated to documenting their transitions and answering questions. From there, I found private online communities. The most helpful information came from a site which served as a type of photo database for trans surgeries and surgeons. Users shared details of their surgery and recovery along with photos throughout the healing process. Each post had a place for other users to comment or ask specific questions, some of which were about navigating insurance coverage, out-of-pocket costs, and having a surgery in another state or country.

My research included nonsurgical options too. Hormone replacement therapy (HRT) is considered a "chemical sex change." Weekly testosteronc injections result in several permanent and semipermanent physical changes. I also learned about medical grade prosthetics, something quite different from items categorized as sex toys.

It was a lot to take in. My emotions ranged from euphoria to defeat and everything in between. The surgeries were major and came with risks, scars, and sometimes complications. Cost and insurance were another challenge, not to mention the time off work required for healing. And some things, like my height for instance, were simply not changeable.

There were so many options to consider, each with its own list of pros and cons. Still, there was no going back. Doing nothing was definitely *not* an option. I'd spent my life trudging ahead, falling in line, fulfilling obligations when nothing made sense, nothing felt right, and everything was unclear. But now I had certainty.

I'd spent decades looking for answers (sometimes looking for the questions too) trying to understand what was "wrong" with me, why being feminine felt so awkward and off-putting, why I felt naturally drawn to some things and repelled by others.

I finally had an answer for all of it. Not a *probable* answer or a *good* answer, it was *the* answer: solid, certain, and undeniable. I knew it on a cellular level, the way I knew my children were my own.

Thanks to AA, I sidestepped what otherwise might have been an existential crisis. Some of my best recovery work was happening during this time. The program taught me to take accountability for my actions and reactions, and, more importantly, to own up to my bullshit. I also learned the importance of daily gratitude. Those two pieces together were game changers.

Although it wasn't immediately obvious to me, AA filled the spiritual void left by my split with Catholicism. The program gave me space to believe in and be in relationship with God, free from dogma. It also gave me space to *not* believe in God and still feel worthy and deserving of a good life. The *AA Big Book* has an entire chapter called "We Agnostics," which explains how atheists and agnostics can frame the concept of a higher power without compromising their beliefs or disbeliefs.

That particular chapter had a profound impact. It showed me that the program was truly nonjudgmental. AA welcomed *everyone* and affirmed their human dignity. I didn't see that in Catholicism. Sure, the church talks a big game with "all are welcome here" and popes like John Paul II and Francis have written some beautiful words about human dignity. Sadly, it's all contradicted by doctrine. While many individual Catholics I knew genuinely embodied a Christ-like mentality, I couldn't find it in the religion as a whole.

The twelve-step program became my spiritual practice, without all of the inconsistencies of organized religion. If I compared my experience with Catholicism to eating a fast-food diet, then AA was eating whole food organic. The program was not easy, don't get me wrong, but it was straightforward and made sense. It was teaching me how to show up in the world as a better person: an active participant in life rather than a despairing, fearful, people-pleaser.

I could have easily been crushed under the word *transgender* and all of the major decisions that came with it. AA provided structure and filled my downtime with regular tasks like calling my sponsor, going to meetings, reading the book, making gratitude lists, and ending each day with a mental review. The mantra "one day at a time" prevented me from getting tangled up in "what ifs" and worst-case scenarios. Friends in the program reminded me that sometimes it's "one minute at a time and that's okay because we've all been there."

The "what ifs" were often far more challenging than staying sober, particularly when I considered going back into the dating world as a man. It was a relief to understand why my relationships with lesbians never worked. They are attracted to women and internally I wasn't one. It was an energetic mismatch. But how would any straight woman want to date me? They are attracted to male bodies, and I didn't have that yet. At some point down the road, I would but then there's the problem of disclosure. Keeping it a secret isn't an option. *What should I say and when is the right time to say it?* I considered a couple different scenarios:

What if a woman approached me for conversation or was flirtatious? Disclosing the facts too early would be presumptive. And weird. Waiting until she developed feelings was not only wrong, but too much like the storyline of a bad romantic comedy. You know, the ones that make you scream at the TV, "Just tell the truth you idiot!"

What if I used dating sites and self-identified as a trans man in the profile details? Would anyone actually get to know me, or would they ask to see pictures of my genitals first? Would someone respond solely out of freakish curiosity? Would strangers overload my inbox with inappropriate questions and rude or hateful comments?

None of those options were acceptable. It left me feeling hopeless and wondering if I'd be alone forever.

This anxious stream of thoughts replayed from time to time, usually when I was alone and reading information about some aspect of being trans. It became a nuisance, an emotional pothole, and I'd had enough. Predictions are not my job; predictions are not trust.

AA helped me to develop the skills to manage these feelings of loneliness or anxiety. I was able to connect to God with genuine trust. I could just focus on doing the things that were within my power to do and believe that the rest would be taken care of. When I started to worry about something or feel anxious, I learned to slow down and check my instincts. I put this into practice many times, talking myself off the proverbial ledge:

Okay, slow down, take deep breaths. Think about where you've been and where you are now. You finally know who you are! Your life makes sense now; too much sense to have it all be for nothing.

Think for a minute, tune in to that deep instinctual knowing... do you really think you'll be alone forever?

No. The answer was a clear and resounding no. I felt peaceful. The thoughts returned on one or two more occasions but each time I was able to guide myself to the same peaceful answer.

Do you really think you'll be alone forever?

No.

Well then you have to be patient and trust in the timing. What if there's someone who is so well-matched for you that it's beyond your imagination?

I had to smile. This felt right, felt solid. I didn't need to be anxious at all because there were no bad outcomes. I stopped worrying about the timetable. It wasn't important. In the meantime, I'd keep working on being the best version of myself.

One evening while finishing up some twelve-step work I thought about the kind of person I wanted to be in a future relationship. *How can I improve?* I wondered. I grabbed my laptop and made a list of everyone I'd been involved with or dated. After each name I answered the following questions: *What did I learn from my involvement with this person? What mistakes did I make; where did I cause harm? What did I do that was reckless, hurtful, or mean? What are my regrets?*

My answers were painfully honest and as a result it was a difficult read. However, seeing it all at once made it possible to connect the dots between offenses large and small. This revealed a bigger story. My selfish behaviors that seemed benign in the moment sometimes paved the way for manipulation. In other cases, they manifested as immaturity and repelled my partner, leaving me confused, hurt, and unaware that I was the source of the problem. In that case I created more issues by feeling like a victim. My most shameful moments involved infidelity and deception, things I wanted to leave in the past and never repeat in the future.

Everything I'd written had already been discussed with my sponsor months earlier. It was done in a different format with a much broader context. I made amends where possible and when doing so didn't inflict more harm on the person I wronged. I learned that in some cases the only amend you can make is to stay the hell out of someone's life.

I closed my laptop. The list was a painful reminder of *why* I drank. Like two sides of the same coin, it was also a list of reasons *not* to drink. And a blueprint for self-improvement.

CHAPTER FORTY-SEVEN

In the spring, I landed an adjunct position at a small community college where my sister worked. It was part time, but the pay was much more than I'd earned anywhere else. I jumped at the opportunity. The class was called Professional Development, a first semester requirement for all majors. It was full of practical skills for surviving college and balancing work, family, and studies. In a condensed format, each class ran for one month and students attended three hours a day, two days a week.

The first month was rocky as I tried to get my bearings and navigate the school's digital learning system. I was off and running in month two and made some improvements to the course content. By month three, the dean took notice and rewarded my efforts by adding a second section of the course, which doubled my income. She also asked me to collaborate with the person in charge of student services to create a welcome session for new students.

Next, I was approached to take part in the monthly newsletter's meet-and-greet section. It was ten questions I'd answer about myself as a new faculty member. Question number ten made me laugh:

10. What is one thing people don't know about you that you'd like them to know?

That was one hell of a final question. I sailed through the previous nine, all of which were pretty standard. The questions and answers would be printed next to my photo, which I'd undoubtedly loathe, with the title "Meet Our New Faculty."

There were so many possible answers to question ten, none of which I could actually make public. At least not now, not with the ongoing divorce battle, the kids in a Catholic school, and my entire family still under the impression I was a lesbian. But it was somewhat amusing to imagine the unprintable truths:

Yes, I like women. No, I'm not gay.

I'm a guy in the wrong body.

I hate my appearance, so, please, don't stare at me.

And then a printable answer popped into my head—

I hate my first name and prefer to be called by my first initial—J.

I turned in the survey and forgot about it until days later when a coworker smiled and said, "Hi, Jay!" I returned the greeting and felt my mouth naturally form a smile. *Wow, how nice of that person to read the newsletter and remember,* I thought. Later another coworker did the same. And then another. They didn't stop to question me about it, they just did it. *Is it really this easy? Holy shit.*

Each time it happened my face broke into a real smile. I was suddenly aware of how few of my smiles were genuine like these. When I was growing up, I regularly heard people tell me to smile. I knew it was meant to be funny or lighthearted, but it was always unexpected and embarrassing. "Smile, it doesn't hurt!" someone would say, or "Don't look so serious; smile!"

The next day at work I ran into my boss, the academic dean, in the hallway. She greeted me by my birth name and began a friendly conversation about my classes. Within a few seconds another employee passed by us with "Good morning, Dean; good morning, Jay."

Immediately, my boss stopped our conversation, placed her hand on my arm and apologized. "I'm so sorry, I forgot to call you Jay! Why didn't you say something?" I assured her no harm was done. I had no way of knowing whether she had even read the newsletter yet, maybe she didn't know. We both laughed politely, and she continued, "Well, I'm horrible with names, and I'm probably going to forget again, but be patient with me—I'll get it right... and if I screw up, stop me."

I never doubted her sincerity as she was known to everyone to be a kind and caring personality. I was impressed by her honesty and willingness to accommodate a statement made in a single sentence of a company newsletter.

It did take her a while to remember, but to the Dean's credit, she always corrected herself. It was her effort and the validation in *trying* that meant the world to me. Obviously, it takes time and repetition to begin calling someone by a different name. I knew that people were not going to get it right in the beginning.

One afternoon I walked into the administrative office to check my mailbox and ran into my sister and two other employees who were having a conversation. My sister greeted me by my birth name and the male employee referred to the fact that I hated that name, as I'd stated in the newsletter. The two of them made jokes about names and people wanting to be called by specific names. I wasn't amused but was trying to remain professional. Suddenly the third person who had been silently observing this exchange spoke up.

"You want to be called Jay, right?" she asked me, very pointedly.

"Yes." I replied.

"Then *I* will call you Jay," she said, her eyes throwing me a lifeline.

I thanked her before she left in one direction and I left in another. Her name was Amanda, the person with whom the dean had just asked me to collaborate. We were introduced on my first day, but that had been two months ago. I didn't know her beyond an occasional "hello" in the office. However, this interaction spoke volumes about her character.

CHAPTER FORTY-EIGHT

In my fifth month of teaching at the college, the dean's project was complete. Amanda and I created a short presentation to be delivered during a portion of one of my class sessions. It all went smoothly, and she was very fun and easy to work with. At some point we revisited the topic of my name, and I confided that I was transgender but not out to my sister or any family members yet, only close friends. She was supportive and didn't seem to flinch at this piece of information. She said it made sense because interacting with me felt no different from interacting with a cisgender (assigned male at birth) man.

Three days a week I taught one section of my course from 9 a.m. to 1 p.m. and a second section from 6 p.m. to 10 p.m. On the break in between I'd go home, get the kids from school, and spend time with them until their dad picked them up. One afternoon I received a text from Amanda that said, "I stole your pen." I remembered she borrowed it that morning when she came into my classroom for the new student presentation. I responded with "Thief," and that was the beginning of our first non-work-related text conversation.

The next day we continued conversing through texts. It was clear there was a spark between us, but I had two hesitations: the first was her age and the second was her sexual orientation. I had just turned forty-three and she was twenty-four. She was straight and had only ever dated men. Would a pre-transition trans man count? Though she maintained that she felt forty and always dated older guys, I mentally labeled our friendship as strictly friendship.

After a few laughs we moved on to talking about life in general. Despite the age gap, I was still ten-to-thirteen years younger than her parents. They were on the younger end of the baby boomer generation while my parents were older baby boomers, which meant Amanda and I were raised with very similar family values. We shared many of the same childhood rules, manners, and behavior expectations.

It didn't take long to see why she was an old soul. She was intelligent, independent, and well-traveled. Her family lived in Germany for a few years and that's where she attended kindergarten and first grade. As a teen she traveled to Spain with her Spanish class and made a solo trip to New York for one of several college visits. She was accepted into a very selective liberal arts university and lived on campus. For six months, she studied abroad, living in Argentina with a host family.

Those experiences were so different from my own. I was twenty-eight years old the first time I flew on an airplane and my only trip out of the country was on a cruise ship. I dreamed of traveling to Spain but that was still a far-off dream. Hell, I'd never lived on my own until two months before my fortieth birthday.

Her life sounded so put together and well-rounded that I was surprised when one of her texts in our conversation said, "I have no idea what the hell I'm doing with my life."

"In your career or in general?" I asked.

"In general. I could go all existential, but I'll save you that."

"Try me," I offered. "I'm a bit of an existentialist myself; I've had multiple life crises." I was intrigued by where this was going. I watched my screen and waited for her reply.

"Fair enough. I just have no idea if I'm settling in life or whether I should be happy. I grew up moving all over and now I'm here, but

I moved down here for my ex-fiancé and that's long over with but I'm still here. I had all these great dreams when I was younger that now seem impractical, but I still miss their presence. I want to go to grad school and was accepted but can't afford it. Really have no friends here (one or two) which is slowly eating away at me... List goes on. Haha. Very irritated how much money influences life and decisions and opportunities."

Even though our conversation was happening through text messages I felt a distinct shift in her energy. I was re-reading before typing my response when a second text came through.

"So then I just start thinking, *well I'll just settle in and live a life of mediocrity like everyone else.* I could get shot walking down the street so I might as well just be happy to be alive. Don't get me wrong, I'm actually super happy most of the time, it's just all very confusing and frustrating."

I felt a strange urgency to tell her not to give up, that anything is possible. There was nothing romantic in my concern, it seemed to come from a feeling of deep friendship—which also didn't make sense because I'd only been getting to know her for two days. I shook off the hesitation and told her anyway.

"Sadly, I totally get it. All of it. Don't settle for mediocrity, trust me on this one. I spent an entire lifetime trying to be and do what people expected of me... my life sucked. I remember being twenty and wishing I was forty and settled. I didn't have the energy to deal with figuring out life. So, I said fuck it and married at twenty-one, gave up and kinda said what you said: Could be worse, at least I'm alive. But it got worse, way worse. So yeah, please consider me one of your friends. I'm happy to be a sounding board. How long have you been in this area?"

She told me about her roots in the area and disappointment at being unable to afford UC tuition to earn her master's in Spanish, and I encouraged her to apply for a paid assistantship at a nearby university. I found myself invested in her dream. She thanked me and added, "Btw, if you're up for sharing I'd be happy to hear more of your story."

Our conversation ended with a tentative plan to talk more over coffee on Sunday if we were both free. I made the offer from a genuine place of friendship as evidenced by the fact it was for coffee at midday on a Sunday. Besides, now that she knew our exact age gap, I figured an overt friend-zone offer would assure her that I had no intentions of chasing her like some sort of creepy old man.

The next day we didn't text at all even though she popped into my mind regularly. Each time my text alert sounded I hoped it was from her, but it wasn't. Part of me still felt a spark while another part of me screamed, *You're too OLD! She's being nice because she's one of those uncharacteristically kind humans.* I silently laughed it off and felt a sense of immense gratitude for her friendship. *Maybe in another lifetime our paths will cross again, and we will be closer in age.*

On Sunday morning I didn't hear from her either. *Okay good, you gave her an out and she took it. We will be work friends and that is enough. It's all good!* Around noon I put my phone in the front pocket of my jeans and got on my motorcycle to go to the gym. Halfway there I felt the buzz of my phone. Instantly and unexplainably, I knew it was Amanda. I pulled into a gas station to check and sure enough her name was on the screen.

"You still free today?" she asked.

"Yes, on my way to the gym but free any time after," I typed back.

"Were you thinking LITERALLY coffee talk somewhere or…?"

"I don't actually drink coffee…" I admitted, "but in general, I meant lounging somewhere with beverages. Potentially food. Ever been to Goodfellas Pizza? Great outdoor patio in the back."

She agreed and planned to text me after running a couple errands. Around 4 p.m. I was still waiting and beginning to wonder if she had changed her mind. I opened Facebook and saw that she had just posted something about shopping for a new outfit. *Holy shit, this is kind of a date,* I thought. I had to rethink my own clothing choices. I couldn't be too obvious, or it would look like *I* was trying to make it a date. I settled on my favorite pair of jeans and a casual button-down plaid shirt. As I pulled the shirt from my closet I remembered wearing it to my first drag audition. *Maybe it will give me better luck on this "date" than it did at the audition.*

She finally texted and we agreed to meet at 6 p.m. I was so nervous that I intentionally arrived early so that I might appear relaxed when she showed up. In a parking lot nearly the size of a city block I sat on my motorcycle and waited, scanning rows and rows of parked cars. I noticed a very attractive brunette heading in my direction and did a double take when I realized it was Amanda. She was wearing a pair of dark wash jeans, a low-cut top with a tiny flower pattern, a black cardigan, and the brightest smile I'd ever witnessed on another human being.

When we sat down across from one another at a patio table I was stunned. *She dresses nice like this at work, and I've always thought she was cute; why does it feel like I'm seeing her for the first time?*

Our pizza dinner at Goodfellas unlocked something I couldn't explain. Our conversations were so easy, and we began talking daily, by text as well as actual phone calls. We still kept a professional distance at work, careful to keep our personal lives personal.

Life was looking up. And so were my finances now that I was teaching additional sections of my course at the community college. I wanted to move into a bigger space where the kids might have their own rooms instead of sharing one. A Facebook friend told me about an old two-story house on the other side of town that her landlord owned. The tenant had just moved out. It was in a great location, so I called and scheduled a walk-through for the following day.

I felt an overwhelming urge to invite Amanda to come check it out with me. On one hand the idea was absurd; we were just two weeks into talking to one another on a personal level. Instead of feeling like I was getting to know her it somehow felt like we were reconnecting after a long absence. At times it was unsettling. I'd mentally question if things were moving too fast or if I was getting ahead of myself but that wasn't the case at all.

I told her about the place and used every ounce of restraint to not invite her along. She was excited and hopeful for me. "Text me after you see it, I can't wait to hear how it goes!" The next day I woke up and got ready for the walk-through. By the time I pulled up to the house, it was all I could do to keep from calling Amanda and asking her to meet me there. I couldn't shake the strange feeling that I was checking it out for the both of us. *What the hell is wrong with me? That makes no sense! It's barely been three weeks!* I thought.

But the minute I walked through the front door it felt like *our* home and I couldn't wait for her to see it. My brain cycled through questions in an effort to keep myself in check. *Am I out of my mind? Am I reaching?* No, I didn't feel like I was forcing anything emotionally or trying to create something that wasn't there. *Am I lonely?* No. In fact I truly enjoyed single parenthood as well as the freedom of doing whatever I wanted when the kids were with their dad. *Am I trying to sleep with her?* Well, I hoped that was in the cards but definitely not yet. There was a very strong attraction that neither of us were denying at this point, but I wanted to go slow. This connection with Amanda was so unlike anything I'd known and had the potential to be something very special. I wanted to stay clearheaded and do things the right way.

CHAPTER FORTY-NINE

Violet and Max met Amanda on separate occasions. In both cases, she was introduced as my friend, which was the truth since we weren't officially a couple yet. There was an evening when I had to take Violet to work with me because Lou was at a doctor's appointment with Max. When my class started, Amanda offered to walk Violet to the breakroom for a slice of pizza. It was no surprise that they hit it off right away. They loved *all* animals even the ones most people can't stand. They were remarkably kind and compassionate, always ready to help others. If someone was being treated unfairly or ridiculed, they spoke up. Both individuals had big warm smiles and a natural ability to make people laugh.

Max met Amanda on a Saturday afternoon when I took him for a ride on the motorcycle. I told him we were going to the park to meet my friend and her dog, Chico. Once we arrived and settled down at a picnic table, Max was quiet. This wasn't out of character for him but twenty-five minutes into the interaction he not so subtly asked me, "Can we go now?" Amanda and I exchanged a look, both of us a little worried that this wasn't going well. We left about ten minutes later and once we were back home, I asked if everything was okay. He said, "Yeah, I was just bored sitting there." I wasn't convinced this was entirely true but dropped the subject rather than push for more.

Amanda and I were still getting to know each other at the time so there was no pressure to forge a connection between her and Max. Objectively speaking, Max was far more reserved than his siblings despite sharing the same sense of humor. It's difficult to gauge what he's thinking; he always looks so serious. But once he lets you in, the kid will have you rolling in the aisles. He *loves* to laugh. It's an instant shift too, as if someone tapped his face with a magic wand: His mouth springs open wide with sound, and his cheeks smash his brown eyes into two cartoonish arcs.

A week or two later, I took both kids to work with me to wait for their dad, who was stuck in traffic. In the car I heard Violet say to her brother, "Maybe mom's friend Amanda will be there, you'll like her. She gave me pizza last time." In the typical way that siblings like to one-up each other, Max shot back, "I know Amanda. She's hilarious! I met her dog too." I breathed a huge sigh of relief.

By the beginning of November Amanda and I were officially a couple. It was time to share that piece of news with the kids. Although I knew they liked her, it was still the first time they would know someone as my girlfriend. The routine of the shared custody arrangement made it easy to separate my "personal life" from my "mom life" and I'd been careful not to mix the two. The boundaries were as much for my benefit as theirs.

I'd also witnessed the ups and downs the kids experienced with Lou's girlfriend. Sometimes they loved her, sometimes they hated her. That was definitely not a situation I wanted to be in although I recognized it was largely out of our control. I leaned into the fact that Amanda was proving to be exactly what I promised in terms of stepmom qualities.

Four days after moving into the two-story house we sat in the backyard around a small fire pit roasting marshmallows. It was a breezy November evening. The kids were energetic and happy in this new place, each with their own bedroom after having shared a room at our previous addresses. We had a real yard with a privacy fence where they could play outside free from speeding cars and strangers.

They were comically excited about having a staircase and an "upstairs." I suppose it was a novelty since Lou's house and the places they lived with me were all single-floor layouts. It reminded me of my own excitement about having sidewalks when my family moved to Kentucky.

The kids loved looking out the upstairs window to see the buildings, lights, and bridges of the Cincinnati skyline. It was a close-up view too since we were just two blocks from the Ohio River, the border separating the two states. It was a very active area with restaurants, a movie theater and entertainment complex, regular fireworks displays after Cincinnati Reds home games, and a steady rotation of riverfront festivals all summer long.

My heart was so full. The kids ran around the yard stopping periodically to roast a marshmallow. Seconds later they burst into laughter and fake panic when a marshmallow caught fire. It seemed the only thing more hilarious was the splat of charred, flaming goo melting off the stick if they didn't blow it out fast enough. Now was as good a time as any to share the news.

"Hey guys, I want to ask you something," I took a deep breath. "How would you feel if Amanda was my girlfriend?"

"YESSSSS!" they shouted together. "Can she come over now?" Max asked.

"Can she bring her dog, Chico?" Violet squealed with excitement. This was the reaction I'd been hoping for.

I texted Amanda the good news and invited her to the marshmallow roast. She lived less than ten minutes away and when she showed up, Violet greeted her with a giant hug and then began making plans. "You can come to Thanksgiving dinner with us, and Christmas, and Easter! Do you want to spend the night sometime? You can bring Chico! We can play games…"

Needless to say, things were off to a great start. The next day brought more good news: My divorce was final. It took three-and-a-half years, but I was no less grateful to have it behind me. When the kids returned to their dad the next day Amanda and I celebrated the events of our first week as a couple.

"Is this real life?" we said with amusement. It felt like a fairy tale. In the conversations leading to the start of our relationship I learned that Amanda had felt the same uncanny familiarity: As if we'd known each other in past lives and were getting reacquainted after a very long absence.

"Well, I've only been waiting on you for the past forty-three years," I teased.

"I know, I'm late for everything," she laughed and put her arms around me.

"It's okay," I said and squeezed her tight. "We're here now and that's all that matters."

CHAPTER FIFTY

With the divorce officially behind me and the love of my life at my side, it was time to start figuring out how to align my outer self with my inner self. It was incredibly difficult to think about going through transition in front of coworkers and students at the community college. As it turned out, I didn't have to. The college was closing its doors permanently at the end of the spring term. Amanda and I would have to find new jobs. With a little luck and strategizing, I'd start the transition process near the tail end of one job and go into the new job as a male even if I still looked more feminine than masculine.

I'd had a full year to research my options and spend some time figuring out what changes I needed to feel at home in my body. Transition is not a one-size-fits-all process. People (trans or not trans) experience gender in their own unique way and express it in the way that's most comfortable and true to who they are. For example, women hold varying attitudes about their breasts and how much or how little attention is drawn to them. Men hold varying attitudes about things like penis size and baldness.

For me, the plan was to start with HRT (testosterone injections) and then have chest surgery. I was still on the fence in terms of which bottom surgery I wanted as there were multiple options. Every aspect of transition required huge chunks of time and even bigger chunks of money. Simple tasks like getting information from insurance companies and finding trustworthy doctors quickly added up to hours of research and phone calls. In the meantime, I'd have to improvise and find other ways to be identified as male when in public.

I'd been wearing men's clothing for a few years now all the way down to boxer briefs. I'd thrown out bras long ago in exchange for the most restrictive, flattening sports bras I could find. On some occasions I duct-taped my chest like I'd done for drag performing despite it being incredibly uncomfortable and painful to remove.

I learned about specialized undergarments called chest binders that are safer and more comfortable than tape. They were cut like a tank top: the front panel of the shirt was several layers of restrictive material while the back panel was a single layer. They weren't cheap but I managed to buy one each payday until I had five. It helped me feel a bit better about leaving the house and flattened my chest easier than tape. On the downside, the binders were so tight that I often needed Amanda's help to get out of them at the end of the day. I read warnings about wearing binders too long and too often because over time they can cause rib damage. The warning made sense: Running or doing strenuous exercise was impossible because it was difficult to fully expand my lungs. But none of that mattered to me. Having the appearance of a male chest relieved some of the mental anguish of existing in the wrong body. I figured it was no riskier than the latest weight-loss drug or weight-loss surgery, just two examples of many high-risk things people do to feel at home in their bodies.

While navigating health insurance requirements for hormones and surgeries, I decided to tackle an easier task: changing my name. It was surprisingly simple. I downloaded a petition form from the Circuit Court Clerk's website, filled it out in about five minutes, delivered it to their office, paid the filing fee of $40 and was told it should be complete in a week.

In a perfect world I would have chosen a new first and middle name but that would require outing myself to everyone all at once.

"Jay" was still technically "J," the first initial of my birth name so I could buy a little more time before telling my parents and kids I was trans. Besides, I had been unofficially using *Jay* for about a year now and was used to it. Unable to settle on a middle name that went with Jay, I dropped it entirely. There are no rules that require a person to have three names anyway.

One week later I was officially Jay DeFazio. I returned to the courthouse to pick up the legal documents and carried them down the hall to the DMV for an updated driver's license. I still didn't like my photo or that it said *female,* but the new name was an exciting start. Amanda and I celebrated this milestone quietly. I told everyone I changed it because I've always hated my birth name, a true fact that was no surprise. I'd wait a bit longer before telling them about the transition.

There wasn't too much pushback around my new name. In my family, most criticism happens when the person being criticized isn't in the room. I tried not to care considering it was out of my control. What I *did* care about, and still do, is that people use the correct name. Obviously, it was going to take some time to get used to since I'd been called something else for my entire life. In fact, I didn't care if my family members and longtime friends got it wrong as long as they corrected it in the moment. I'm trans, not heartless.

Name changes take time to get used to, but they also take practice and a willingness to try. It's not a foreign concept and people do it willingly in other situations. Think about a person who goes through a difficult divorce and reclaims their maiden name. Anyone who cares about that person will make considerable effort to use the correct name. If they slip up, they will apologize and self-correct on the spot. Why does any good person make such an effort in that scenario? Because they know the former name brings some level of pain and is a reminder of a person and an identity their friend or family member left behind.

I had two confrontations over the use of my new first name: one with Lou and one with a close family member. Immediately after the change I sent Lou a simple text saying, "I legally changed my first name to Jay since I've always hated my birth name." After a minute or two my message was marked "read" although he did not reply, nor did I expect him to. A few weeks later I received his monthly court-ordered payment in a check made out to my old name. I said nothing and let it slide in an attempt to assume (or pretend) it was a simple oversight. The next month the check was again made out to my former name. This time I sent a text asking him to please remember to correct it next month. No reply, no surprise. A month later a check arrived, *again* made out to the wrong name. I could no longer pretend this wasn't malicious. I had to send another text threatening legal action because my bank was not going to let me cash checks to a name that didn't match my ID. Only then did I start receiving payments made out to Jay DeFazio.

The confrontation with my family member also took place several months after the change. She had started calling me Jay in social settings where everyone else called me Jay but every time I saw her at a family function, she used my birth name multiple times without correction or any acknowledgment that it was accidental. Even when my parents would get it right, she made no attempt. On the third or fourth time this happened I could no longer contain my irritation.

"You call me Jay in public but that's still my name when you see me here."

"Well, if that's what you like to be called, I guess," she answered.

"It's not *what I like to be called*, it's my name…" I pulled my driver's license out of my pocket and held it up, "it's on my driver's license. It's my actual legal name."

I couldn't imagine what it was going to be like when I told everyone I'm transgender.

****

In February, Amanda moved in, both of us certain we'd found our forever partner. She was a pro at switching pronouns: referring to me as "she" only when in conversation with the kids and using "he" all other times. Amanda said it felt weird to refer to me as "she" in those moments, and I admitted it was weird to hear, although we both knew it was necessary for now.

I felt so incredibly lucky. A year earlier I was dreaming about the person I'd meet and now here she was, everything I wished for and everything I didn't know to wish for back then. In those moments alone and unsure, my thoughts were straightforward. I wanted to be with someone who *really* loved me as much as I loved them. I wanted someone who was crazy about me.

I never thought to specifically wish for someone who saw the real me beyond the physical body, but Amanda did from the start. When we started dating and the relationship became physical, I asked her how it was possible she still saw me as a man given the fact that my body, the body lying next to her each night, was pre-transition. I'll never forget her answer nor the love and sincerity with which it was spoken: "The body lying next to me each night is the body of the person I love more deeply than anyone I've ever loved. You've always been male to me from the beginning; I feel it and I know it. To me, your body is just *you*, even if you don't feel comfortable in it. I love it because I love you and everything about you."

We were both very aware that the rest of the world didn't see it that way. Amanda had always dated men and identified as straight. But when we were together in public people saw us as lesbians. It was a new experience for her and one that gave her a new appreciation for what I was dealing with as a trans person.

"It's hard not having control over how people perceive you and how they define you. Even when it's a stranger on the street, someone whose opinion doesn't matter, it's still hard," she confided.

I started to apologize, knowing I was the sole reason people assumed we were a gay couple. She shut it down immediately.

"Don't you dare apologize. I'm proud to be seen with you; you're my future husband! I'll go anywhere with you. I can't say that I know what it feels like to be you, but I can at least understand, on a much smaller scale, the frustration of not having control over how you're perceived. It sucks and I'm sorry you experience this and have *been* experiencing it for so long."

She meant every word. I knew it because she always walked with her head up, proud to be seen with me. There has never been a time she's avoided going somewhere or shown even an ounce of shame or embarrassment. In fact, she's been quite the opposite.

On one occasion we were sitting across from each other in a restaurant. Everything seemed fine. I was talking about something when I noticed her facial expression became more serious. Her eyes kept looking off to the side at something behind me to my right. After a few seconds I stopped talking and glanced over my shoulder. "Keep talking" she said, bringing my attention back to her. It was clear she was pissed off. She explained while still glaring at something or someone behind me: "There's a nosey old woman who keeps staring at you like she has a problem." I noticed she hadn't bothered to lower her voice.

"What? Like staring how?" I whispered.

"Staring like she doesn't know how to act in public, like she has a problem." Amanda answered, definitely not whispering.

I was too amused to be offended by the staring stranger. It was the first time I experienced someone being protective of me in a healthy way, free from possessiveness or jealousy. It wouldn't be the last time.

Going to restaurants is something I've always enjoyed, but by far the worst part was always the interactions with the server: "How are you ladies doing today?"

"Good afternoon, ladies."

"Would either of you ladies like a refill?"

"Are you ladies ready for the check?" And on and on. It was unbearable. Once in a while I'd get lucky, and a server would see me as a male and begin taking our orders. He or she would start with Amanda and then turn to me and say, "and for you, Sir?" I'd start ordering only to have the server interrupt with, "Oh, I'm sorry! Ma'am…" One of us would correct the person and say, "It's Sir." Sometimes it stuck, sometimes it didn't.

On one occasion we were on a weekend trip out of town when we went to an upscale steak restaurant. The waiter called me sir until I started to give my order, at which point he switched to ma'am. I politely corrected him, but he was belligerent for the rest of the meal, insisting on addressing me as ma'am each time he returned to the table. I shut down after the second time it happened, but Amanda was furious, talking over him each time and correcting him. We had to ask for our food to-go and left the restaurant.

CHAPTER FIFTY-ONE

No, we don't treat *transgenders.*" Wow. Nothing like being reduced to a *thing*, a broad category of awfulness like "the lepers" in the Bible. I imagined a 21st century New Testament: live Fox News coverage of Jesus hanging out with *the transgenders* while righteous viewers curse and shake fists at their TVs.

It was my third failed attempt at finding an endocrinologist. I scratched out the number and went to the next one on my list. A friendly voice answered the phone. The doctor was not taking new patients, but her nurse practitioner could see me and the doctor would oversee my care. Did they offer transgender HRT? Yes. Finally, a *yes.* The next available appointment was in three months. I was bummed but grateful to have found a provider.

Amanda's eyes lit up when I shared the news. She hugged me tight with an assurance that three months would go by quickly. Not ten minutes later my phone rang, and it was the endocrinologist's office. There was a last-minute cancellation, and the receptionist asked if I would like the appointment. I agreed, hopeful it would be in the same week. "Well, it's today at 1 p.m. Do you think you can make it?" she asked. I looked at the time, it was 12:20 and the office was thirty minutes away.

"Yes, I'm on my way, thank you!" Amanda and I stared at each other in disbelief.

"Oh my God, go! I'll stay here with the kids, go!" We laughed as I scrambled for a change of clothes.

The nurse practitioner was a kind man who looked to be a few years older than me. I gave him a letter of endorsement from my therapist, Carol. I'd been holding onto it for months, knowing it was a requirement for HRT. We discussed my medical history, the effects of testosterone, risks, as well as my expectations and concerns. My primary concern was how the drug might affect mood, considering my complex mental health history.

Since the overdose in 2012 I had been on the same dosage of a single medication, an antidepressant. It had been working without any side effects or issues. I was still seeing Carol once a month, sometimes twice if things felt particularly difficult. My work in AA helped me be proactive with the practice of daily personal inventories: reviewing any bumps in my day and examining my role in it first, before placing blame elsewhere.

The practitioner explained that while some patients take one shot every two weeks, he recommended splitting the dosage into weekly shots which helps keep the medication levels more stable in the bloodstream. I would start at a smaller dose for the first two weeks and then increase to the standard dose. This sounded like a good plan. He explained how to do the injection and then handed me my first prescription. I'd return in a month or call sooner if there were any issues.

At each traffic light on the way home, I glanced at the prescription paper on the passenger seat. It seemed unreal, almost magical. I felt like Charlie with the Wonka golden ticket. *This is actually going to happen.*

When I walked through the door Amanda threw her arms around me and we laughed in disbelief. "That was so fast!" she said.

"I know! Just a couple hours ago I was going down that list of numbers with no luck at all and then thought I'd have to wait three months for the appointment."

"And now it's in your hand! Where will you get it filled?" she asked.

"Well, I have this discount card which I'll definitely need to use. Looks like it will save me almost half the cost. We'll head out after Lou picks up the kids."

A few hours later, our celebration was interrupted at the pharmacy counter. They didn't have the drug in stock. "Man, I didn't expect that," I said, "but let's go to the one a few blocks from here."

At pharmacy number two they had the medication but not the right needle sizes. And they didn't accept the prescription card. We got back into our car, and I was beginning to lose patience. "What the hell?"

"Okay, no need to panic; we'll just sit here in the parking lot and call the next one before we drive there," Amanda assured me.

I was grateful we lived in an urban area with multiple major pharmacy chains. But our choices were narrowing, and stores were closing. At 9:40 p.m. we walked into our fourth pharmacy of the night. Over the phone they had confirmed they had exactly what I needed and accepted the discount. We got to the counter and were greeted with a smile, the same employee from the phone call. But when I handed her the paper prescription her smile disappeared.

"Ohhhh, this was written in Ohio."

"Yes, but I live here in Kentucky. My doctor is over there." This was typical, living on the border of two states.

She shook her head apologetically, "Right but testosterone is a controlled substance and there are specific rules. Your doctor has to write the prescription on a different pad, it should be blue, and it will have a different set of numbers printed at the top."

"You've got to be kidding me," I said, defeated. Amanda squeezed my hand.

The employee appeared genuinely sympathetic. Her tone softened. "Your doctor can rewrite it for you, just tell him you're getting it filled in Kentucky. Then bring it back tomorrow and we'll get you all set up."

I nodded and thanked her as she handed the prescription back to me.

"Wait!" her eyes widened. "There's a twenty-four-hour Walgreens on the west side of Cincinnati. You might be able to get it there tonight, would you like me to call and see if they have it?"

Twenty minutes later we entered pharmacy number five and left with vials, syringes, needles, and a box of alcohol wipes. Back on the road and headed for home; we put the windows down and turned up the radio.

"Holy shit what an adventure!" Amanda said with a laugh. "But you have it!"

We laughed off the stress together. I couldn't imagine doing this alone.

****

At home we carefully unpacked the white paper bag. Until this moment I had no fear or concerns about giving myself an intramuscular injection once a week for the rest of my life. Of course, that was all before the shaky needle was hovering over my thigh. I learned to give this type of injection when I was nineteen, in nursing school. Surprisingly the instructor's words were still there on the hard drive of my brain: *Hold the syringe like a dart, 90-degree angle to the surface of the skin... don't hesitate.... go straight in, quickly and firmly, with one smooth motion. If you try to go slow and easy, you'll nick the capillaries and cause more bleeding and more pain.*

Sometimes a good memory isn't all that helpful. I moved the needle in a dart-like motion toward my thigh only to have it stop an inch above the surface. I tried again. The same reflexive stop. *What the hell?* My arm had gone rogue, it was having no part of driving a needle into my leg. Amanda watched with concern. "I don't know what's wrong," I said. "It must be some protective subconscious response or something. It's bizarre."

For the next thirty minutes I wrestled with the shot. I cursed; I got up and walked around, changed positions, closed my eyes and took deep breaths, and even pulled up YouTube videos to see if anyone had any secret strategies. Finally, it just worked. It didn't even hurt.

"That was intense…" Amanda said nervously, "but you did it!" I relaxed into her arms, feeling an immense relief and a wave of gratitude for her, the medication, and the changes to come.

CHAPTER FIFTY-TWO

The start of HRT was like a get-out-of-jail-free card in terms of menopause. I'd never have to deal with it down the road. It simply disappeared from the menu, and I couldn't have been happier. Of course, in exchange for cheating menopause I'd have to go through male puberty.

It's okay, really. Given the choice again I would never hesitate to choose puberty. It was actually kind of comical. Less than two weeks after starting HRT, I took a job at Target unloading trucks and restocking the store from 4 a.m. to 11 a.m. It was physically demanding to say the least as the unload happened in an assembly line fashion. Each person moved quickly to grab boxes as they rolled down the line then placed them on the correct pallets, sorted by department. Once the truck was unloaded, we moved the pallets out into the store and began the tedious task of restocking shelves and breaking down cardboard.

In the interview and hiring process I presented myself as a man and corrected anyone who referred to me as *she* or *her*. The human resources manager was the only person who knew my driver's license still identified me as *female*. I explained that I was working on it, and it would take a few months. I also asked for reassurance that this information was private and not to be shared outside of HR. She was professional and kind.

It sucked to constantly correct people when they assumed I was female, but at least I was new and didn't know anyone. It was a challenge to do the job while wearing a chest binder but at this point, I was determined to wear it daily until I could get surgery.

Fortunately, the effects of HRT happen quickly. I'd had no more than three or four injections when I noticed how much more I was sweating. It was to be expected, and I'd read as much. What came as a disturbing surprise was that I was sweating from parts of my body that had never before produced sweat. Instead of sweating at just my hairline, it was my entire head. Amanda sent her usual morning greeting to me as a text, "Good morning! How's your day so far?" to which I replied, "Okay except that my kneecaps are sweating. Wtf?"

On the upside, the physical workout was perfectly timed for the first couple months of HRT. I was building muscle mass quickly and my body fat was redistributing into the typical male pattern: lean hips and thighs, less fat around my eyes and jawline, stomach fat moving higher up towards the diaphragm, and shrinking breast tissue. (For trans women estrogen does just the opposite.)

I dealt with some acne, but it was manageable with the right skincare routine. My appetite increased but so did my metabolism. There were no mood swings and things stayed even keeled save for an increased libido, although even that was well-timed for being in the honeymoon stages of a new relationship.

There are some changes that happen slower than others: male pattern baldness, voice deepening, facial hair, and increased body hair. I knew those were on the way which meant it was time to come out of the trans closet. I had been agonizing over this moment for more than a year and a half, but it didn't feel any easier.

How the hell do you tell your kids you're trans? Stringing together the right words was only part of the challenge. I knew the language would be different for Randy and Megan because they are adults. Violet had just turned twelve and Max was ten. In any case I'd stumble through.

The bigger problem, the heart of my fear, was the *impact* of my words. There was no way to predict how this might change my relationship with each one of them. Would they pull away? Hate me? Would they be ashamed of me? Would the younger two start asking to stay with their dad on days they were supposed to be with me? I was terrified. I didn't want to hurt them, yet it was unavoidable. Even if I gave up and attempted to go backward it wouldn't work. If I somehow tried to look like the mom they had had four years ago, I'd be only that: a physical shell familiar in appearance but unrecognizable in personality.

The clock was ticking, and I had to tell them. Multiple times a day it entered my mind like a gut punch, the same sickening feeling that buckles your knees every morning after you've lost a loved one or gone through a major breakup. Each time you wake up you remember it's real, not a bad dream.

"You are still their mom, and they *love* you," Amanda reminded me. "I see it so clearly just watching you interact with them."

I hoped like hell she was right.

Writing these words years after the fact I can't say that I remember much of those conversations. With Max and Violet, the talk took place in our living room with Amanda by my side. I tried to explain it in terms they could understand, focusing on the fact that I had always felt different from the time I was a little kid. I tried to be what I was expected to be but never felt comfortable and never liked myself.

The most difficult part was the part I have the least memory of: actually telling them I was going to transition. The only thing I can recall now is trying to explain some of the effects of HRT. For example, I would eventually grow facial hair and have thicker arm and leg hair. I believe one of the kids made a comment about the arm hair, that they were bothered by it.

I reiterated over and over that I was not changing on the inside, that I'd always be their mom and would never make them call me dad because they already had one. When Amanda and I married I'd be her husband; I'd be a son, son-in-law, a brother-in-law, and an uncle. If Randy and Megan had kids, I'd be a grandpa.

I promised that it would never change the love I had for them or how I treated them. I'd still hug and kiss them the same, still play the same silly games and have the same silly jokes. I wasn't changing *who* I was, I was changing the container, the body that was on the outside.

No one cried, at least not in front of us. I had no choice but to ask them not to tell their dad yet because I wanted to tell him first. I hugged them, told them I loved them and if they had any questions, they could come to either one of us and ask.

Telling Randy and Megan may have given me more options in terms of language, but it certainly didn't make it any easier. I told Megan first because we had always been close. As far as I was concerned, she was also one of my kids. When she and Randy started dating in high school, Max was a baby and Violet was a toddler. In my mind I've always had four children.

But as with the other conversations, I remember very little. I know I told her first so that I could get her opinion on how Randy might handle the news. I also wanted her to be prepared for Randy's reaction and not be blindsided. Overall, I left feeling positive and somehow strengthened for the next conversation.

I had a lot of emotion when it came time to talk with Randy. I was still carrying a great deal of guilt from what he went through with all of my mental health hospitalizations, drinking, and near death from overdose. Yet here I was about to tell him I was transitioning. I'm sure until that point, he probably thought he'd seen it all.

Again, I don't recall my explanation. But I remember quite clearly his response: "I don't understand it, but I love you, and I want you to be alive and happy."

CHAPTER FIFTY-THREE

"Have you ever watched this show?" my mom asked as her channel surfing stopped on *My 600-lb Life*. She went on to explain, "This doctor helps these poor people. I feel so bad for them, can you imagine? People stare at them when they leave their house; they're depressed. It's just awful, I can't imagine how hard that must be."

I realized this was perhaps the *best* possible time to tell her I'm trans. But I didn't want to take away from the show that had now started. She was explaining some other episodes she'd watched and the plight of those individuals. I was caught between the drama unfolding on the television and the potential drama that would unfold when I opened my mouth. The clock kept ticking.

I'd been there for nearly an hour before the show started. We'd talked about the kids, Amanda, my siblings, our family members in West Virginia, and my dad who, to my surprise, wasn't home. He'd gone out with coworkers to celebrate someone's retirement. This was the second time I'd stopped by hoping to break the news. My dad wasn't home the last time either, he was at karate class. This trip was going to be the one though, we'd just have to bring him up to speed later.

But so far, I'd been unable to find the right point in the conversation to drop the news. What exactly was I going to say anyway? *Oh hey, you know this whole lesbian thing I've had going on for a few years now? Well never mind all that, I'm actually a straight man.* That's probably not the right approach. I continued searching my brain for the right words.

The show was wrapping up and a graphic in the lower right-hand corner of the screen said there was another episode "coming up next." I had to spit out my news or risk sitting through a marathon of *My 600-lb Life*. With no lead-in whatsoever I blurted out one awkward question: "So would you disown me if I had a sex change?"

I had eighteen months to prepare for this moment and that's what I came up with. *Jesus Christ.* I don't remember the words of her response, only her obvious confusion. I also don't remember the clarification I gave. But then my brain stopped buffering and started recording memories again when her next question was "What about Amanda? Does she know?"

I almost thought she was joking but then started to really understand the depth of this secret I'd been keeping. "Yes, of course she knows. She's straight, Mom. She's never dated women."

From the look on her face, I could see that my words added zero clarification, in fact the opposite. I felt a wee bit of panic creeping into my chest as if my lungs were packing up to leave this disaster. I saw them like two cartoon balloons unplugging themselves from my trachea, shaking their cartoonish heads in disappointment. One says, "Can you believe this shit?" and the other says, "I know, right? Let's go get a beer, I can't watch."

My mom was on to another question. "What about Terry and Jim? Which one of them is a woman?"

"Well... neither, Mom. They are just two gay guys. They're men."

"What about Sandy and Sue? Which one is the man?" she asked, still confused and calling to mind my gay-couple friends she'd met over the years.

"They are both lesbians. They're women."

I never imagined how absolutely foreign this transgender concept might seem to someone like my mom who probably never considered that gender and sexual orientation are two different things. Of course it was completely confusing to her, she had zero point of reference. This was certainly the most unprepared I'd ever been. For anything. I felt awful.

The rest of the conversation is foggy. I may have attempted to explain the difference between sexual orientation (who you are attracted to) and gender (who you know yourself to be), although if I did, I'm sure it was just as muddled.

My dad had yet to return. I told my mom she could fill him in, or I'd come back over and tell him myself, and then I left. Crash and burn complete.

Amanda was waiting at home. Given the length of time I'd been gone I knew her expectations were too high. I relayed the events. When I got to the part of the story where I asked my mom if she'd disown me if I had a sex change, Amanda nearly fell out of her chair. "BABE! Oh my God!"

In the following weeks I had one more conversation to tackle and that was with Lou. We met at a bar and grill type restaurant where I wasted no time getting right to the point. Much like my other stress-inducing "coming out" conversations, my memory of this one is also spotty. However, it was made somewhat easier by the fact that he was (at least at one time) aware of my life-long struggle with self-loathing.

I explained the situation to the best of my ability as he listened. He didn't make any disparaging remarks and was polite throughout. At certain points of the conversation his expression appeared confused as if he was struggling to make sense of what I was saying. Who wouldn't be? It was similar to what I'd experienced in telling other people. Hell, it took more than forty years to figure it out myself.

My primary concern was how much of his opinion he would openly share with the kids. I explained that they had known for several weeks and asked that he redirect any of their questions and concerns back to me or Amanda. Deep down I felt it was a pointless request but worth trying. We parted ways and about thirty minutes after our meeting he sent me a text, one sentence that read, "I'm glad you've found happiness." I was shocked and sent a *thank you* reply.

I'd love to say it was all smooth sailing after that but that's not how things go. Transitioning and being trans was one more point of contention in the rotation of recurring problems between divorced coparents. If I weren't trans, it would be something else. Luckily coparenting has a shelf life and we were more than halfway there.

As for other coming-out conversations, it was a mixed bag of reactions. Some people, like my sister, found out from my mom or other family members which was fine by me. I planned to tell my brother personally but before I could do so he shared a news story on Facebook about a trans celebrity and then posted a negative comment. I contacted him and outed myself while also defending the celebrity. He said he had no issue with my being trans, so I dropped it and moved on.

I never did circle back to talk about it with my dad. My mom told him later that evening when he returned, but I never heard or asked the specifics. I did however email some educational infor-mation for them to look over: a one-page resource about the effects of hormone replacement therapy for female to male transition and a YouTube video made by a young trans man who was five or six years into the process. It was a montage of weekly photos he'd been taking since beginning HRT. I felt it would give them a pretty good idea of what changes to expect and how quickly it would happen.

About three months after that initial conversation with my mom, I was invited by a nonprofit organization to give a talk about gender identity and my experience. It was open to the public and took place at one of the local library branches nearby. I invited my parents, siblings, Randy, and Megan to attend. They all showed up in support, except for my brother who had a scheduling conflict and couldn't make it. It was well-received, and I felt very fortunate, loved, and thankful for their acceptance and understanding.

Outside of this closest circle of family, I eventually lost a couple friends and relatives. I suppose that was to be expected, statistically speaking, although it was still difficult. There were plenty of supportive reactions too but none quite as memorable as Samantha's. She was actually the very first person I told, right after figuring it out for myself that eventful afternoon in my living room years earlier. I'd called her the very next day.

"So, here's a funny story…" I started the conversation. "What would you say if I told you I'm not actually a gay woman, I'm a straight man?"

"Wait, what?"

"I've had this all wrong. I'm not gay. I'm not even a woman. That's why this has been such a shit show for so long. But I finally figured it out: I'm a *man*. A straight man."

"Okay. Wow… that's…" she chuckled. "You're a straight man. Okay!" she laughed some more.

"I know, it's a lot to digest. It's okay."

"No! No, I'm sorry I'm not laughing *at* you or anything like that. I just totally didn't see that coming in the conversation."

We were both laughing now. "Yeah, that's fair. I probably could have given a little more of a lead-in before blurting it out."

"Yeah, ya think?" she said sarcastically with a belly laugh. There was great comfort in her laughter; it was so characteristic of our relationship. She continued, "Well, okay. You're a guy! How'd you figure it out?"

I told her what happened the day before and how I put it all together. She listened intently as I went back through the years, listing all of the indicators I'd missed. Since she was such a big part of my childhood it was easy for her to see how all the pieces fit.

"So now what, what's the plan? Are you going to tell the kids? Get surgery?" she asked.

I explained the need to keep things quiet at least until the divorce was final, probably longer. I wanted to go slow for the kids, knowing it would be too jarring to change a bunch of things overnight. "I don't know… that stuff is still way off in the future at this point. You're the first person I've told."

"Awww, well thanks! I'm glad. And I support you one hundred percent of course but wow, my mind is blown. It's going to take me a minute to process."

We shared a few more laughs as this piece of news settled upon our thirty-four-year friendship. "Woah, I just thought of something" I interrupted. "One day I'll show up at your house for a visit and I'll look like a guy. Won't that be crazy? Can you imagine? I wonder what I'll look like?"

"Oh my God! That IS crazy!" she agreed.

"Wait, wait! This is even crazier, holy shit…" Realizations were coming to me faster than I could speak them.

"What??" She said, impatiently laughing.

"Okay, this one is really out there. I could literally show up to your house—shirtless. Like hanging out in the summer with no shirt and a hairy post-surgery man chest."

"Ohhhh. My. Gawwwwd! My brain just exploded."

That one took us over the edge. We laughed because there was genuinely humor in it but with full awareness that this was bigger than anything we could yet imagine.

CHAPTER FIFTY-FOUR

The start of HRT and the difficult coming out conversations that followed were the first big hurdles I cleared. The weekly shots were still challenging but Amanda stepped up and started giving them to me. As my physical body began to change, I was slowly becoming more comfortable in my skin. In October of that same year, I took Amanda on a trip to West Virginia to meet my second family: Samantha, her sister, niece, and mom. It was an extra special meeting because they helped set up a surprise marriage proposal complete with a celebratory homemade lasagna dinner. We still look back on that trip as one of the best memories we've ever made.

The wedding date we picked was two years away because we had so many things happening. Amanda was getting her master's degree in teaching and taking long-term substitute positions at some of the local high schools. Strangers were no longer calling me ma'am or miss, and I'd completed the legal process of changing my birth certificate and driver's license to a male gender marker. I felt safe to finally leave my part-time jobs and start applying for high school teaching positions.

The kids were adjusting to the transition as well as can be expected. There were difficulties along the way, and we all did our best to navigate them. They still called me mom, which was fine until we were in public. The trans bathroom debate was all over the news and I was nervous. I had to delicately explain to Violet and Max that when we are out shopping, they can't yell "Mom" across the aisles to me. It was a tough conversation. They felt a bit hurt and understandably so. Yet the reality was that it could potentially draw stares from people, and I was fearful of someone approaching us or making a hateful remark.

The transition in general seemed to be most difficult for Max, the youngest. One evening the two of us had an intense conversation about it. I struggled to explain that I was still his mom, still the same personality but no longer pretending to be something I wasn't.

"But you're my *mom!*" Max said.

"Yes, I am. That is not changing; it will never change. With the exception of giving birth and having that very special physical bond with you, all of the things that we think of as "mom tasks" can be done by anyone. What about kids who don't have a mom? Or their mom dies? Or is in the military and stationed somewhere far away? That kid's dad or grandparent or aunt or big sibling would be the one taking care of them and doing all the things their mom normally does right? A person doesn't have to be female to style hair, paint nails, cook meals…"

"But you're my *mom!*" Max repeated.

"Nothing is going to change the way I care for you and the way I love you. My appearance will be what's different and I know that's really difficult. I'm not downplaying that at all buddy. I'm sorry this is so messy and hard to understand."

We sat in silence for a moment. I felt a tremendous weight of guilt knowing that my personal needs were in opposition to his and to his siblings as well. Moms are naturally programmed to put their kids' needs first, particularly when it protects them from anything emotionally painful. *I'll be a better mom if I'm a whole person and not a deeply depressed recluse,* I reminded myself.

My heart hurt. Obviously, I knew this was well beyond what his adolescent mind could understand but I was desperate for a way to assure him that being a man did not prevent me from being his mom.

We all did the best we could in those tough moments and had a lot of fun times as well. Amanda was building relationships with both kids, finding things in common with each one. She had a comical way of tucking them in at night, securing each one into a tightly bundled blanket "burrito" for laughs. We somehow managed to get cheap bicycles and took family bike rides around town. In the summer we watched huge firework displays and walked down to the riverfront festivals to eat funnel cakes and listen to live music. We were settling into a familiar rhythm and routine for our family of four.

Other hurdles of transition were big ones. Surgeries brought a great deal of satisfaction as well as scars. I've purposefully left those stories out of the book. Gender affirming surgeries, as they're called, are incredibly personal topics and one of the only parts of my life I don't openly discuss with anyone except Amanda. More importantly, surgeries are not the measure or end goal of being transgender. Assuming that every trans person wants *every* surgery (or any surgery) is no different than assuming *every* cisgender woman wants a boob job. No one should be judged either way; a person should do whatever makes them feel at home in their body.

In some ways, I suppose I was almost too focused on changing my body to match my internal identity. It was easy to believe it was the ultimate fix that would make everything perfect somehow. I never considered some of the realities that come with functioning as a man in society: a whole new set of labels, expectations, and social norms.

There were several surprises I encountered in the beginning, as my appearance changed and I became just another average white guy in the landscape. One morning as I stocked shelves in the toy department of Target, a woman and her preschool-aged daughter started down the aisle. The little girl had picked out a fluffy stuffed dog and had it wrapped in her arms with a big smile as they browsed. We made eye contact, and I spoke to the girl, "What a cool puppy you have there! Does it have a name?" Before she could answer her mom shot me a disapproving look and steered the two of them quickly past without saying a word. I was puzzled for about five seconds before I realized that *as a man,* I could no longer make friendly conversation with moms and their kids.

Well, I'm a guy but I'm also a mom, I thought. Changing my body to match who I am inside doesn't erase my life experience. It was a difficult realization. A few weeks later I received a phone call from the kids' school and was told that Violet was sick and needed to be picked up. I went to my manager and explained that I had to leave because my daughter was sick. She looked at me and asked, "Where's her mom?" I answered in a way that wasn't a lie but also didn't out me as trans: "At work. I'm sorry I need to clock out and go."

Now I was irritated. As a mom, I was always the first emergency number. I was always the one who stayed home when a kid was sick because I wanted to and because sick kids want their mom. Being seen for my authentic self was great but I was not about to change how I cared for my kids.

That's not to say there aren't dads out there who stay at home with their kids or are the first emergency contact. I'm sure there are kids who want their dad when they are sick. My irritation was with the notion of gender roles and societal norms that create the *assumption* that a man couldn't possibly be the one to leave work and go home to care for a sick child.

There were other hard lessons. One morning I finished my shift and stopped at a restaurant for breakfast. I ordered a diet drink, a pancake, and sausage links. The waitress looked at me with surprise and said, "That's it? You better eat more than that, hun!" Nothing like this had ever happened to me before. "I'll start with that and add on if I need to," I said, a little confused. It wasn't until she walked away that I realized *men* don't place tiny food orders. Sure, I wanted the big breakfast of eggs, hashbrowns, pancakes, and sausage but I was too self-conscious to order a large meal. A lifetime of body image issues and fat shaming would never allow me to do so without feeling embarrassment. I laughed, feeling as if I won some kind of food lottery or permission to order large portions with no shame. The waitress returned with my drink, and I changed my order to the big breakfast combo. "That's more like it!" she said. But moments later I had another realization, and I wasn't laughing: In our society no one questions a large plate of food in front of a man. Why is that not the same for women? This was total bullshit.

It was a disturbing epiphany. I naively believed that coming into my authentic self meant freedom from labels and preconceived notions. Let me quickly acknowledge what an obvious and immature oversight that was on my part.

What was wrong with me? Was I stuck in some sort of brat mentality of wanting something, getting it, and then finding fault with it? Again, I recalled standing in front of the mirror two years into HRT and thinking I wanted to go out into the world and be physically recognized as a man... just not a fat, bald one. I was working hard to move past that, but it seemed I just moved on to being a brat about other undesirable things that come with the territory.

Like men's public restrooms. In my experience, most are disgusting on a whole new level. I also didn't like my new position in social situations. Where the men are congregating in one area (the grill, watching sports, etc.) and the women in another (the kitchen, keeping an eye on the kids' activities), I was now relegated to the men's group. My discomfort had nothing to do with being a man and everything to do with the things men talk about and the way in which they communicate. Let me clarify, this is not a cheap shot at men. There's nothing wrong with talking about sports, I just don't watch any except for women's basketball.

Given my past experiences in life I had no tolerance for homophobic, transphobic, or sexist jokes. I didn't want to hear guys talk shit about their wives, brag about affairs, or make fun of women they declared ugly, overweight, or stupid. Again, this is not a broad generalization on my part; I've actually heard those things and had to walk away from the conversations.

I began to realize what male privilege means, not to mention white male privilege. I worked jobs where a customer had mistaken me for the manager because I was the oldest white man in the room despite being in the same exact uniform and performing the same exact tasks as my brown-skinned coworkers. It's fucked up.

"Sometimes I don't know where I fit in in the world, you know?" I said to Amanda. "I'm not doubting my gender, that's at least one certainty I have going for me. I'm a guy and people see me as a guy, which is everything I've wanted. But there are so many things that come with the territory, things I don't want people to assume about me."

She put her hand on mine and squeezed. "Like what?"

"Stereotypes I guess. I don't want people to see me, a white, middle-aged man, and make an assumption about who I voted for, or whether I'm a racist or a womanizer. Do you know an older woman at work pulled me aside and started asking me about this problem she's having with her car? I told her I really don't know anything about cars, and she looked at me like I had three heads and said, 'Well don't you drive that silver Mustang in the parking lot?'"

Amanda laughed. "What did you say? Yeah, but I don't work on it?"

"No, I told the truth: Yeah, that's my wife's car. She just said 'oh' and walked away." I shook my head and couldn't help but be amused.

"Well, there's no denying you're different in some of those stereotypical ways but keep in mind those are *stereotypes* and those exist for every type of person and every type of situation. And they aren't true in every case. Besides, most of them are negative anyway so it's good that they don't apply to you!"

She was right. I'd already spent my entire life worrying about what other people think of me. Maybe it was just going to take a while to deprogram those old thought patterns and be myself.

CHAPTER FIFTY-FIVE

O ur family was growing. I became Grandpa Jay in June of 2017 when Megan gave birth to Layla. She carried her well past the due date and I missed the birth, having flown out of town for transition surgery. As soon as we returned home, we headed over to their house to meet the new baby. I'll never forget the first time I held her. The feeling was so much like the connection I had with my own kids. There is something miraculous within shared DNA that bonds mothers, children, and grandchildren.

Layla arrived just in time to be part of the wedding party. Amanda and I were married in October of that same year. This wedding was decidedly *not* in a church. Through AA I found a path to peace in my spiritual life, one that did not involve organized religion or the typical god concept.

The turning point was pretty straightforward and actually came from the gospels, attributed to one of Jesus' teachings: an analogy of a tree and its fruit. In my early twenties I heard a priest give a talk about discernment. He referenced this particular teaching and said that if you're unsure about an action you're going to take or a person you're going to trust, consider "By their fruits you will know them." Specifically, ask yourself what is the fruit of this thing I'm about to do? He took it a step further and suggested that if you are unsure whether something is coming from God or your own mind, again consider the "fruit" or the outcome.

In my AA recovery work, I remembered that talk and it stayed in the back of my mind over the years as I wrestled with religious dogma and the man-made rules that are in opposition to the teachings of Jesus.

What was the fruit of my transition and self-acceptance? I'm a different person, a more loving and accepting person. I have greater empathy and feel more connected to everything in the universe.

In contrast, before I realized I was transgender, I was deeply depressed and consumed with morphing myself into what other people or systems said I should be. I wasn't living the truth of who I am on a soul level.

I thought back to the novena prayer—purify my marriage—and the events that followed, setting me on a totally different path. The good fruits of that relationship were my children. The other fruits were not good: anger, distrust, criticism, selfishness. In that sense, it was easy to look back and see that it had run its course, and it was time for Lou and me to part ways.

The fruit of my AA work focused on a higher power, a universal oneness, rather than a religious god concept. It also made me a better person, a whole person, one who could love himself enough to see and accept the truth of who he was. The fruit of that acceptance opened me to the entirely new experience of love and partnership I found with Amanda. In that relationship, love was expansive, not constricting. It was selfless, not possessive; it was kind, not cruel.

Amanda was the person I'd dreamt about long ago when I was in undergrad and imagining a different life someday. She was the stepparent I promised to Max and Violet, the one who would be funny, love to laugh, and love them as much as I did. She was the person who was so well-matched for me that I couldn't comprehend it but trusted our paths would meet when the timing was right. She saw me when I couldn't bear to see myself.

And I got to marry her.

The book could end here with its "happily ever after" but that would be misleading. Life is a wave of ups and downs. Weddings come with mishaps and things that don't go as planned. For one, I didn't try on my tux after picking it up. It was a rookie error on my part—I had a fitting, so I assumed it would fit.

Three hours before the ceremony, I looked in the full-length mirror of the fancy changing room and felt nauseous. The vest was too big because I'm so short. I put on the jacket, and it was also too big, the sleeves covering my hands to the last joint of my fingers. I looked like a kid playing dress-up in my dad's closet.

I was furious with myself. *What the hell was I thinking? Why didn't I try the damn thing on at home the day before? Why didn't I ask about sleeve length?* I took the jacket off. Maybe I could just wear the vest. I adjusted the little strap on the back of it as far as it would go but it still looked ridiculous. The arm holes were huge, and it was too long. I tossed it aside. *Fuck it.* I put the jacket back on. There was no fix, I was going to look awful on the one day that mattered most.

One of Amanda's best friends, who was also in the wedding party, was sent to check on me. I was so swept up in my clothing crisis that I was late for pictures. He remained calm as I blurted out my problem and then said one sentence that changed my focus: "Your bride is waiting, and she looks gorgeous." He pinned my jacket in a couple places and sent me on my way.

As I walked to the ceremony, I took in this huge wedding celebration of family and friends—people who traveled from as far away as New York and California. Some we'd known since childhood and considered them equal to blood relatives, like Samantha and her mom. There were people there who knew me long before I became Jay, like Lou's mom and sister; and people who didn't know me until after I became Jay, like my new in-laws, our coworkers, and our friends. They were all there to celebrate us and our commitment to one another.

For an artist or writer, the art is the process; that's where the magic happens. Art is about creating something, whether it's a painting, a song, a performance, or in this case, words. In the process of writing my vows I found the most beautiful, magical perspective of my life at that point in time:

Many times, I jokingly ask you, "Where have you been my whole life?" And your answer is, "Honey, I'm late for everything."

But in reality, your timing was impeccable because I'm one of the few people in this world given the gift of living two totally different, consecutive lives in one single lifetime.

You came to me when I was starting to bridge the gap between those two lives. You looked right through my awkward physical disguise and recognized me. And I recognized you.

Together with my four children who are standing at our side today you walked with me fearlessly into this new life, this new existence, sharing a love, familiarity, and strength that defies all explanation.

And now, here in front of all our friends and family, I promise to keep walking fearlessly beside you into everything that lies ahead. To be your rock, your strength, your laughter, and to never leave your side. While I can't promise that the journey will be easy, I can promise that I will hold on tighter when it gets tough.

EPILOGUE

I followed Amanda through the restaurant to the back patio and up a set of stairs to a covered deck that had a few empty tables. She put two large sodas down in front of two chairs and I placed a plate of pizza next to each.

"Cheers to ten years!" she said, raising her cup.

I raised mine, "To the date that wasn't a date!"

We reminisced about that September evening so long ago, right there at the very table we were sharing. Every fall we celebrate this anniversary in addition to our wedding anniversary in October. We'd been a couple for three years before getting married, so it definitely warranted two celebrations.

Amanda shook her head, "We made it through some serious stuff, babe. Career changes, surgeries, financial ups and downs, PTSD therapy, raising Violet and Max."

"No kidding. I remember feeling like coparenting with Lou was never going to end. I'm pretty sure I would've fucked up my relationships with the kids if it weren't for you talking me off the ledge in some critical moments."

She smiled and said, "Well, I'm glad something good came from surviving my own parents' divorce. I never dreamed that perspective would be so useful, even with my students too."

Her input had been far beyond useful. Shared custody with Lou was anything but easy. Amanda had a way of recognizing many of the pain points the kids dealt with and could communicate those to me so that I could tread lightly and avoid making things worse.

Somehow, we made it. Max was now nineteen and preparing to move into his first apartment with his girlfriend. Violet had recently turned twenty-one and was out on her own as well. The only time Lou and I were in the same space was at Layla's birthday parties or extracurricular activities. He never initiated conversation in those moments but if I started talking first, he opened up.

I was shocked to get a text from him recently asking to meet and talk. He assured me it was nothing bad, so I agreed, still unsure of what the conversation would entail. I knew that he'd been trying to get Violet and Max to go to church with him, but neither were interested. I thought he might ask for my help to encourage them to go so I was prepared to tactfully decline. We met at the local chicken wing bar, and I wasted no time getting down to business. "What's up?" I asked, internally rehearsing my stance against our adult children being strong-armed into religious practice.

I couldn't have been more off the mark. He brought up Rylie's death and apologized for not staying in the hospital with me at any point during the four-week ordeal but particularly the final three nights when I tearfully begged him to stay. I was dumbstruck.

He had been carrying a great deal of guilt over how he handled the entire situation: his absence at the hospital, his immediate return to work when I was discharged, his refusal to ever visit the gravesite with me, and for not allowing me to see a therapist when the grief was overwhelming. He explained that he looks back on the ordeal with disbelief and regret. "If Randy or Max were in that situation and acting the way I acted, I'd get on them, tell them to pull their head out of their ass, and do the right thing."

I didn't know what to say and was shocked that he had been carrying this for years. I accepted his apology. Out of habit I attempted to rationalize a little bit of his absence by pointing out that he had been still fairly new on his job and that Randy had baseball practices and games. To his credit he didn't take the outs I offered. He said his new employer was more than accommodating and would've given him as much time off as he needed, that Randy could have easily stayed with my parents and gotten rides to practice with his best friend who was the coach's son.

We talked at length and eventually moved on to other topics, like the loss of his mother in 2018 and the type of family drama that sometimes happens after a death. There was lighter conversation and even some laughs when we shared current stories about the kids.

After two hours or so, we parted ways. He offered to talk again if I thought of anything that needed to be resolved. I thanked him and we agreed to move past the tensions and difficulties experienced over the years.

I don't believe that conversation would have been possible a few years ago. He and I have some very dark history. But out of our dysfunction and immaturity came life. Four of them to be exact, three living and one who was only here briefly.

****

Amanda gave me a quick kiss on her way out the door. "Good luck today; you're going to be great. Text me after and let me know how it goes." I gave her my word and headed to the bathroom to get ready. Stepping in front of the mirror I took notice of the gray whiskers in my beard and crows'-feet near my eyes.

"High five. Be nice," I thought, taking a deep breath. I tapped my raised palm to the glass and studied the reflection. It's the daily practice I learned in a book by Mel Robbins, *The High 5 Habit.* The premise is to high-five your reflection in the morning when you

wake up. It seemed silly at first, but I soon realized that starting my day with one act of compassion or kindness toward myself adds up over time.

Over the course of three years, it seemed the high five made a little crack in the foundation of hatred I'd been building since childhood. I credit the habit for an important realization that came to me one day in conversation with Amanda. We were discussing various struggles we had in our respective childhoods, her parents' divorce, my family's move to Kentucky. Throughout our conversation I noticed how much compassion we expressed for our adolescent selves. I imagined having a time machine and going back to give that lost thirteen-year-old a big hug and say, "You're okay... you're not going to hell; you're not weird."

Those thoughts came to mind the next time I looked in the mirror and high-fived. *Why is it so hard to be compassionate to my present-day self,* I wondered. Logically, a few years into the future I might look back at this day and feel compassion or kindness toward the reflection in front of me now. I'd see a middle-aged guy trying to find his way in the world, trying to make a living, trying to be a good husband, a good parent. I'd want to tell him, "Hey, go easy on us man. You're okay. You're doing the best you can. You're a good guy."

I brushed my teeth, got dressed and made my way to the kitchen. I was actually ahead of schedule, there was time to eat a quick bite. I opened the fridge and stared for several moments, unimpressed with my options. My attention drifted to the artwork hanging on the door of the freezer: a crayon drawing of me and Layla that she'd made as a birthday card months earlier. In the handwriting of a seven-year-old it said, *Happy birthday Grandpa Jay. You are the best. Love, Layla.* It hung between her school photo and her gymnastics team photo.

Being Grandpa Jay is one of my greatest joys. When Layla was around three years old, she began to understand the concept of family relationships and titles. Like all kids that age, she started to understand which grandparents were mommy's and daddy's parents. She asked Randy, "Who is your mommy?" His answer was simple, "Grandpa Jay is my mommy." She did a double take. He said, "Grandpa Jay used to be a girl." Like a typical three-year-old she repeated it back as a question, "Grandpa Jay is your mommy, and he used to be a girl?" Randy said yes, and she accepted it and moved on to the next topic.

Her reaction is not surprising to me. For a three-year-old anything is possible, and the world is magical: Stuffed animals talk, she drinks imaginary tea from toy cups, puts on a costume and becomes her favorite Disney character. The fact that Grandpa Jay was once a girl is neither shocking nor impossible.

For a few weeks after learning this piece of news she integrated it into her world regularly. One afternoon Megan sent me a short video of Layla pushing a large toy jeep around the room. It was stuffed with dolls. Megan stopped her to ask, "Who's in your jeep?" Layla named the two dolls in the front seat and then pointed to a stuffed Batgirl doll in the back seat and said, "This is Grandpa Jay when he was a girl." Then she zoomed off.

When my former self wasn't being Batgirl, I started to show up in her drawings. The best one of all time was drawn inside Megan's Mother's Day card. She opened the card and asked Layla, "Oh is this me?" The answer was, "No, that's Grandpa Jay when he was a girl." I was a floating head, smiling, no facial hair, and a halo over top.

I closed the fridge and opted to skip food and get to my presentation a few minutes earlier than planned. I was giving a self-portrait workshop for transgender folks, a project I started during the pandemic with a grant from the city's biggest public art organization. I called it Inside Out because being transgender is a transformation that begins on the inside as we work to align who we are internally with what we look like externally. Participants create a self-portrait, write a short artist statement about it, then I take a high-resolution photo, and it's added to the project website.

I knew firsthand the pain of creating a self-portrait. I'd created a few after transition and it was a completely different process than mirror portraits two decades prior. While there were still glaring imperfections, the male face I saw was 100 percent me. It was empowering, and I'd hoped to bring that experience to others as well.

I arrived at the venue and began the process of unloading my art supplies and setting up for five participants. I'd done this project with as many as sixteen people in a group and as small as a single person. The results were always positive.

Minutes later I stood before five nervous faces. "Well, let's jump right in and get started."

A soft-spoken trans woman raised her hand and said, "I've never drawn anything before. I'm pretty sure I haven't even touched crayons since I was a little kid and I'm now fifty-seven."

"That is totally fine. This project requires no previous experience with art. None whatsoever. I'm first going to explain a little bit about the project. We'll do a warm-up activity and then I'll introduce the materials and demonstrate a simple technique you can use if you'd like."

She smiled and nodded. With no other hands in the air, I started the presentation with a personal introduction and story of how the project came to be and why it's self-portraiture.

"Self-portraits are difficult even for seasoned art professionals. So, I'm sure you're wondering why I'd ever think it's something a trans person wants to create—particularly since, by definition, there is a disparity between who we know ourselves to be (gender) and the body we're born into (sex)."

Heads nodded in agreement.

"But let me tell you why, as trans people, we are perfectly suited for this project. We possess a level of bravery, authenticity, and resilience that is unheard of. *Transition* is not a short list of tasks and changes then, boom, it's done. It is an upending of your entire life, every aspect. It's like being tasked with a cross-country trip but you've been handed a unicycle instead of a car or plane ticket. Right?

"We take on some monumental stuff. In fact, I think I can safely say that we are all much stronger than we give ourselves credit for. Trust me when I say this self-portrait will be a breeze in comparison."

I passed out some small blank booklets and started a writing activity as a warm-up exercise. "There's no need to be nervous for this part because what you write is for your eyes only. I won't ask anyone to share. This is simply to get your brain moving and ready to create.

"I first want to acknowledge that we are all in different places on our individual journeys here. In general, I've found that we all struggle to be kind to ourselves, particularly when our brains keep a running monologue of our imperfections. We are going to try to push pause on that tape for the time being. You've already taken a huge step in doing something nice for yourself by showing up here today!"

I began the warm-up by asking each person to write about their hobbies, favorite colors and seasons, people who inspire them, and what their closest friend or partner would describe as their great qualities. That last question is the most important. I hoped each person's response would steer them toward objectivity in how they view themselves.

"There are multiple ways to do a self-portrait. Your portrait doesn't necessarily have to have your face in it. For example, a guitar player or a surgeon or a sculptor might want to focus on their hands. Or you could create something symbolic or metaphorical. You could draw yourself as an animated character, an animal or flower, or even a building. You have some options and can pick one that feels right for you. But please know there is really no wrong way to do this. There are no set rules."

Each person seemed to relax a little.

"What aspect of yourself do you want to highlight? How do you want to be seen on paper?

"You are the creator, and it is entirely up to you to decide."

****

At some point in this journey, I began to worry that I wouldn't find my place in society. I felt a bit like Mowgli in *The Jungle Book*, awkward among my kind. So, what's the verdict? Where *is* my place in the world? I've learned that when I embrace the ups and downs I'm exactly where I'm supposed to be; there's no box to fit into or sign to stand under. My life is too full of love, beauty, and awe to believe otherwise. I am a human—a hybrid of sorts: a male soul/essence/brain who started this incarnation in the vehicle of a female body.

We are all on the same journey, broadly speaking. Most people travel by one mode of transportation for the entirety but I, and others like me, are not built for that. What starts for us as a very long nonstop flight in coach with no leg room and no windows becomes an emergency landing and layover. Our golden ticket is for the second leg of the trip: a luxury car ride with open windows, fresh air, winding roads, and an ever-changing view.

How incredibly lucky I am for these two routes of one journey, two lives in one lifetime.

ABOUT THE AUTHOR

Jay DeFazio is an educator, artist, and trans activist. Through classrooms, workshops, and guest lectures, Jay breaks down the concepts of gender identity and sexuality to non-LGBTQ+ audiences.

In 2020, Jay received the ArtWorks Emerging Artist Award to launch *Inside Out*, a transgender visibility project in which participants create a self portrait. The project's success helped earn another award: Northern Kentucky Pride's 2021 Artist of the Year. The portrait gallery can be viewed at: www.insideout-transart.org

For more great books from Pride and Joy Press
Visit Books.GracePointPublishing.com

PRIDE & JOY
publishing

If you enjoyed reading *You Only Live Twice,* and purchased it through an online retailer, please return to the site and write a review to help others find the book.